THE COMPLETE GUIDE TO
SCULPTURE, MODELING
AND
CERAMICS
TECHNIQUES AND MATERIALS

THE COMPLETE GUIDE TO
SCULPTURE, MODELING
AND
CERAMICS
TECHNIQUES AND MATERIALS

CONSULTANT EDITOR
BARRY MIDGLEY

CHARTWELL
BOOKS, INC.

Consultant editor
Barry Midgley

Contributing editors
John Calcutt
Trevor Crabtree
Andrew Fyvie
David Harper
Dan King
Liz Lydiate
John Maine
David Morris
Rod Murray
David Nash
Sean Rice
Janet Rudge

A QED BOOK

Published by Chartwell Books Inc.
A Division of Booksales Inc.
110 Enterprise Avenue, Secaucus, New Jersey 07094.

First published in the United States 1982.
© Copyright QED Publishing Limited
ISBN 0–89009–471–3

Library of Congress Catalog Card No 81-66993

This book was designed and produced by
QED Publishing Limited
32 Kingly Court
London W1

Art director **Alastair Campbell**
Production director **Edward Kinsey**
Editorial director **Jeremy Harwood**
Senior editor **Kathy Rooney**
Editors **Nicola Thompson, Judy Martin, Catherine
Carpenter, Elbie Spivack, Carol Cormack**
Designers **Caroline Courtney, Nick Clark**
Illustrators **Chris Forsey, David Mallot, Simon Roulstone
Lorna Turpin, Sally Kindberg.**
Special photography **Jon Wyand, Paul Sawyer**

Filmset in Great Britain by Tradespools Limited, Frome, Somerset.
Colour origination in Hong Kong by Hong Kong Graphic Arts Limited.
Printed in Hong Kong by Leefung Asco Printers Limited.

QED would like to thank the many individuals and companies who
have given invaluable help during the preparation for this book.
Particular thanks go to Alec Tiranti Ltd for supplying materials for
photography. We would also like to thank the following: Candle
Maker's Supplies Ltd, London; Ruth Franklin and Sally Somerville,
Barbican Arts Group; Fry's Metals Ltd, London; BL Pattern and
Foundry Co; Mr Shelton of Podmore Ceramics; Pitt and Scott Ltd; and
Dufaylite Developments Ltd; and the Stone Firms, Portland, Dorset.

CONTENTS

FOREWORD

An understanding of materials and a respect for their qualities is as relevant to sculpture today as it always has been. This book is intended to introduce the reader to techniques commonly employed by sculptors – some traditional and others firmly anchored in the twentieth century.

Craftsmanship cannot be seen as an end in itself and a poor or ill-considered idea will not be rescued by good craftsmanship. But knowledge of techniques and materials will help the reader to explore ideas and so begin to understand the relationships involved in the creative processes of sculpture, modeling and ceramics.

Barry Midgley
December 1981

PRINCIPLES OF SCULPTURE

Above The rugged stone carvings at Mount Rushmore in South Dakota can be seen from miles around. The huge sculptures took many years to complete, and were indeed finished by the son of the artist Gutzon Borglum, who began the work. One of the fascinations of sculpture is that it can encompass works on a very large and very small scale.

MAIN TECHNIQUES

Sculpture is an art form which deals directly with real space, unlike painting which creates fictive space on a single plane. Sculpture, being three-dimensional, must occupy, interact with or enclose actual space. A form may be compact and solid or armed with projections intruding into the surrounding environment. It may be hollow, linear or pierced, giving access to its own internal space. Because sculpture has to have a real existence, however temporary, in a complex and cluttered world, a sculptor must be able to sctch perception and imagination with practical, technical skills.

Sculpture in the round demands a coherent combination of many different design elements, as it will be seen from several different view points, and ideally each view should be equal worked out. Relief sculpture presents quite di ferent design problems, since a complicated seri of actual spatial relationships may have to indicated within a relatively shallow depth material. The particular challenges to a sculptor capabilities may be overcome by learning or instinct, but, inevitably, it is only in practice, n in theory, that the solutions are found.

The three basic methods of creating sculptu with raw materials are carving, modeling a construction. Carving and modeling are the olde methods, and the basis of sculptural tradition whereas construction has only been fully e ploited and accepted in the twentieth centur Casting is a fourth basic technique, but this is process of reproduction, not of original shapin

8

CARVING

Carving is a subtractive process. This means that a solid mass of resistant material is shaped by cutting, chiseling and abrading the exterior to reduce the mass and create a particular form.

The outer limits of a carved sculpture are set by the shape and size of the mass of raw material. Wood and stone can be used for small- or large-scale work, and blocks of these materials can even be joined together if the form so demands. Carvings in ivory and precious stones are always small-scale.

The texture and substance of the material determine certain characteristics of the sculptural form. A soft stone may be too crumbly to be carved with any delicacy. Exhausting physical work is required to shape quite simple forms in a hard stone such as granite. Marble is relatively hard, and can be shaped into detailed forms, but could splinter during the carving process. Because of the lack of tensile strength—or the ability to withstand stress—in stone, the carving of slender, projecting forms is extremely precarious, since an ill-judged blow can fracture the whole piece. In many figurative stone carvings, arms are carved close to the body, and where a shape narrows, at the ankles for instance, there is often a supporting weight of stone, disguised as drapery, a tree trunk, or some other detail suitable to the subject. The instinctive confidence of Michelangelo (1475–1564) and Bernini (1598–1680) in handling their medium is evident from the intricacies of formal detail and their widely different approaches, which can be seen clearly in many of their works.

The fibrousness of wood gives it rather more tensile strength. Openwork designs and fragile, detailed forms are more commonly seen in wood carvings, such as beautiful Gothic altarpieces. A modern approach is that of the British sculptor Henry Moore (born 1898) who uses juxtapositions of space and mass in both wood and stone carvings.

MODELING

Modeling is an additive process—the form is directly built up in a soft, malleable material, such as clay or wax, over a minimal supporting structure of rigid material. Modeling provides the sculptor with a greater freedom of expression than carving. The modeling material can be molded and formed at every stage of the sculpture, giving complete control of both the inner and outer structure of the form, and if the work is unsatisfactory, part or all of the material can be pulled off and the process started again.

The size, shape and extension of forms in modeling is also more variable than in carving. Providing the supporting armature is strong and well balanced, no external supports are needed for the forms.

Hollow building in terracotta is a different type of modeling technique. There is no inner support, so the form must be more compact and self-supporting. Hollow-built terracottas are dried and fired to make the material more durable, and can be decorated with colored glazes for surface detail and shine.

Models in wax or clay are often cast in metal, to give a finished, unbreakable version of the sculpture. Casting gives perfect reproduction of the form, but obviously alters the surface texture and color of the original material.

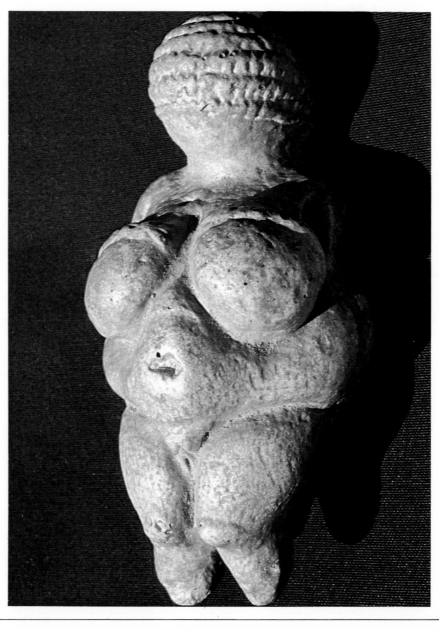

Below The *Venus of Willendorf* probably dates from 27000 BC. Carved with crude and clumsy tools, the roughly hewn generalized forms, especially the swelling breasts and belly, nevertheless convey an impression of sensuality and fecundity. The figurine was probably used as a fertility symbol.

Stone quarrying

Regardless of the area of sculpture which you are working in, it is important to remember the origins of the materials you are working with. For instance, the natural fibers of wood have a bearing on the ways in which the material can be used. Similarly, the fact that resins and glass fiber are synthetic materials affects how they are employed by the sculptor. Stone is a natural material. But, unlike wood, it has to be hewn out of the ground. Unless the sculptor is working on a very small scale, it is likely that the stone will have come from a quarry. Marble has traditionally been one of the most popular types of stone for sculpture.

Some of the most famous marble quarries in the world are at Carrara in Italy. This is where Michelangelo obtained his stone. Here stone workings at the top of Monte Altissimo (1) can be seen. The exact methods of quarrying may vary according to the type of stone. At Carrara a network of wires which are used to cut the stone can be guided into position by pulleys. The stones are cut into large blocks (2). The huge size of the blocks can be judged by the tiny figures of men standing on top of them, using drills to split them into smaller pieces. Another way of splitting blocks of stone is using wire in conjunction with carborundum stone which acts as an abrasive (4). In this instance, granite is being cut. Water is used to lessen both the heat caused by the friction and the amount of dust created. Holes have to be made in the stone so they can be lifted and transported (5). Here the nip holes are being made, before lifting, while other stones are being lifted in the background. Most quarries have their own large stockpiles. The blocks of stone are heaped on top of one another. For this, heavy gantries and lifting gear are essential (6). The blocks of stone (9) are stacked in the stockyard to await sale. Like most stockpiles, the marble stockyard at Carrara (8) contains pieces of stone of many sizes. When selecting a piece of stone to work on, make sure you assess its possible structural weaknesses as well as whether the shape and texture suits the effect you wish to achieve. Drills are used to split the stones (7) even when they are very

7

large. Wedges and pressure may also be used. Stone has poor tensile strength and so will split reasonably easily if pressure is exerted through it, by means of wedges, for example. Stones come from many different parts of the world. This spectacular picture (**3**) shows the Rock of Ages quarry in New York state, in the United States. The stones are piled to a great height. Granite is one of the hardest stones to work on and requires special tools.

Sculpture with stone is one of the oldest sculptural media. Some of the earliest relics of artistic achievement include small stone carvings which may have been used as religious fertility symbols. Although the techniques of stone sculpture may have changed little over the centuries, the subjects and treatment by the sculptor have constantly changed to ensure that stone sculpture is one of the most popular and enduring areas of sculpture.

8

9

Above Gianlorenzo Bernini was one of the greatest Italian sculptors. This statue of St Longinus is made from terracotta which was later covered with gesso and gilded. This was a smaller version of Bernini's marble statue of St Longinus which stands in St Peter's in Rome. Bernini worked in many different sculptural media.

Modern techniques of lifting, joining and supporting heavy materials have removed some of the traditional restrictions on sculpted forms, and opened the way to very different descriptions of the relationships between space and mass. Transparent plastics give access to the internal space of a sculpture, even if it is enclosed. Industrial welding techniques are used in metal sculpture which thrust out huge, heavy projections, unsupported in space.

Preformed shapes and whole found objects can be joined together and combined with raw materials to function in a new context. Motor mechanisms and electrical circuits are incorporated in works that move through space or cast out light. The scope offered by new materials and techniques has also prompted artists to re-examine the possibilities of natural materials, even reshaping them in their own environment to form giant earthworks.

CASTING

Casting processes are for reproducing a sculpture in a different, usually more durable material from that of the original. With some methods, the original work perishes during the casting process and, again depending on the technique, it may be possible to produce several copies of the original or only one. A mold or impression is built up around the original form, and used as the pattern into which the new material is set.

The traditional technique of casting is the lost wax method for casting bronze. Small models may be cast solid, but larger ones are usually hollow. Metal has considerable tensile strength so that fragile and extensive forms can be cast which would be impossible to work in stone, or liable to fracture in either stone or hardened clay. Since bronze is poured into a mold in liquid form, it settles into every detail and sets in a completely faithful copy in which all the intricacies of form in the original are preserved. Complex compositions can be cast in several sections and later constructed into the whole. The qualities of bronze have always been highly regarded for their own sake—the rich, reflective surface, its natural color and the heavy patination which it forms are all elements which can be held in mind when the original model is made.

Plaster is a cheap and readily available material for casting, but is somewhat crude for finished work. Glass fiber resin is a relatively new material which can be used to cast both modeled and constructed forms. Special pigmentation enables the sculptor to cast directly in bright color, or even produce a surface imitative of bronze. A great advantage of the material is that, when cast hollow, the sculpture is quite lightweight.

CONSTRUCTION

Construction refers to the process of building a whole sculpture from various component parts, which may be all of the same material or of different substances. This is largely a twentieth century development, brought about by the sudden increase in materials and techniques which have become available through scientific and industrial research. Constructions may incorporate traditional sculptural materials, such as wood, stone and metal, but these are used to develop quite new ideas, which may, perhaps, be combined with modern materials such as plastics and glass fiber.

DEVELOPMENTS

any of the tools, materials and forms of sculpture have changed little through centuries of activity. The earliest evidence of a deliberate carving process is the tiny *Venus of Willendorf*, dating from about 27000 BC. The simple curving shape of the figure indicates the problems of fashioning a form with primitive stone tools. Early artefacts were usually made from small lumps and fragments of material which could be easily carried and worked.

Small bone and stone sculptures, as well as clay figurines and pots, survive from the Paleolithic periods, but wood sculptures appear to have perished. Much evidence exists to prove that the impulse to create decorative and expressive form in natural materials was a very early feature of human development.

The significant early development in the history of sculpture was the discovery of metal working techniques. This at once provided a new material for sculpture, and far more efficient tools for cutting and carving. Abrasion techniques, equivalent to sandpapering wood, were well established, but these were laborious and imprecise. Metal tools were a much quicker and more accurate means of shaping, making possible delicate detail and intricate decoration.

The basic principles of carving, working in clay and bronze casting in use today were known in ancient Greek and Roman civilizations, and neither the tools nor the techniques have greatly changed. Their particular use has been subject to fashion and personal preference, and this has had considerable bearing on the developing styles of sculpture through the ages. In carving, for instance, each different tool gives a characteristic mark. The relatively deep holes formed by a punch, used in much decorative detail on Egyptian sculpture, set a very different style from that of the criss-cross texture and curving surfaces formed by claw chisel work. Although many of Michelangelo's sculptures are highly finished and polished, his mastery of chisel work is often clearly visible.

The marks on a clay model are an extremely personal expression of individual skill, since they are often formed with the fingers in a very direct engagement with the material. Although much clay sculpture was smoothed and neatened in the pursuit of 'perfect' form, the work of the modern French sculptor Auguste Rodin (1840–1917), with its massive forms and craggy, organic texture, clearly illustrates the vitality of the medium. The task of a sculptor is to cooperate with the material to achieve his or her ideas, rather than impose a predetermined form upon it. For instance, it is senseless to try to imitate the plasticity of clay in rigid stone. The finest sculptors have always controlled their medium while paying due respect to its own inherent qualities. This can be seen in a traditional view of carving which holds that the sculpture lies already imprisoned within the block, and the sculptor works to recognize and reveal the true form.

The human figure was the primary subject for sculpture until the twentieth century. Ancient and medieval sculpture was created mainly for religious or celebratory purposes, to portray gods and goddesses, figures from myth and legend, and ordinary mortals in pursuit of a higher plane of living. Animals also appear frequently, with particular significance in pre-Christian, Eastern and tribal cultures. In relief sculpture, where quite different rules of space and form apply, some elements of architecture and landscape are shown in a rather condensed view.

Below This glazed figure of a mounted drummer is an example of Tang dynasty ware. This time—from AD 618 to 906—was one of great excellence in ceramic wares. The modeling on this figure is very detailed. The color of the fired clay can be seen in places where the glaze has chipped off.

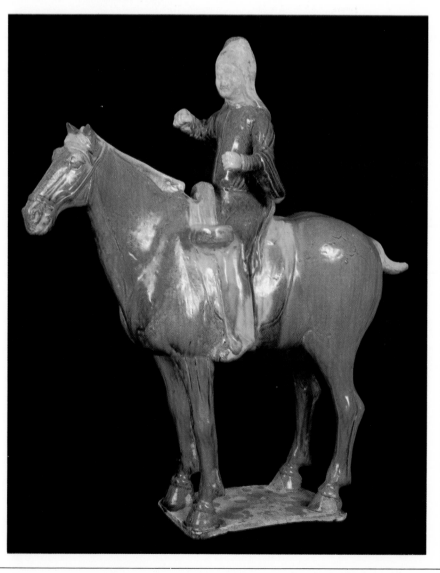

The twentieth century has seen many changes which have revitalized sculptural activity. Industrialization has produced man-made materials and mechanized tools which sculptors have eagerly grasped and put to their own uses. Communications are so efficient that virtually an international conversation has occurred between artists, resulting in an unprecedented and rapid evolution of ideas.

From tentative beginnings, pure abstraction came to be the dominant mode of artistic and sculptural form in a space of only 50 years, after centuries of figurative tradition. Picasso (1881–1973) was a remarkable innovator in both painting and sculpture. His analysis of form in his Cubist paintings introduced a new concept of volume, mass and space in visual terms. Reducing a form to a series of basic planes and angles, and combining several viewpoints simultaneously, he examined the interior and exterior structure of solid mass, without regard to its 'realistic' surface appearance. Picasso also first introduced the use of found objects and humble materials as appropriate components of sculpture.

The French artist Marcel Duchamp (1887–1968) went further, exhibiting everyday, functional objects, unaltered, as works of art. The lofty plane of sculptural tradition was questioned in the context of commercialism, industrial design and the immense social, political and philosophical upheavals occasioned by the First World War. The Dada and Surrealist movements investigated futility and fantasy, illustrating their visions as artistic form. Futurism and Constructivism attempted to define an art appropriate to the age of machines and urban development. Abstract art after the Second World War declined to grapple with social or political messages and concentrate on the full expression of the physical qualities of artists' materials, and pure visual sensation.

The images of Pop Art in the 1950s and 1960s entered into direct combat with the images and products of a consumer society, placing the form in a fine art context. Minimal sculpture returned to pure form, allowing the characteristic qualities of the materials full reign, and artists even took to the land, working natural materials in their proper environment, and importing contrasting man-made elements.

Lightweight man-made materials, such as plastics and glass fiber resin, have reintroduced color as an important feature of sculpture, as have paints developed for industrial and commercial use, which can be applied to metal and plastic. Heavy metal sculptures by the American David Smith (1906–1965) and the Briton Anthony Caro (born 1924) gain vibrancy from their bright color which matches the impact of the innovative forms. The whole basis of Smith's technique was learned directly in the workshop of an auto factory. The celebration, by Pop and Superrealist sculptors, of the vigor and vulgarity of modern life would be far less effective if they did not use materials invented by the consumer society.

Mechanized tools and lifting gear have banished restrictions on sculpture originally imposed by the weight and substance of the materials. A new attitude to scale, both real and symbolic, has emerged. The human figure has been ousted from its dominant place in the subject matter of sculpture by the rapid adoption of abstract styles and concepts. Sculpture has achieved architectural scale in constructions and inflatable forms, and rivaled the immensity of landscape by treating it as both studio and gallery. For instance, the *Wrapped Coastline* in Little Bay, Australia, project of the sculptor Christo (born 1935), could only be a twentieth century feat, a redefinition of the natural form of the oldest sculptural material, stone, by literally packaging a coastline in plastic sheeting. On a smaller scale, sculptures have been produced which, in different forms, examine the space within which they exist. The *Corner Reliefs* by the Russian sculptor Vladimir Tatlin (1885–1953) are simple wooden constructions fitting into a 90° angle in a studio or gallery, from which curving metal rods reach out and touch the walls to create the sculptural area. *Palace at 4am* by the Swiss artist Alberto Giacometti (1901–1966), made of glass, string and wooden rods, defines the whole space of a building on a small scale by means of open linear framework.

Below One of the most exciting breakthroughs in sculpture this century has been the advent of plastics as a sculptural medium. This work by the Italian artist Gino Marotta is entitled *Rhinoceros*. It is made from acrylic sheet. Acrylics are often used in conjunction with light because of their translucent qualities.

PREPARATIONS
DRAWINGS

rawing is the common medium of all visual rtists, and a common purpose is shared when rawing is used as a means of noting visual npressions quickly in a sketchbook or on a rough eet. In many ways, however, the drawings of a ulptor may differ from those of a painter or aphic artist. Sculptors are not bound to two- mensional space and need not spend time eveloping complex systems of perspective, im- ense vistas of landscape or crowded figurative enes. Studies for a sculpture are quite likely to e self-contained images within the picture plane, nd may be anything from a minutely careful amination of form from life, to a broadly etched impression of the basic idea for a rticular work. Color plays a less important role, nce the immediate problem is to define three- mensional structure, as in an architect's draw- g. Many sculptures use the natural color of the aterial, and, if not, ideas about surface finish ay arise directly from the execution of the form.

Many beautiful line and hatched ink drawings xist which demonstrate the preoccupations and orking methods of major artists such as lichelangelo, Leonardo da Vinci (1452–1519) nd the German wood carver Veit Stoss (c1450– 533). Small, broken studies of anatomical detail, e outline for an equestrian statue or an intricate esign of a whole altarpiece show how drawing cords the progress from original research to a sion of the completed form.

The lovely wash drawings of Rodin indicate the assive, vital forms of his models by means of elicate overlapping tones. The modern sculptors avid Smith and Alexander Calder (1898–1976) ade bold abstract drawings with brush and int, which are not necessarily a plan for a rticular work, but provide the essence of their pproaches to sculptural form. Christo and merican Claes Oldenburg (born 1920) both mbine collage with drawn images to describe ge outdoor projects, whether in town or land- ape. Some of Christo's collages are like shallow liefs, and Oldenburg sometimes adds photo- aphs to suggest the three-dimensional reality.

Constructed forms, such as kinetic sculpture ith motor power, or a transparent plastic sculp- re with internal lighting, cannot be thrown gether. Accurate drawings are needed which an out both the aesthetic form and technical tail. In figurative work, disciplined objective udies of human form are made, to observe and nderstand the structure before the sculptural edium is approached.

In any artist's work, no theory or formula can provide an adequate substitute for careful and continual observation, and drawing is the quick- est way to record this experience. In sculpture, however, the usefulness of drawing is limited as the final form of the work will depend upon the different experience of the physical qualities of the material, which cannot be accounted for entirely in advance.

This being said, it is also true that drawing media—like pencil, charcoal, pastel, ink or gouache—have characteristic material qualities of their own which may themselves suggest visual properties for the work. The importance of draw- ing for sculpture is often overlooked in the emphasis on three-dimensional form, but the sculptor's range can extend to cover the materials of both painting and sculpture, giving a very broad area of visual expression to be explored.

MAQUETTES

Drawing alone may be inadequate as a prep- aration for sculpture, since the crucial question is what the work will look like in a solid form, in real space and from all viewpoints. A useful way of checking the balance and volume of a sculpture is to make a small-scale model in which all the ideas for the larger work can be tried and tested. This is known as a maquette. It is a traditional aspect of carving and modeling work and, with drawing, has historically served the purpose of demonstrating the sculpture not only to the artist, but also to the patron who may have commis- sioned the work. In modern techniques of con- struction, the practice is not always suitable, since the forms are often arrived at through work in progress, suggested by the shape, texture and scale of each component piece. The ideas may be developed in small-scale sculptures which are important works in their own right.

Clay, wax or plaster can be used to make a maquette for a carved or modeled sculpture. A maquette can be scaled up mechanically to match a stone block by a technique known as pointing. This involves taking careful measurements of the forms and transferring the proportions to the stone via a metal structure with adjustable arms. This does not always produce a good result, since the large work may be a dull copy of the model, exhibiting no real relationship between the carver and the material.

The emphasis on direct engagement with ma- terials, which has been a feature of twentieth century art, somewhat outmoded this academic tradition. Nevertheless, it may provide the means of understanding a form more completely than is possible in drawing, without the danger of wast- ing expensive materials.

The studio This diagram (**left**) shows a possible layout for a sculptor's studio. Important factors in working out the design for a studio or working space are good light (both natural and artificial), good ventilation to expel gases and fumes, as much working surface as possible, a well as clear floor space for working on large-scale pieces and for ease of movement and safety. It is also vital to have a sink and running water near at hand as well as large bins for trash. Storage is another major consideration. You should try to keep the studio as tidy as possible, even though sculpture tends to produce large amounts of trash. It is also vital that different types of material ar kept apart. For example, clay should be kept well away from chips of stone. Plaster, which needs to be kept dry, must be stored away from clay which has to be damp. Tools should be kept tidy to prevent them from being damaged. Safety factors should also be considered. These vary according to the materials used, but a good fir extinguisher is always essential.

Natural light

Large cupboard

Spotlight

Racks and shelves for materials and tools

Floor space kept clear

Fire extinguisher

Pin board

Extractor fan

Ventilation

Drawers for stora

Cupboards for stora

Artificial lig

Strong flo

Working surfa

Natural lig

Extension le

Si

Large airtight container for cl

Large doors for transporting large piec

THE STUDIO

The social role of the sculptor has changed considerably over the centuries, and, in addition, the conditions in which sculpture is produced have also changed. Medieval and Renaissance sculptors worked closely with other craftsmen, and the links between sculpture and architecture were particularly strong in church building and decoration. The workstore was a busy place, where apprentices helped to carry out the more mundane aspects of the physical work, while the master sculptor added refinements of form and detail. In the Renaissance, secular patronage from a ruling elite at first widened the scope for grandiose sculptural projects. However, developments in trade and commerce and subsequent urban development caused gradual social changes, which ultimately stifled many opportunities for sculptors. Sculpture has never found much of a home in small-scale domestic interiors, and, during the nineteenth and twentieth centuries, the sculptor has been gradually forced into isolation, depending upon an audience created through public and private galleries and relatively few commissioned civic projects. Many contemporary sculptors must continue to work without immediate benefits from exhibitions or sales. Studio space is vital, and, since a well-equipped, large workstore may not be an economic reality, the next best environment must be found.

PRACTICAL STUDIO REQUIREMENTS

A garage, loft, basement, spare room or disused warehouse can be equipped to form a suitable studio space. The basic necessities are good lighting, storage space for tools, materials and finished work, and access to running water for cleaning and mixing.

The ideal studio for large-scale work would be at ground floor level, with large doors to give easy access, a strong, solid floor and equipment for lifting and moving heavy weights. More realistically, the architecture of a room or basement will probably restrict the scale of work and possibly even the type of materials which can be used.

Sculptural processes involving solid materials inevitably make some mess, whether fine dust from cutting plastics, crumbly chips of stone, wood shavings, drips of plaster or the clutter of raw materials gathered for a construction. Different activities must be segregated or the materials may be spoiled. Fragments of stone or plaster, for instance, must be kept away from an area where fresh clay is modeled or stored. Used materials, which cannot be recycled, need not be kept lying around. Fresh materials must be stored in the proper conditions—wood or plaster, for example, can be ruined by damp, whereas clay must be kept moist.

Tools and equipment stored tidily on shelves or in a cupboard are more likely to stay in prime condition and can be found quickly when needed. Sharp tools should be kept well out of the way when not in use, in wall racks or a cupboard. This is for safety reasons, and to avoid blunting them with unnecessary wear. If a jumble of materials is kept in a studio for construction work, valuable tools may be easily mislaid.

A heavy wooden bench or table is very useful for most types of work. According to the materials being used, a modeling stand, a banker or a well-supported plastic or metal worktop may be additional necessities. Each material has characteristic properties which dictate the range of equipment needed, so the studio can either be made into a versatile workstore with a place for everything, or specially equipped for a particular medium.

Good, general lighting is a minimum requirement, and can be supplemented with spotlights if a particularly strong, angled beam is needed. The studio should be well ventilated whatever the type of work, but some materials, such as glass fiber resin, give off extremely unpleasant fumes and an efficient extractor is essential. Electric wall sockets, conveniently placed, are also vital if power tools are used frequently. An extension lead is a useful item, but wires which trail across a room are a hazard, and the lead should be coiled when not in use.

Particular safety requirements, as for resin or electrical equipment, must be carefully noted and observed. The same basic safety precautions must be taken in a studio as in any home or place of work, with due reference to the tools, equipment and processes used in the area.

Below This picture shows the artist Henry Moore at work in his studio. He is working on *Interlocking No 10*, a two piece sculpture. He is using plaster and has a variety of tools at hand – riffler, brush and an ordinary household grater.

CLAY

Above This Sumerian clay sculpture dates from between 2750 BC and 2600 BC. It was discovered in a temple at Nippur in Iraq. The image and the modeling techniques are fairly simple, although the image is, nevertheless, expressive. It is noticeable that more attention was devoted to the heads and faces than to the lower part of the work.

Above right This figure of a recumbent man was modeled by the sixteenth century Italian artist Vicenzo Danti. The marks of the modeling tools can be detected on the surface. The hair and face are quite well developed. Contrasting techniques have been used on the hair, flesh and drapery. Danti worked for most of his career in Florence.

HISTORY

Clays, in common with materials for carving, have been used for sculptures since earliest times. Most cultures have adopted pottery techniques for making sculptures. Sculptural objects are usually made up hollow from coils, slabs or tubes of clay which are then fired. Sometimes the outside surfaces are decorated either with clay modeling or by colors and glazes. Clay sculptures have also been formed by the technique of press-molding, in which fresh clay is pressed into previously fired clay molds. Whichever technique is used, the final material of the work is clay, and objects modeled in this way are referred to as 'terracotta' work. This term means 'baked clay'.

As early as the third century BC, the Greeks made their now famous Tanagra press-molded terracotta figurines, which they painted with non-ceramic colors. In the Tang Dynasty (AD 61 906), the Chinese made decorated and glaz press-molded terracottas, whose excellence ow a great deal to the qualities peculiar to t ceramic techniques of their time and place. T potters of Pre-Columbian America, before t sixteenth century, and those in China and Gree made terracotta vessels or sculptures often corating them with non-ceramic colors. In t fifteenth century, the Italian della Robbia fam revived the use of press-molding to create dec rated and glazed sculptures. However, the m eloquent and successful sculptures, like the p trait of Giuliano by Andrea Verrochio (c 143 1488), does not depend on great technical soph tication for its effectiveness. Even though t portrait may not have been possible without t Tuscan knowledge of earthenware, it is not e bedded in the potter's practices with clay a glazes in the same way as, for example, Ta sculpture was.

Right This is one of the 7000 life size terracotta warriors found in the excavations at Mount Li of the mausoleum of the First Emperor of Ch'in. The figures were made in about 200 BC. The heavy clay found in the region of Mount Li enabled life size portraits to be made, and a striking feature is that no two warriors have the same face. More standardization is evident in the making of the torso, where molds were probably used. Individual details were probably sculpted in afterwards, and the final statue brightly painted.

During the early Renaissance in Europe a new emphasis on visual naturalism developed. Bronze casting technology was revived. This, in turn, changed the way in which clay was used. It now became a transitional medium and no longer the end product of sculptures. It was used to model sculptures, which would later be cast in another medium like metal and, in more recent times, concrete or plastic resins. It was also used to make molds for ceramic press-moldings or simply as a material for preliminary studies. This second tradition of clay sculpture ran parallel with that of terracotta.

The sculptures made by contemporary sculptors who have used clay as a transitional medium, like the Italian Giacomo Manzù (born 1908), owe much of their liveliness in bronze to the qualities of clay, but nothing at all to ceramic technique. However, there are signs that sculptors are beginning to use ceramic techniques once again in new and creative ways.

Reconditioning clay 1.
Unfired clay is broken down into pieces and dropped into a shallow bath of water. From time to time, it is stirred around until it absorbs water and softens to a thick sludge.

2. It is then scooped out onto plaster bats which absorb excess moisture.

Storing clay Keep clay in a large trashcan, covered with a damp sack and plastic. Keep the bin airtight with a well fitting lid.

2

Keeping work damp 1. If the model is left overnight or for any long period during the work, spray it with water.

2. Wrap a damp towel around the model, taking care not to damage the modeling work already done.

3. Cover the whole thing in a large plastic bag and tie it tight around the base. This will keep the clay workable.

3

CLAY AS A TRANSITIONAL MEDIUM

In this way of using clay, the sculpture is treated just as if it were to be the final object. However, after the modeling is completed, it is used as the source for molds of different types, depending on whether the final object is to be a casting in metal, concrete, plastic resins, press-molded in terracotta, or a plaster cast. The clay is never allowed to dry out, and when mold-making is completed, it is stripped away from the internal supports, reconditioned and stored for reuse.

MATERIALS

Clay is one of the most commonly available materials, and if you happen to have access to deposits of suitable clay, you could dig your own. But few naturally occurring deposits yield clays that are sufficiently uniform, plastic and fine textured for sculpture purposes, so most sculptors buy the cheaper varieties of clay sold by pottery suppliers. Clays can be smooth or rough, depending on whether or not the clay contains sand and grog—clay that has been fired and ground up. For modeling rather than ceramic purposes, the choice is largely a matter of personal preference. The smoother varieties are better for small, finely detailed work, but grogged clays are easier to reprocess, because of their greater porosity, and have a ruggedness and resistance in handling that the smooth clays lack.

Clays are most conveniently bought already mixed, rather than as dry powder, and, since they are usually sold in plastic bags, they can be bought in any quantity and stored for long periods provided the bags remain airtight. Most sculptors use large galvanized bins with improvised airtight covers to store large quantities of clay for immediate use. Since these can be very heavy when full, it is useful to have them on small, wheeled dollies or trucks for mobility. A separate bin should be kept for clay which is being reconditioned. To recondition clay, chop or break it into small lumps and wet it down.

Modeling clay in optimum condition should be sufficiently plastic to be modeled easily, but not so wet that it becomes sticky. To maintain clay in this condition, a plaster of Paris slab of the sort made and used by potters for wedging (kneading) clay is best. These slabs or bats usually measure about $20 \times 20 \times 4$in $(50 \times 50 \times 10$cm). When dry, the porosity of the bat will soon dry out any over-wet clay which is kneaded and left in contact with the bat. Bats are also useful for kneading clay to which plenty of water has been added to make it more plastic, since the wet clay will not stick to the plaster for long. Bats are best supported on strips of wood, 2–3in (5–7.5cm) above the surface they rest on, so that air can circulate.

Modeling stands, important for working with clay, come in a variety of sizes and shapes. They normally consist of a turntable or a top which can be rotated. The heavier tripod types sometimes incorporate a means of using the platform at an angle for small relief work, and the tops are adjustable for height. For larger, heavier work, fixed-height turntables called bankers are used.

The easiest way to maintain the dampness of clay during periods of working is by using a household water sprayer. Between sessions, the sculpture should be draped with a damp towel and wrapped securely in plastic sheeting.

Back iron for quarter life-size figure The construction of this back iron is similar to the larger one but it is small enough to be used on a tripod.

Back iron for life-size figure A large support such as this must be firmly screwed down on a heavy wood base. As it will take some time to model the figure, the stand may be mounted on wheels and moved around.

Tripods These modeling stands can be adjusted in height and have rotating heads on which the baseboard of the model is fixed. The head of the tripod shown on the right can also be tipped at an angle for work on relief modeling.

Banker The banker is sturdier than a tripod. Again the top rotates, allowing access to the whole work.

ARMATURES

There are few hard and fast rules for making armatures, since their configuration must vary with the job in hand. The simplest type is that used for heads or busts, called a bust peg. Another simple armature is the sort used for modeling reliefs. It need only consist of a rigid board studded with round-headed galvanized nails driven a short way in. For larger reliefs, it is advisable to provide a grid of galvanized wire running from the top of one nail to the top of another, giving more support to the additional weight of clay.

Most figure armatures are based on similar principles, and the larger the work, the sturdier the metal supports must be. These armatures usually have a strong, rigid wooden base, somewhat larger than the area to be occupied by the sculpture. The base is battened on two opposite sides of its bottom surface to make it easy to handle, and, if appropriate, the battens are spaced so that the base fits snugly over the top of a modeling stand. This base is the foundation onto which 'back irons', cranked, mild steel bars furnished with flanges, are screwed or bolted. This main support must be sturdy enough to

remain perfectly rigid after all the clay has been added. Further main sections of armature can be made either from screwed piping or welded steel. The advantage of the pipework type is that it can be dismantled from inside a waste mold, providing the threads are packed with heavy grease before the clay is added, but the welded type can sometimes be more convenient, and is more easily adapted to follow the center of the modeled forms.

Fastened to the main support are secondary supports, which can be made of flexible materials. Most commonly used is square-section aluminum wire, which is available in various sizes. Secondary supports must be fixed to the main irons as firmly as possible, since armature pieces that rotate around one another are useless. The extremities of the supports should be fixed down wherever possible to avoid whipping and to give firm support to the clay.

In designing armatures, there is no real substitute for experience and common sense. After a while you develop an intuitive sense of where strength or flexibility will be needed for making a sculpture.

In the case of large sculptures, one of the functions of the armature is to provide a skeleton onto which bulking materials can be securely wired. These can be blocks of wood, polystyrene foam, or any suitable non-absorbent material such as cork. To help the clay to stick to these materials, the surface can be studded with galvanized nails or enclosed in a layer of chicken wire. A useful device for supporting the weight of clay between major armature members is called a butterfly. This is a small X-shaped object, usually made by crossing and binding two short wooden laths. The butterfly is suspended by a wire from the nearest point of the armature. Because of the tendency of clay to sag, it is helpful, when working on a large scale, to start in the center of the form with clay which is slightly harder than usual, and build up to the outer layers with progressively softer clay.

Learning to model with clay can be difficult and frustrating, as the clay has no resistant form of its own, and because its tendency to sag can lead to distortions. Its very responsiveness can yield spontaneous and delightful effects which may turn out to be irrelevant for your purposes. Thus it is vital to get to know the material, to gain experience in the ability to work out clear sculptural forms, to find out when to exert control and when to exploit the happy accident. One of the keys to developing control of clay is the practise of building outward from the armature with fairly definitely shaped rolls, strips or blocks of clay, working outward toward the final surface gradually and all over.

Relief modeling A special armature is needed for relief work. Drive round-headed nails into a wooden board at regular intervals. If the work is quite large, link the nails with wire to support the weight of clay.

The armature provides a rigid skeletal structure inside a modeled sculpture. It should follow the main axes of the sculpture and is especially crucial if there are projections of the form which are otherwise unsupported. Twisted wire forms the basic lines of the armature and the component parts must be securely bound at the joints so they cannot slip. If a particularly heavy weight of clay is to be applied, the structure is bulked out with blocks of wood or polystyrene, bound to the wire. The armature should be firmly fixed to a heavy wooden baseboard so that it cannot topple over.

Construction of an Armature 1. Pieces of square-section aluminum wire are bent into shape and bound together with galvanized steel wire.

2. The armature is secured to a back iron for support, again tied tightly with wire.

3. The bottom of the armature should be anchored to the base with nails hammered in and bent over the aluminum.

4. Small detailed shapes, such as hands, are constructed in wire and bound to the main armature.

5. To reduce the weight of clay, the armature is bulked out with wood which should support long sections but leave the joints free.

TOOLS

The main tools used for modeling are hands and fingers, and try to think of other modeling tools as specialized extensions of them. In selecting or making tools, a good rule is the fewer and simpler the better. A good assortment would consist of paddles or blocks for consolidating large masses, a variety of simply shaped wooden or metal modeling tools, and wire loop-ended tools. A useful cutting tool for dividing large lumps of clay can be made by twisting two strands of fine brass wire together and fastening a short stick or dowel to each end of the resulting 'wedging' wire. Most modeling is done with wooden tools, but metal ones can give a distinctly different quality. Metal tools are usually made of mild steel. The best wooden tools are made of boxwood or holly, but many sculptors make their own from any compact, fine-grained hardwood—particularly apple, pear or other fruit-woods. Experiment with wood and metal tools will show which suits your needs.

TECHNIQUES

Modeling is a complementary procedure to carving. Instead of removing stone or wood from the block in order to arrive at the sculpture's surface, the modeler works toward the surface from the core. The responsive nature of clay encourages a degree of flexibility in the sculptor's thinking that is not always possible in carving. But, whether modeling or carving, the work demands that the sculptor has a fairly definite concept in mind before beginning work on the final object. The degree of comfortable certainty will vary among sculptors, and the nature of the sculptural idea is usually the result of preliminary drawings, maquettes and studies on a smaller scale. When used on a large scale, clay needs good internal supports, which can put broad limits on the range of

Tools for clay modeling Remember that modeling tools should be thought of as extensions of the hands and fingers. The effects produced by many of the tools pictured here closely resemble those which can be made by different parts of the human hand—finger tips, palms or the sides of the hands, for example. Tools come in a variety of sizes and shapes and most of them are made of wood, usually boxwood or holly (**7**). Plastic tools (**4**) are also available and are certainly valuable for the beginner.

The variety of tools to be found in craft stores can be overwhelming, so remember the principle that, in selecting or buying tools, the fewer and simpler the better. Experiment with as many tools as you can until you discover which best suit your personal needs. A sturdy baseboard (**6**), usually made of plywood or a similar material, is an essential for everyone— amateur or professional. It must be sealed to prevent water absorption. Purpose-made tools are not always preferable to items which

you can probably find around the house. A rolling pin (**I**), wooden spoons (**2**), a plant spray (**3**)—vital for maintaining the moisture of the clay—kitchen knives (**10**), a penknife (**12**) and a plumb-line (**5**) will all prove to be invaluable. Broken hacksaw blades (**11**) are often used to create flat areas and as cross-scrapers to remove indentations. For measuring you will need a tape measure, as well as outside calipers (**8**) and inside calipers (**9**) for calculating exterior and interior measurements.

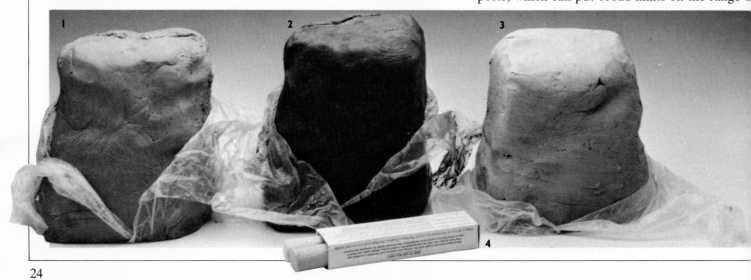

exibility in the sculptor's thinking. It is possible, f course, to make a major change at some point uring the final work, but this might mean ismantling the sculpture, altering the armature nd beginning again—an uneconomic procedure.

In developing toward the final surfaces, the nportance of good lighting cannot be overstated. oth a good general level of lighting and port-ble, directional light sources are needed. The arying play of light over modeled surfaces has nportant effects on how the form is perceived, nd work in progress should be studied frequently nder different lighting conditions. Lighting con-itions are particularly crucial in the way relief culpture is perceived, and, for this reason, any elief modeling must always be done, as nearly as ossible, with the clay in the same relationship to e eye as in the final siting.

How the final qualities of form and surface are eated is a matter to be resolved by experience. owever, there are some important factors to ear in mind. Firstly it is useful to have a nowledge of and, where possible, first-hand cquaintance with as many examples as possible f what has already been achieved. Secondly, it is nportant to consider the particular qualities of e underlying form and what seems most appro-riate to reveal them at the surface. The visual aditions and uses of the material in which the culpture will be cast should also be considered. further important factor is what is appropriate oth to the subject and to the sculptor's percep-ons of it as these emerge in the working process. bove all, the artist should always use new ossibilities as they emerge during the develop-ent of specific works or sculptural interests.

In a sense, clay used as a transitional material ontains few particular instructions or guides to ow it should be used, apart from those men-oned. However, the sculptor should constantly ear in mind the qualities of the material of the nal cast—whether bronze, lead, or plastic resins.

ypes of clay The type of ay (**left**) chosen for odeling depends upon the ture of the finished work. When clay is used as a ansitional medium, in a odel which is to be cast in a ore durable material, a gray ay body (**1**) or natural clay) may be used. It should be a suitable texture and asticity to be worked into e required form. A model in rracotta (**2**), a dark red clay, finished by firing, and it is nportant to keep the clay ee of impurities. Sticks or ocks of modeling clay which rden without firing (**4**) are so available.

Right Arturo Martini's *Clair de Lune* was made in 1932. It is an example of terracotta modeling and shows how Martini tried to recreate aspects of classical art in a modern idiom. The figures convey an impression of stillness and calm. Martini was trained as a goldsmith and a potter before he took up sculpture in 1906. In 1945, shortly before his death in 1947, he gave up sculpture in favor of painting. He felt that sculpture was no longer a living medium.

Modeling with clay 1.
Construct a suitable armature for the model. Here a bust peg with central butterfly is used.

2. Build out the armature with large lumps of clay pressing firmly around the stem and filling in the rounded head.

3. Give the model volume and basic form by patting on thick rolls of clay, rounding out the shape.

4. Work over the surface with your fingers drawing the clay rolls together into a single mass.

5. Continue to rough out the model with your fingers before adding detail. Develop the rhythm and contour of the form.

6. Add more clay to the surface and start to define features on the head and face.

7. Use a modeling tool to work into the shapes of eyes, nose and mouth, adjusting the forms by scraping off or adding clay.

8. Work the model to a stage where a basic representation of the subject is achieved.

10. Work continuously over the whole form, adding detail to the portrait and bringing up the characteristic lines and shapes.

11. Develop details of clothing or drapery by patting on small rolls of clay and modeling them into the broader shapes.

12. Add small dabs of clay and model them into the surface. Keep the texture active without losing coherence in the form.

TECHNIQUES

Solid forms A heavily grogged clay body can be made into a sculpture which can be fired solid without hollowing out, provided that adequate time is allowed for the drying process and firing is carried out very slowly. The drawbacks are the weight of the sculpture and the long drying time. But the real hazard is the danger of cracking, and the greater the contrast between thicker and thinner forms, the more likely it is that the clay will crack in the drying process. As a general rule then, terracotta sculpture should be made as uniform in thickness as possible.

Another rule is that the clay should contain as few air pockets as possible, particularly in the case of smooth-textured clays. For this reason, and also to ensure that all the clay to be used for the sculpture is of about the same consistency, it is necessary to wedge or knead the clay in the way that potters do, using a plaster bat as a kneading surface.

Hollow forms A form with a large, flat bottom surface can be modeled directly and later hollowed out with a wire-loop tool when the clay has nearly reached the leather-hard stage and can be handled safely without distortion. Other forms can be prepared by forming a slab of clay over

9. Draw into the clay surface with a modeling tool to develop texture in the hair.

Observe the subject closely as you work.

13. There are no hard and fast rules in clay modeling. The skills are best acquired with practice, adapting techniques to suit the final result you wish to achieve.

ound of sand and later joining the slabs together ith clay slip. Slip is made by mixing powdered ay with water until it reaches a thick soup-like onsistency. Another method is to model directly ver a simply shaped armature, and, when the ay is leather-hard, cut it into sections with a edging wire and carefully remove from the rmature. The armature must be designed with is in mind, so that the clay is not trapped on gid projections. Since some shrinkage will occur etween the completion of modeling and the time hen the clay is leather-hard, a rigid armature ould be bulked out with a soft material such as ewspaper, which is easy for the clay to compress ghtly as it shrinks. After the sculpture has been it and removed from the armature, the pieces e reassembled after roughening the surfaces to e joined and painting them with slip. The ulpture is wrapped up to protect it from drying ut any further until the moisture from the slip as equalized with the general condition of the st of the clay, after which drying can continue irly rapidly. Any walls which enclose a cavity ust be perforated to allow the air inside to xpand during firing without damaging the sculp- re. The thickness of the final walls can vary om ¼in (6mm) to 1in (2.5cm) or more, depend- g on the size of the sculpture and the coarseness f the body. But the sculptor must bear in mind

Left Isamu Noguchi's *Even the Centipede* (1952) consists of 11 pieces of Kasama ware, each approximately 18in (46cm) wide, mounted on a wooden pole 14 feet (4.25 meters) high. It demonstrates Noguchi's individual contribution to the world of sculpture. Although born and trained in America, he spent his childhood in Japan, and this combination of influences gives a special quality to his work, which, as well as sculpture, includes theater and costume design, garden plans and playgrounds. For Noguchi the essence of sculpture is 'the perception of space'.

Hollow modeling

Working with a hollow form is more satisfactory than modeling solid, especially where the work is so large that drying out would take too long or cause cracking. Hollow forms can be made directly and hollowed out when the work is leather-hard. Other methods include forming a slab of clay over a bed of sand or using a simple armature.

Hollow building 1. Wedge the clay thoroughly on a plaster bat or flat work surface covered with clean hessian or canvas.

2. Draw out the kneaded clay into a long, thick roll.

3. Place the roll on the hessian and hit it with the side of the hand along the length to flatten it out.

4. Work over the clay with a rolling pin to even out the thickness.

5. Guide the rolling pin over the wood battens placed either side of the clay. This ensures even depth to the rolled clay.

6. Pick up the clay pancake at one end and turn it over. Use the rolling pin again.

7. Cut the clay with a sharp knife guided along a straight-edge. Make pieces of suitable size for the intended sculpture.

8. Curl the sheet of clay around to form a hollow tube, and model along the edges to form a seam.

9. Hold the tube upright and draw it down with your other hand to narrow and lengthen it into the required shape.

10. Make all the sections needed for the work in the same way and leave them to dry out on a bed of grog until they are leather-hard.

11. Hold the pieces in place and make marks on the clay with a knife to locate the joints.

12. Roughen the clay surface by scoring with a knife. This provides a key for adhesion in the joint.

13. Roughen all the other surfaces which form faces of the joint. A plastic comb is useful for this.

14. Paint clay slip over the roughened surfaces. This acts as an adhesive on the clay.

15. Lay a small roll of clay along the marked joint. This can be used to model around the seam lines.

16. Press the preformed shapes into place and smooth clay over the joint to secure the sections.

17. Use a modeling tool to work into spaces inaccessible to the fingers. Seal all cracks at the seams.

18. Fit all the pieces together in the same way to construct the basic shape of the model.

at uniform wall thickness is the key to minimiz-
g the stresses that are set up in the clay during
rying and firing.

Another important factor in working with
ollow forms is timing. The clay must be kept in
e optimum condition of dampness for each
age of work, and no part of the sculpture should
e allowed to dry out to the leather-hard stage
efore any other. Working with quite large forms
ay prove to be an exception, as it may be
cessary to start at the bottom and build up-
ards in stages. In this case, the lower sections
ust be allowed to dry enough to support the
eight of the next stage or section, but not so
uch that joints might become insecure from too
eat a difference in moisture content. If cracking
curs at the leather-hard stage it can seldom be
paired successfully. A lower section can be
lowed to dry out slightly without danger, if the
p edge is kept damp with wet paper or cloths.

Hollow sculptures are usually worked and fired
a a bed of sand or grog, so that the form can
ntract freely on its base or kiln shelf. From the
mpletion of shaping through drying and firing,
terracotta will have shrunk by about 10 per cent.
size is critical, this will have to be allowed for by
orking on a slightly larger scale from the outset.
the sculpture is fairly large and is likely to be
vkward to move or handle before firing, it can
worked on a grogged kiln shelf and placed
rectly into the kiln after drying.

In addition to the armature method, the main
chniques for making ceramic sculpture are the
same as those used by potters: building a form
with coils or slabs; press-molding; slip-casting (for
quantity production); and throwing on the potter's wheel, all of which are covered in the section
on pottery (pp 32–53). Each technique has its
own particularly rich possibilities and vocabulary
of forms.

There are some limitations on the size of
terracotta sculptures which should be borne in
mind. The problem of portability for firing can
sometimes be circumvented by building a temporary kiln around the sculpture, if the time and
effort are warranted. However, the size of available kilns should always be considered. This need
not really be a limitation, providing that the
sculpture is cut into sections at the leather-hard
stage. Since the sections will then shrink and
distort independently, a slight mismatching of
form along the joints must be taken into account.
Another consideration is that, after firing, the
rejoining will have to be done using adhesives or
cement grouts, and this too must be taken into
account, since such joints will almost always be
visible.

There is one important aspect of ceramic technique which is not often mentioned in relation to
sculpture. It is in the nature of clay-working and
ceramics that objects are made in quantity, and
rejects are common. The lesson for the sculptor is
clear: until you know the medium well through
personal experience, it is a good idea to make
more than one of a sculpture, or at least several
variations on a theme.

TERRACOTTA

The term terracotta simply means baked clay and is used by most sculptors to mean any sculpture in which clay is used as a final material, which is fired to achieve permanence. There is also a more specialized usage, where terracotta specifically means fired clay sculpture, characteristically made in red earthenware bodies, which are comparatively soft and usually not fired to over 2332°F (1277°C). Today, however, much ceramic sculpture is also made in stoneware clays. These are harder and typically lighter in color, sometimes as light as pale buff, and fired at temperatures which are much higher. Pure white porcelain clays and bone chinas are also used by a small number of specialists. The technical scope of ceramic sculpture can be as vast as the ceramics field itself, whether in the matter of shaping techniques, surface treatments, colorings, glazes or firing methods, and anyone approaching it from a sculptor's viewpoint is well advised either to cultivate the friendship of an experienced potter, or to take the time to become one.

The workplace in which clay is to be worked and fired must be kept very clean, as must the clays, tools and materials. Any foreign materials, especially plaster, must be stored and used elsewhere. If any bits of plaster are present in a clay sculpture during firing, they will cause small explosions of steam, which will mar or destroy the work, and can even damage the kiln.

MATERIALS

The clays available for terracotta sculpture are the same as for pottery, ranging from the red earthenwares through the salmon or pinkish mid-temperature clays to the paler, toast-colored or buff stoneware bodies. The texture of any of these can be varied by the addition of sand and grog up to about 25 per cent, and this has the effect of reducing the amount of shrinkage and warping that all clay undergoes during drying out and firing. If a coarse texture is not desired, however, some increase in the stability of even a very smooth clay can be obtained by wedging in some sand or grog, which has been passed through a fine sieve. Although this will reduce the plasticity of the clay somewhat, it need not necessarily increase its roughness. Beyond this, the technically minded might become interested in the enormous range of possible colors and textures that can be produced by adding special texturing materials and coloring oxides.

Ceramic materials and techniques, of all those available for sculpture, provide probably the most varied and wide-ranging field of artistic pos-sibilities. However, simplicity and directne should be the sculptor's aims until enough exper ence of the technical possibilities for any immed ate sculptural purposes has been achieved.

In beginning, it is wise to choose either smooth or textured earthenware body, sometim called earthenware sculpture clay, or a texture stoneware body, called a 'crank mixture'. T choice may depend less on individual preferenc which should always be determined by looking fired samples, than on the type of firing faciliti available. Clays should normally be fired to the correct maturing, or vitrifying, temperatures, a some kilns are designed for higher operati temperatures than others. The two fundamental different types are oxidizing and reducing kiln and each has characteristic effects on the color fired clays and glazes.

Right This picture shows the fired model. It is considerably lighter in color than the unfired clay. It is important to fire the clay at the right temperature. It is very important to check the type of kiln and the temperatures to which it operates before firing any work.

Following a terracotta model 1. The armature used for this model was padded with newspaper to reduce the weight of clay.

2. Model the form in the usual way. When the model is leather-hard, cut it loose from the base with a long knife.

3. Mark a seam line over the model and cut it into sections, preferably two. Pull them away from the armature.

4. Hollow out inside the form with a wire-loop tool. The clay must be firm but not too dry.

5. Work on each part of the model in this way, leaving even clay walls of about 1–1½in (2.5–3.8cm) in thickness.

6. Roughen the seam lines with a comb or knife, and paint them with clay slip.

Place the sections of the model on a bed of grog and press them together, matching the seams exactly.

8. Wipe away surplus slip and model fresh clay over the seam to conceal it.

9. Once the seams are covered, finish the model to its original state. It is now ready for firing.

POTTERY AND CERAMICS

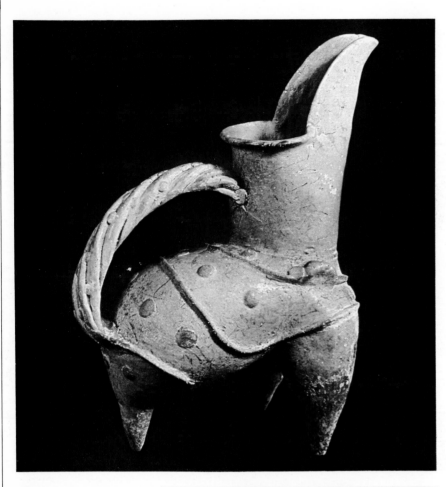

Above This earthenware tripod jug dates from the second or third millenium BC. The handle is made from twisted strips of clay. The other decoration is simple, consisting of raised strips or circles of clay. Pottery has been a popular craft since earliest times, and there are many fascinating traditions from all over the world. The development of glazes and kilns around 4000 BC made it possible to create durable, glazed ceramic vessels.

HISTORY

Pottery is one of the oldest and most widely practiced crafts; it is unique and exciting. It is a tradition that has come through time with man and ranges from the purely ornate to the truly functional. Clay has unique characteristics and the beginner needs to understand some of these to be able to work with the clay intelligently. The term ceramics covers pottery and anything made from clay which has been hardened by firing.

Clay in its fired state is fragile and easily broken, yet is imperishable and it does not corrode or rot. For this reason, ceramic artefacts remain as a continuous record of man's development from earliest times. The museums of today are full of ceramic objects showing a rich profusion of styles and techniques.

The earliest ceramic objects date back to 6000 BC. These were no more than modeled clay images of men and animals baked hard in the sun and probably used for magical or religious purposes. Clay occurs over most of the earth's surface and many different societies possessed the basic knowledge and techniques needed to use it. It is not known when man first discovered that,

when clay was fired, it became permanent an durable, but it is thought that man's involvemen with fire and its maintenance helped, perhaps b accident. Pottery making developed when ma stopped the wandering nomadic life of a hunte and started to cultivate and farm. This explain why the parts of the world that first develope identifiable social patterns, such as Egypt, Indi China and the Middle East, should be place where the earliest known ceramics come from.

Around 4000 BC potters in these countri developed kilns which allowed them to produ high quality pottery with glazed surfaces. Th coincided with the development of metal smel ing. Even at this early date, the practice borrowing forms and decoration from oth media was common, and, as early bronzes wei rarer and more valuable than pottery, it was on natural that they were copied. As pottery d veloped into an industry, trading contacts i creased and so helped spread new ideas ai techniques rapidly. The rise of warfare betwee nations played a role in this too.

When Greece became a new center of pow and wealth, pottery forms produced were classic and owed little to the natural quality of clay b more to aesthetic ideals. The subject matter f decoration was superb illustrations of warrior gods and classical myths, carried out in a sty called *terra sigillata*, which involves applyii colored slip—liquid clay—over the ware ai scratching the design through from the bas Later the Romans, much influenced by Greek a and culture, helped to change the simple potte of Europe to a more sophisticated style ai quality. When the Roman Empire collapse much of the technology they had introduc lapsed.

China also possessed a long, unbroken tr dition in ceramics. But the Chinese found enjo ment in the spiritual rather than the physical, ai this quality is evident in much of their potter The Chinese also buried ceramic models ai vessels with their dead—the figures and anim: which date from the Tang period (AD 618–90 and Sung period (AD 960–1279) are renowne for their excellence and demonstration of supe skills and techniques. China's greatest sing contribution to the advancement of the craft is more purely technical feat—the invention white translucent porcelain probably during tl Tang dynasty.

The spread of Islam from the seventh centu marked a new phase in the cultures and arts Asia, North Africa and parts of Europe. pottery, Islam readily accepted the traditions ai techniques of Near Eastern potters. Howeve trade and cultural contacts with China provid influences that can be seen in the ceramics of bo ltures, one being the use of copper-blue to corate ceramic wares. Persian influence was ident in Spain due to the invading Moors from orth Africa. It was through Spain that the Near stern techniques passed on to the European tters, tin glaze being one technique, which, gether with enamel painted decoration (in Italy led 'majolica'), was to dominate European ramics until the eighteenth century.

Around the end of the fourteenth century other significant technical innovation took ace in Europe—the discovery and development saltglaze stonewares in Germany. This process volves throwing salt into a kiln during firing. e salt combines with chemicals in the clay body form a glaze. The process is little used today r safety reasons. This is particularly because it oduces dangerous fumes.

Above The development of ceramics in the Near East was greatly boosted by the spread of Islam after the seventh century. This charming figure of a bull (**left**) was made in Syria around AD 1200. Persia had several important ceramic centers. This earthenware bowl (**right**) dates from around AD 1000, and comes from Nishapur in eastern Persia. The geometric design and decoration with various colors of slip are typical for the culture and period.

Left The invention of the potter's wheel—probably in Mesopotamia between 3000 BC and 4000 BC— determined many of the potter's working practices for centuries after. This eighteenth century engraving by Thomas Bewick shows a potter's workshop. The wheel is being turned by the craftsman's foot.

Top This jar is an example of Chinese Yueh ware, dating from between the third and sixth centuries AD. It has a stoneware body and a celadon glaze. This important type of Chinese glaze has a greenish color. This is caused by iron which colors the glaze during firing.

Above Pottery developed in the Americas isolated from any of the influences which have characterized Western and Eastern ceramics. This jar, showing a seated man with beads around his neck, is an example of early Mexican orangeware.

Right Staffordshire saltglaze ware was extremely popular in the eighteenth and early nineteenth centuries. Thanks to the use of molds, many ornate and unusual shapes could be made. This lively, colorful bear jug is an early nineteenth century example. It has overglazed, enamel-painted decoration.

In the seventeenth century large quantities of Chinese porcelain were imported into Europe. The search for a match for this white clay body was to prove to be a great stimulus to innovation and technical advancement in the production of European ceramic wares.

Social and economic conditions began to change rapidly in the middle of the eighteenth century. The population expanded and demands for mass-produced products increased. In Britain the development was brought about by individuals, often sponsored by dukes or royalty. In this way Josiah Wedgwood (1730–1795) and his contemporaries helped to develop the manufacture of ceramics. These processes remain broadly similar today.

Far left This distinctively shaped vase is an example of Chinese Sung Lung ware. Toward the end of the Sung dynasty, invasions from the north by Tartars forced the Emperor to move south. This meant that the town of Lung Chuan became the center of the production of celadon ware. Much Lung Chuan ware was mass produced, the lower quality articles being reserved for the export market.

Left This colorful ceramic jar is an example of Russian eighteenth century pottery. It has simple, stylized figurative decoration.

Below Willow pattern is one of the best known patterns on domestic china. It dates from around 1819 and became popular because the pattern could be transfer printed. This meant that the decoration process was both quicker and cheaper, and so the ware was accessible to a very large number of people. The process of transfer printing was a great success commercially in the nineteenth century. Willow pattern china has been made by many manufacturers, this example comes from Wedgwood.

MATERIALS

Clay is a material difficult to define accurately, a all clays are mixtures of minerals. In genera terms, clay is the natural result of the decompos tion of granite and igneous rocks. There are tw main types of clay. 'Primary' clays are foun where they are formed and are therefore white and purer than the other 'secondary' clays. Se ondary clays have been moved by water, wind glacial activity. This movement reduces the pa ticle size and increases the plasticity of the cla Plasticity refers to the ability of a clay to b malleable and yet to retain its shape when it h been modeled. It is a major consideration selecting clay and the degree of plasticity vari from type to type. However, impurities a picked up as the clay moves and these affe shrinkage and drying. They also give the clay darker color.

Above *Ceramic Head* by Glenys Barton is an excellent example of the use of mold-making in ceramics. The stark, simple shape and intricate figures, which form an integral part of the image, produce a striking effect.

Right Elizabeth Fritsch, one of Britain's leading ceramicists, acknowledges the influence of music on her work. *Optical Pot with Swinging Counterpoint* (1978) is an example of what can be achieved using coiling.

Far right Another hand-building technique which contemporary potters are exploiting is pinching. This delicate, crackle glazed pot was fashioned by Mary Rogers, who uses natural forms as one of her main inspirations.

TYPES OF CLAY

Natural clay This is clay that has been mined, cleaned and can be used without additives.

Red earthenware This is also known as terracotta and is normally an iron-bearing, secondary clay. It is red in color, quite soft and has good plasticity and strength. Red earthenware is excellent for modeling, hand building and throwing.

Ball clay This secondary clay is blue or black in color and has a high drying and firing contraction. Ball clays provide a high plasticity and strength to clay bodies. A clay 'body' is a type or mixture of clay.

China clay or kaolin China clay or kaolin is a primary clay. It is a washed kaolin formed from decomposed granite and has very little plasticity, is less vitreous than ball clay and has a low firing contraction. It turns white on firing. China clay is used to provide the necessary working properties of the body and to act as a bond. China clay is the main source of whiteness used in preparation of most bodies and may be used as a glaze source of alumina and silica.

Fireclay Fireclay gets its name from its heat resistant nature. Its physical characteristics vary, some are plastic while others are coarse and granular. Fireclays generally contain some iron and are associated with coal deposits. They are used for insulating brick, hard fired brick, kiln furniture and also as additives to stoneware bodies to give a certain plasticity and the ability to withstand high temperatures.

Stoneware clay Smooth plastic sedimentary stoneware clays withstand high temperatures. They usually appear light buff, gray and light brown in color. Stoneware clay needs additives before being used.

Bentonite This is an extremely fine plastic clay of volcanic dust origin. Bentonite is added to clay bodies to improve plasticity.

Types of clay
These are some of the clays which will prove useful to the potter—many because of their good plasticity.

Stoneware clay withstands extremes of temperatures, even very high ones.

China clay acts as a bond and is the main source of whiteness.

Fireclay is extremely heat-resistant and is often added to stoneware to increase plasticity.

Blue ball clay is used to add strength and plasticity to clay bodies.

Bentonite also adds plasticity to clay bodies.

Natural clay can be used without additives.

Red earthenware is usually called terracotta and is very soft.

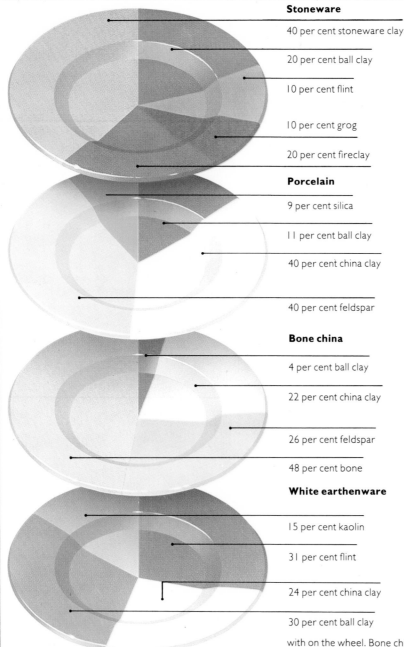

Stoneware

40 per cent stoneware clay

20 per cent ball clay

10 per cent flint

10 per cent grog

20 per cent fireclay

Porcelain

9 per cent silica

11 per cent ball clay

40 per cent china clay

40 per cent feldspar

Bone china

4 per cent ball clay

22 per cent china clay

26 per cent feldspar

48 per cent bone

White earthenware

15 per cent kaolin

31 per cent flint

24 per cent china clay

30 per cent ball clay

Clay bodies Clay, always a mixture of minerals, is basically the natural result of decomposition, usually of igneous rocks and granite. A mixture of clays or a mixture of clays with other ceramic materials is referred to as a 'clay body'. These bodies can be obtained in one of two ways: they can either be purchased directly from pottery or craft supply centers or be dug up and mixed by the potter. The latter method will of course be quite difficult for the amateur. An understanding of the qualities and characteristics of the material to be used is of paramount importance before work is begun. Four of the main types of clay body in general use are broken down into their component parts above. Stoneware bodies have a very high plasticity and are suitable for hand-building and throwing. Porcelain has a low plasticity and it therefore tends to be difficult to work with on the wheel. Bone china, although the chief body used in industrial manufacture of ceramics, has a plasticity which makes it difficult to handle. It is very brittle before it is fired. White earthenware is also frequently used for industrial work; it is often avoided by the amateur because it is difficult to hand-build and to throw. Texture, color, durability and plasticity must be considered when choosing a clay body with which to work. Bear in mind that these bodies can be mixed according to personal specifications.

CLAY BODIES

A body is a mixture of clays or a mixture of clays with other ceramic materials to give a working basis for the type of pottery required.

The important qualities of all clays as far as the potter or sculptor are concerned are plasticity, texture, color and durability, both when green—or unfired—and during and after firing. Clay bodies can be dug up and mixed by the potter or can be purchased from pottery suppliers. These suppliers stock most types of clay bodies or will mix a body according to personal requirements. It is important for the potter to choose the right clay for his or her needs and to understand the physical and aesthetic qualities of the material involved.

The main types of clay body on the market are stoneware, porcelain, bone china, white earthenware and red earthenware.

Stoneware A basic stoneware body consists of 40 per cent stoneware clay, 20 per cent fireclay, 20 per cent ball clay, 10 per cent flint, a mixture of ground flint, china clay and quartz, which helps to stiffen the body. Stoneware also contains about 10 per cent grog. Grog is clay which has been biscuit fired—fired just enough to dry it out—and then ground up. It adds texture to the clay mixture and helps give strength during firing. This combination gives the stoneware body its buff color and high plasticity, which makes it very suitable for hand building and throwing. It has a low temperature of about 1832°F (1000°C) for the first or biscuit firing, and around 2336°F (1280°C) for the second, high gloss firing. When fired at this higher temperature, the body is very strong.

Porcelain The main ingredient of porcelain is china clay. A typical porcelain body might contain 40 per cent feldspar, 9 per cent silica, 40 per cent china clay and 11 per cent ball clay. This mixture gives the body a blue-white color and translucency when fired at a high temperature, but its plasticity is low. It can be difficult to work with on the wheel, and so practice is needed to work well with this clay. This mixture has a fairly low biscuit-firing temperature of 1940°F (1060°C) and a gloss firing temperature of about 2336° (1280°C).

Bone china This type of body is normally used in the industrial manufacture of ceramic wares. The mixture of about 48 per cent calcined bone, between 25 and 30 per cent feldspar, about 22 per cent china clay and up to 4 per cent ball clay gives a pure white, translucent body. When fired, it remains strong even if it is very thin, but it is brittle in its green—or unfired—state. Its plasticity makes it difficult to handle.

White earthenware This is a second type of clay

...dy predominantly used in industry. A mixture ...' ball clay, china clay and flint, it has good ...hiteness, but is not translucent. It is difficult to ...row or hand build, but suits industrial pro-...sses.

TOOLS

...he range of tools used in the production of ...ramic forms is vast and the variety endless. ...ome can be made without much difficulty or ...lapted from household utensils, while more ...pecialized tools for specific skills or techniques ...n be purchased from pottery suppliers. They ...ll broadly into two categories—shaping or mod-...ing tools and cutting tools.

...The modeling tools can be made in wood, ...etal or plastic and also come in a variety of ...lapes and sizes. They are used for a wide range ...f functions from texturing clay to smoothing it or ...erving as extensions of the fingers. Cutting tools ...t the clay in one form or another. These include ...ires which are used for cutting forms off the ...heel-head or slabs from a pancake of clay.

Ceramic tools
A small array of some of the vast range of tools used in the production of ceramics is shown here. They range from ordinary household utensils to those designed for specific tasks. Most ceramic tools falls into one of two types: those used for modeling and those used for cutting. Included here are: battens (**1**), rolling pin (**2**), hessian (**3**), turning tools (**4**), sponge (**5**), rubber kidney (**6**), cutting wire (**7**), knife (**8**), plastic comb (**9**), brush (**10**), wooden spatula (**11**), and various wire-loop tools (**12**).

Insulating bricks

Vent with brick

Pyrometer dial

Electric heating elements

Spyhole for watching pyrometric cones

Pots stacked for biscuit firing

Heat input regulator

On/off indicator

Heat fuse

This electric kiln is stacked for a biscuit firing. Clay pots are allowed to dry out and are then biscuit fired at a fairly high temperature. A small electric kiln can be operated from normal domestic electric points. The temperature in the kiln should be carefully checked throughout the firing, using pyrometric cones and a pyrometer dial. The cones are placed inside the kiln and will soften and fall at a certain temperature, while the pyrometer records the temperature inside the kiln.

1100
1000
900
800
700
600
500
400
300
200
100
0°C

At 1100°C the particles of clay are bonded and it is non-porous.

At 1000°C bonding has begun in the clay but it is porous.

At 600°C chemical changes have begun in the clay which are irreversible.

As clay dries out it shrinks.

Spiral wedging Knead the clay on a flat worktop. Pull it up and around with one hand, while wedging it down with the other.

Wedging 1. Form the clay into a large loaf and slam it down onto the workbench to remove any pockets of air.

2. Draw a cutting wire through the clay loaf to cut it into two pieces.

3. Pick up the top half of the loaf and turn it over. Throw it down onto the lower half. Repeat the process a few times.

Wedging Before working with clay make sure that it has the same consistency throughout. Wedging is the name of the technique for achieving this. It involves shaping the clay into a loaf and slamming it repeatedly on a table.

Protective clothing such as an apron is useful to avoid any mess.

Use the full weight of your body when pressing down.

The surface should be lower than the height of a normal table, and must be slightly absorbent.

Keep your feet well apart so that you can rock back and forth, adding weight to your work.

TECHNIQUES
PREPARATION

Both pre-mixed, purchased clay and clay that you have mixed yourself must be thoroughly prepared. The importance of this cannot be stressed too highly. Only with correct preparation will the clay give the results you desire. The preparation may seem rather laborious, but it is well worth the time and effort which it takes.

Wedging Wedging is a technique of mixing kneading moist clay in order to make sure that the clay has the same consistency throughout. Wedging can be done in several ways. A simple method is to form the clay into a loaf-like shape by slamming it repeatedly on a table or bench. Then using a wire, cut the loaf in half. Turning one half slam it down onto the other until the two halves are combined. The continual cutting and slamming will eliminate lumps, inconsistencies and air bubbles.

A more difficult way used by professionals is spiral wedging. Clay is again formed into a wad loaf which is then kneaded; both hands lift and move the clay from the outside of the mass toward the center. The left hand rotates and guides the clay while the right hand does the kneading. The squeezing and turning forces the clay into a spiral pattern.

It is important to realize that wedging is done not only with the hands but with the entire body. Your feet should be planted firmly apart, so that you can rock back and forth, using the weight of your body when pressing down. The time taken for wedging depends on the condition of the clay. When the clay feels dense and tightly structured it has been wedged sufficiently. Wedging should take place on a slightly absorbent surface, lower than a normal table height. The surface should be wood for clay which is already of the right consistency and plaster slab for wet clay.

Clay that has become hard to work with can be collected in a plastic tub and then covered with water. The clay absorbs the water and softens after a day or two, and it can then be piled onto a plaster slab to be air dried before wedging again to get the correct consistency. If large amounts of clay are to be processed, a machine such as a pug mill can help take the hard work out of clay preparation.

Storing clay Clay should be stored in a damp atmosphere if possible. Clay can keep for months wrapped in plastic and stored in an airtight container or plastic bin. The plasticity of freshly blended clay improves if it is left to age for a week or two. Never allow clay to freeze, as this breaks down the fibers.

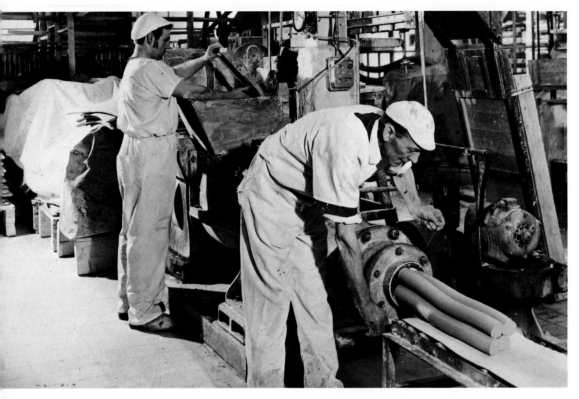

Keeping clay moist

When working with clay, pay attention to its moisture content. Clay should be kept damp before work begins and while work is in progress. Garbage cans (**1**) and plastic buckets with lids (**2**) are useful for keeping clay damp and storing it in its raw state. It can be kept for months in this way, but it must be wrapped in plastic before being stored in these airtight containers. While work is in progress, many potters find plant propagators (**3**) to be a useful means of keeping clay damp. A damp cupboard with a plastic or nylon curtain which zips shut (**4**) provides a slightly more sophisticated method of maintaining moisture levels for work in progress.

FORMING TECHNIQUES

Hand building Hand-made forms have a character that is determined by the irregularities of form and surface. There are no great problems to overcome in making a pot by hand, because clay is pliable and stays where it is put and also because it can be easily added to and extended. The techniques of hand building are essentially simple and easily mastered.

Pinching Small pots may be formed directly from one ball of clay. Roll the clay into a ball about the size of a fist and insert your thumb into the center. Then apply pressure with the thumb of your right hand, if you are right-handed, and left hand, if you are left-handed, on the inside and fingers on the outside. Squeeze the clay thin, as your other hand rotates the pot. If this procedure is repeated rhythmically taking care not to make one area thinner than another, delicate forms can be made. The scale of pinched pots is rather limited by the length of the fingers. For beginners, the most common fault is small cracks which develop on the edge of the pot. Damping your fingers or turning the pot upside down on to a damp cloth until it regains moisture will help prevent this.

Pinching 1. Pick up a lump of clay and shape it into a ball by patting and rolling it between both hands.

2. Insert one thumb into the center of the clay ball and press down firmly.

3. Support the pot in your palm and draw the walls out and up with the thumb and fingers of the other hand.

Below These ceramic figures by the British sculptor Ruth Franklin show a way of using ceramic techniques in a decorative rather than practical way. The shapes for the two figures were suggested by the shape of the clay when it was initially rolled out. The figures were glazed and fired in the usual way.

oiling Coiling is one of the most basic methods ' clay construction. Its main advantage is that actically any shape can be made. Coiling is a chnique using long coils or ropes of plastic clay, proximately the thickness of a person's thumb. owever the thickness of the coil is determined y the size of the form. These coils are formed by lling a piece of clay on a table using the palms d fingers, gradually extending it to the desired ngth and diameter. The rolling should start at e center of the sausage of clay, sliding your unds outwards along the clay as you roll. Try to event the coil from flattening by letting the coil ll free after each rolling motion and by keeping ur fingers slightly arched upwards. Several of ese coils can be made at a time and covered ith a damp cloth until you are ready to use them.

To make a coiled form, first cut out a circular se from a slab of clay the correct thickness for e size of the form. Score and moisten the edge the clay disc with water and position the first il. Work clay down from the coil into the base ith a modeling tool or the tip of your finger. Lay e next coil in the same manner. To curve a form twards, each coil should be slightly offset ward the outer edge of the coil beneath. To ake a form curve inwards, each coil should be t on the inside of the coil underneath it. ontinue these processes until the form is com- ete. It is best to build large forms in stages, lowing each stage to dry, and also preventing e piece becoming distorted or collapsing. But ways ensure that the top coil remains damp, so at it will bond to the subsequent layers. It is portant to work the clay of each coil firmly and noothly into the coil beneath.

Coiling 1. Make small sausages of clay and roll them out thinly. Use the palms of your hands and keep fingertips turned upwards.

2. Make a base for the coil pot. This can be cut from a slab of clay or formed by making a flat spiral of coils.

3. Put the base on a turntable. Roughen the edges and coat with slip. Place the first coil around the base.

4. Add more coils to build up the walls, keeping an even thickness. Set the coils to slant in or out as required.

5. Use a modeling tool to draw the coils together and blend them down into the base.

6. Continue to work on the surface of the clay, supporting the walls of the pot with your free hand.

7. A coil pot has not the smooth, even finish of a thrown pot, but it is a simple and satisfactory process without use of machinery.

Far left This lamp stand was made using the coiling method. The grooves are emphasized by cobalt blue, which was rubbed into them and then sponged off. The pot was finished with a clear glaze.

Slabbing Slabs are sections of clay that have been pounded, rolled or cut into flat pancakes. Working with slabs can be very exciting, and this is one of the most versatile of all clay processes. Some potters work with templates or paper patterns of the forms they are about to make, while others use a totally spontaneous approach, however this needs detailed knowledge of the process.

The first basic method of slabbing is to roll out clay using a rolling pin onto a wooden board covered with hessian or powdered, fired flint. This helps prevent the clay from sticking. For this process, it is best to use wooden guides which will help give an even thickness of clay. The slabs should all be made at the same time and allowed to stiffen, retaining just enough moisture so that they are firm to handle yet capable of being stuck together. The required shapes can now be cut out of the slabs and joined together. To do this, roughen the edges with a fork in a cross-hatch pattern, coat them with slip and press together. The joints can be further strengthened by pressing a roll of clay into the inside joints or by beating them carefully to ensure a perfect bond. The joints are the weakest points in slab-built forms and must be watched for cracks and warping as the clay dries out.

Slabs can also be used at the plastic stage, the plasticity allows it to be bent and formed in different ways. However, in this state, the clay is prone to tearing and cracking, but with careful use of supports these problems can be overcome.

Below Alison Britton makes inventive use of slabbing. *Caged Stork* is an example of a slabbed earthenware jug. In slabbing, it is possible to use both patterns or templates and to work freely. It is an extremely versatile process which can be used to good effect by potters of all standards.

Slabbing 1. Place a thick roll of clay on hessian and beat it with a rolling pin. Roll it out to an even thickness.

2. Make paper templates of the shapes required for each side of the pot. Lay them on the clay and cut around them with a knife.

3. Chamfer each edge of the slabs to form a neat joint. If preferred, the edges can be left flat and a butt joint made.

4. Roughen the edges by scoring across them with a knife and paint them with clay slip to act as adhesive in the joint.

5. Press the edges together to form the first joint, holding the slabs upright.

6. Smooth down any slip which has escaped from the joint. Then clean and seal the outer seam.

7. Reinforce the inside of the corner seam by pressing in a small roll of clay along the joint. Model it to the walls.

8. Repeat the process to form the whole shape of the pot. A thrown section may be added to create a neck on the pot.

Using the wheel
Throwing on the wheel is perhaps the most difficult—and usually the most challenging—skill which the potter must learn. Each potter develops a personal style for throwing, and various techniques are demanded by the type of wheel, as well as by the size of pot to be made and the type of clay being used. Throwing can be generally defined as the technique of using the hands to shape a ball of clay on a rotating wheel, guiding and controlling the clay as the spinning of the wheel throws it up and outwards. The three main steps involved in throwing are centering, coning and raising the walls of the pot. There are many versions of the wheel, but the two basic types are pictured here: a kick-start machine (**left**), and an electric wheel (**below**). The kick-start wheel shown here is chiefly used by professionals. Unlike the electric version below, the potter stands at it while working.

It is important not to hold yourself too tense when using the wheel. Rigidity can interfere with the fluidity of the work.

sponge, turning tools, and ire for pulling the pot off the heel should be kept close at and.

Protective clothing, such as an apron, should always be worn.

A basin holds the water necessary for maintaining the moisture of the clay.

Electric models operate with a simple on-off switch.

This wheel is equipped with a pedal used for altering its speed.

Throwing on the wheel 1.
Make a lump of clay into a smooth tight ball, patting it between both hands.

2. Throw the ball down hard onto the center of the wheel, so that the base flattens and adheres to the wheel.

3. Start the wheel and keep hands wet. Draw the clay to the center of the wheel, pressing with both hands.

4. Cup hands around clay and draw it up into a cone. Keep arms braced against the wheel tray throughout the process.

5. Cup hands over the top of the cone and press it back down. Repeat the coning until the clay is smooth and centered.

6. Press one thumb slowly down into the center of the clay and move it outwards to form the base and walls of the pot.

7. Support the outer walls with one hand and raise the walls from the inside, drawing them up with the fingers.

8. Continue working in the same way until the pot is the width and height required.

9. Curve the walls of the pot by applying finger pressure inside against the knuckles of the other hand outside.

10. Narrowing or collaring the neck prevents the top from splaying out under pressure from movement of the wheel.

11. Shape the neck and rim between the fingers. Apply pressure gently and keep hands steady.

12. Hold a turning tool lightly against the rotating base to trim it. Stop the wheel and cut under the base with wire.

USING THE WHEEL

Throwing Throwing on the wheel is the most difficult challenge facing the amateur potter or ceramicist, and it requires considerable patience and practice. There is no one way to throw, each person develops his or her own style, while the type of wheel, clay and size of pot may also call for variations in technique.

Throwing is basically the technique of using the hands to shape a ball of soft clay on a rotating wheel. The hands guide and control the clay as the spinning action of the wheel throws it up and outwards. The process is restricted to making round or symmetrical forms.

Clay for throwing should be plastic and not too dry—or 'short'—or it may crack. It should also not be so finely grained as to prevent it from supporting itself. The clay must be well wedged. Take small lumps of clay and pat them into balls between 4in (10cm) and 6in (15cm) in diameter. Take one ball and cover the rest with plastic while you practice. Throw or press the ball of clay with force as near to the center of the wheel as possible. When the clay is in position, pat it into a cone shape and squeeze sufficient water to act as a lubricant between hands and clay. Set the wheel spinning fairly quickly. With arms firmly resting on the edge of the tray or braced against your body, press your hands onto the clay ball. The aim is to coax the clay into the exact center of the wheel. This first step is called 'centering'. It is extremely important, as no forms can be thrown successfully until the clay is correctly centered.

The next stage is 'coning'. With arms still resting on the tray, both hands can be enclosed around the clay, the thumbs opposite each other. Pressure from the hands causes the ball of clay to rise into a cone which is then pressed down with the palm of the hand. The coning should be repeated several times to achieve an overall consistency. The final press down leaves the clay running smoothly, perfectly centered on the wheel.

Once this has been achieved, place your right thumb onto the center of the clay and press down to about ¾in (1.8cm) from the wheel-head. The thumb is then forced slowly outwards. This forms the bottom of the pot.

The next step is to raise the walls of the pot. This is done by using the thumb on the inside and fingers on the outside. Keeping an even pressure between the two, a ridge of clay can be drawn up from the bottom of the pot leaving behind the thickness required. This method is fine for small cylinders and bowls which—together with centering and coning—are the most useful forms for the beginner to practice. To check the quality of your

...rowing, cut the pot in half longitudinally using a ...ire. The section should be fairly thick at the ...ottom tapering to an even thickness.

Care must be taken to relax the hands as you ...each the top of the form, as the spinning action ...f the wheel has a tendency to flare out and split. ...his can be countered by 'collaring' the clay, ...hich is done by closing cupped hands around the ...ay, constricting it back into shape. When the ...rm is finished, it can be cut off the wheel-head ...ith a taut wire drawn under the pot from the ...ack to the front. It should then be possible to lift ...e pot carefully off.

The technique of throwing—shaping a ball of clay on the wheel using the hands—is one of the most important techniques for the potter to master. With practice, a wide variety of shapes and forms can be made. The visual effect of thrown pots can be enhanced by the use of glazes. The cheese dish (**above**) was thrown and then glazed with an off-white glaze with iron sprayed on. Metallic colors are used in glazes, and they react in various ways according to the type of glaze employed. The teapot (**left**) has a thin Tenmoku glaze. This is a dark brown type of glaze. The vase (**far left**) is an example of the technique known as agate, in which two different colored clays are mixed and thrown. The glaze is clear, in order to enhance the colors of the clay.

Turning 1. Trim the base of the pot when it is leather-hard. Center it upside down on the wheel, wedged with damp clay.

2. Hold a turning tool inside the base to cut a foot ring on which the pot will stand.

3. Use a broad turning tool to pare down the weight of clay in the base center.

4. Complete turning so the base is neatly shaped. Clear the trimmings from the wheel and remove the pot for firing.

Turning Turning is the trimming off of the excessive thickness of clay from a thrown form, usually from the base, while it is held in a chuck or fixed with clay directly on to the wheel-head. It generally sharpens and gives more definition to the form and can be used to add texture.

Standard turning tools, such as steel profiles and wire loops, can be purchased from pottery suppliers. However, with a little thought and imagination, it is possible to make your own. Turning must take place when the clay is near to leather-hard, as the trimmings should come off in long, unbroken ribbons. The pot must be centered onto the wheel by tapping. This is a skill in itself and takes considerable practice. It is important to study the inside of the pot carefully before turning, in order to determine how much to turn off relating the outside to the inside. The thickness can be gauged by tapping the pot with your finger and noting the tone. In fact this aspect of ceramics—like so much else—in the end depends on developing touch, which can only come with practice.

MOLDS AND MOLD-MAKING FOR POTTERY AND CERAMICS

Mold-making is generally recognized as an industrial technique, and in most studio potteries it is considered too time-consuming to produce molds, unless at least a dozen identical pieces are required. It is, however, an underestimated technique which can be used as a means to an end by the craftsperson and which, with imagination, can be utilized and exploited to create interesting and varied forms.

The basic material for mold-making is plaster of Paris. This is an incompletely hydrated calcium sulphate produced by heating or boiling gypsum stone, after it has been ground. When mixed with water usually in the proportions of about 2 pints (1.1 liters) water to 3lb (1.5kg) plaster, to a thick liquid, the plaster will set fairly quickly in about 20 minutes. After drying, it will be absorbent. The plaster needs to be contained round the object or model being molded. This can be done with any strong non-porous material, such as plastic, wood or soaped plaster slabs, that will easily release from the plaster when it has gone off.

Basic mold-making The mold is made from a master or model which is the shape or form finally intended from the cast. The model is usually solid and has to be longer than the finished size because of shrinkage. It is usually made from clay or plaster, but could be made from almost anything or any material. Designed forms can be turned in plaster from a block on a lathe or mechanical

wheel. However, it is best for the beginner to start by making a simple model with plastic clay. All these models except the clay ones need to be coated with a releasing agent to prevent the plaster from sticking to the model. Common releasing agents include soft soap for plaster and varnish or wax for wood.

The simplest and most common type of mold is the one-piece variety which releases the form without the need for divisions in the mold. However, the more complicated the model, the more complex the mold. The main problem is one of undercutting which should be avoided if possible. If not, it is necessary to make sure that each piece will withdraw freely. These pieces must be notched together so that they will key together once the model has been removed. For a more detailed examination of molds and mold-making see pp 64–75.

Press-molding This can be done in several ways but the most efficient and widely used is to fill the press mold with a slab of evenly rolled clay. Having rolled the clay onto canvas or hessian, lift both together and turn, supporting the clay so that it lies down in contact with the plaster. Remove the canvas and gently ease the clay into the shape of the mold. When in position, the clay can be pressed more firmly. Trim off any unwanted clay with a knife and, when the clay is leather-hard, it can be removed.

If the clay has been pressed over a mold, care must be taken to avoid letting the clay shrink onto it, as this will crack the form or prevent releasing. Many variations of this technique exist and any number of pieces can be stuck together to make more complex forms.

ip casting In slip casting, like press-molding, olds are used to reproduce forms. For this ocess, the clay should be in a liquid form. This done by mixing dry or plastic clay with water d deflocculants in given proportions. Defloccul- ts usually consist of sodium silicate or soda ash, so known as electrolytes. These separate the ay particles from one another and, in so doing, ep the slip fluid.

The slip, clay made liquid by mixing with ater, is poured into a plaster mold. As the mold absorbent, it gradually draws water off the slip aving a clay skin on the inside of the mold. The ickness of this layer of clay depends on the time e casting slip is left in the mold. It is possible to e when the deposit is the correct thickness by ting the mold slightly. The excess slip can be ured back into the container. The mold should inverted and tilted slightly to prevent drips om forming on the inside. When the cast has st its sheen, trim off the surplus clay while the st is still in the mold. This helps to prevent stortion. The cast should be taken out of the old when it is firm enough to keep its shape; ditions can be made at this stage using casting p or water. At the leather-hard or green stage, e seam marks or unwanted parts can be fettled scraped away and sponged. The cast is then ady for firing.

Press-molding I. Roll out a large sheet of clay onto a clean piece of hessian.

2. Lift the hessian keeping the clay supported and turn it down onto the press-mold.

3. Start to ease the clay into the shape of the mold with palm and fingers. Press gently to avoid tearing the clay.

4. Press the clay firmly into the mold and smooth it against the cavity with a rubber kidney.

5. Hold a knife flat across the top of the mold and trim off surplus clay, leaving a clean edge around the shape.

6. When the clay has dried, hold a board flat over the top of the mold and turn it over carefully, releasing the cast.

ip casting I. Slip is liquid y made by wetting it down th water. Make a suitable antity to fill the mold.

2. The slip should be of a thick, creamy consistency. Pour it in to fill the mold right to the top.

3. Leave the slip for about 20 minutes. Tilt the mold and check that a thick skin of slip has formed on the inside walls.

4. Pour out excess slip and let the mold stand until the clay skin loses its shiny surface.

5. Trim the cast and strip away surplus dried slip, so that the shape has a neat edge.

ft Mold-making is a quently used industrial amic technique, as it is an cellent way of producing ltiple pieces. The mold, m which this coffee pot is ng removed, is made of ster of Paris. This vessel uired a two-piece mold.

6. Carefully dismantle the mold to extract the finished cast. It is quite thin and will sag if not sufficiently dry.

7. Here are the three stages of a slip cast—the plaster mold, the green clay cast and the glazed version.

Glazes

Here is a small selection of the extremely extensive range of glazes which can be purchased for working with ceramics.

Far left to right: Row 1 basalt, iron-red on-glaze, lemon on-glaze, pale blue-green glaze; **Row 2** speckled white stoneware, manganese dioxide, ilmenite chun glaze, red sculptors' glaze; **Row 3** reed-green on-glaze, white opaque glaze, jade-green celadon, yellow celadon matt; **Row 4** blue-black tenmoku glaze, azure blue on-glaze, reactive crater slip, matt off white dolomite glaze; **Row 5** satin matt blue dolomite glaze, northern celadon glaze, chun-blue glaze, orange on-glaze. The colors reproduced here are similar to those which you will purchase. These are the colors of raw glazes, and the color will often change completely during the firing process. On-glazes, however, retain their original colors. Remember that glazes can be dangerous if taken internally and also be careful not to get them into the eyes. Remember that it is very important to keep glazes scrupulously separate from each other and from other equipment, as mixing them, even in small quantities, can cause serious problems when firing.

Right Isnik ware is one of the most important types of Islamic ceramic ware. Isnik is situated near the west coast of Asia Minor, and the pots produced there have brightly colored painted decoration. These dishes are typical of Isnik ware, and were made during the heyday of Isnik ware, in the sixteenth century. Its main characteristics include white ground, clear, thin glaze, and finely drawn images, and stylized scrolls around the circumference of the vessels.

GLAZES AND FINISHES

whole range of materials, glazes, colors and echniques are available to the amateur potter. hese can be purchased from the pottery suppliers in dry or liquid form, however some nowledge and understanding of them is necessy, as well as the means of application and firing eatment. There are several good books on the hemistry of glazes which go into greater detail.

Glazes are glassy materials used to cover eramic forms, either to make them impervious to oisture and dirt or to change their appearance ecoratively. The glazes and colors are fused on or into the article by the action of heat. When poled, they should have a thermal expansion milar to that of the clay. They are a mixture of inerals, oxides and chemical compounds and, e clay, contain substantial amounts of silica. uxes are added to help lower or give more ontrol to the temperature at which these glaze aterials will fuse and melt. The most common ethod of classifying glazes is by their maturing firing temperatures. Majolica has a low maturg temperature range of 1492°F to 1922°F (900°C 1050°C). Earthenware glazes have a firing nge of 1832°F to 2102°F (1000°C to 1150°C). reclay or sanitary glazes mature at 2192°F to 82°F (1200°C to 1250°C), while porcelain or oneware glazes mature at 2282°F (1250°C) and er. With reference to glazes the term 'maturing' eans that the glaze has melted and flowed noothly over the surface of the article.

There are many ways of applying a glaze and ese vary according to the size of the work and nount of liquid glaze available. Glaze can be pplied to unfired or greenware, but this practice s many disadvantages and therefore should be oided by the beginner. The most practical and mmon procedure is to glaze in the biscuit state. e amount of glaze put onto the ware is critical. o little will result in starving the ware, while o much will make the glaze run off the ware and ck to the kiln furniture.

pping The outside of a pot be evenly covered with ze by dipping it into a large cket of glaze right up to the n. Brace the fingers inside e neck to hold it firmly.

Spraying glaze This requires special equipment—a compressor and paint spray-gun—and must be done in a spray booth which has an extractor to remove fumes and glaze spray.

Dipping Dipping is the most popular method of glazing. Its main drawback is that a large amount of glaze is needed. The pot is held by hand or a pair of tongs and totally immersed in the glaze for a second or two. It is then taken out and left to dry, and excess glaze cleaned from the base.

Pouring Take the article, pour glaze into the inside and then quickly empty it out. Next, stand it over a large container and pour the glaze over the outside. This should be done with speed and precision. Make sure the article is evenly covered. The advantage of this method is that only a small amount of glaze is required.

Spraying Spraying has two disadvantages. Firstly, large amounts of glaze are wasted and, secondly, some form of fume extraction is needed to avoid inhaling toxic substances. Its advantages are that the glaze coating is easily controlled, using small quantities of glaze, and larger and more complicated articles, such as figurines, can be glazed. Spraying does, however, need time, skill and patience to know exactly how much glaze to apply.

Brush application Painting on the glaze can prove to be very difficult, as getting an even thickness is almost impossible using this technique. However, it is useful for repairing areas which may have been missed, and for decorative purposes.

All methods of glaze application can be used together on one pot. For example, on one vessel it is possible to combine pouring the inside, spraying the outside and using a brush decoration on top of this.

Colors Colors for glazing are metallic in origin and react differently in different glazes. Basic oxides and carbonates can be used, although pottery suppliers sell prepared body or glaze stains and enamel colors for under-glaze or on-glaze painting for the various types of bodies. These are the main types of color application in glazes. In under-glaze painting, the color is applied directly to the unfired vessel, while, for on-glaze work, the additional color is applied to the glazed ware. A third method, in-glaze, involves applying color to raw or gloss fired material which is then fired or refired so that the color actually blends into the glaze.

Pouring I. The inside of a pot may be glazed by pouring glaze into the pot up to the brim.

2. The glaze is poured out to leave an even coating over the inner walls of the pot.

3. To glaze the outside balance the pot on battens over a bucket and pour on glaze from a large jug or bowl.

Above Glaze is best applied with a brush when decorating, especially when creating detail.

Kiln furniture
It is important to stack ware correctly in the kiln, so that the maximum amount can be fired at one time. Kiln furniture is used to support and separate the objects in the kiln. Biscuit and gloss firings have different loading requirements. Useful pieces of kiln furniture include tile cranks (**1**), props (**2**), props with castellated tops (**3**), stilts (**4**) and saddles (**5**). Kiln furniture is made from refractory body, so that it can withstand the very high temperatures inside the kiln.

FIRING AND KILNS

The kiln is the most vital piece of equipment i the potter's studio. It is possible to make a variet of ceramic pieces by hand, but a kiln of one typ or another is needed for the ware to be perma nent and functional. There are various types of kilns and each has its limitations and uses. Cost of fuel is one of the main factors when deciding o the type of kiln to install. The main types use today are electric and gas, but oil and solid fue kilns can be bought or built.

Electric kilns The electric kiln usually takes th form of a steel box lined with refractory brick with a door at the top or front. The heat radiated from wire elements not unlike those of an electric heater. They are set in the walls, floo and sometimes doors of the kiln. Its advantage are more evenness of control together with grea ter safety and greater cleanliness in firing.

The atmosphere in an electric kiln is neutra and there are usually oxidizing ventilation hole in the roof and door, which allow steam to escap and enable the inside of the kiln to be observed The input of current to the elements is regulate by switches which control the rate of increase i the rising temperature.

Gas kilns Gas kilns are generally favored b studio potters because of their wide range of firin techniques they will cover, from earthenware t porcelain, through to oxidizing to reductio They are reasonably cheap to run and requir little repair. The kilns are usually brick structur with a steel box, unless built on site, where only framework is needed. The main disadvantage are the initial cost and the need for adequate flu ventilation to carry away the burnt gases. Burne provide the heat source, these are fed by gas pip fitted with regulators.

Oil fired and solid fuel kilns Kilns using oil for fu are generally similar in design to gas kilns, on different burners are required. Solid fuel kiln burning fuels such as wood, consist basically of chamber into which clay articles are placed t receive the heat which is generated in fire mout situated around or beneath the chamber. Co stant attention and care in stoking is essenti throughout the firing, making it a long an arduous task.

Control of firing It is advisable for the kiln to hav some form of temperature indicator or control, s

Right Pyrometric cones are used to indicate the temperature inside a kiln. They are made from clays which melt at specific temperatures, thus enabling the temperature inside the kiln to be judged. Most kilns also have a thermocouple an pyrometer. The temperatur gauged by the thermocouple is indicated on the outside o the kiln by the pyrometer.

at the temperature of the kiln can be determined at any time. The most common is the thermocouple and pyrometer. The thermocouple protrudes inside the kiln while the temperature is indicated on the pyrometer. Pyrometric cones are also used inside the kiln. These bend at certain temperatures and by constant observation the temperature of the kiln can be gauged. The packing and firing of the kiln is an important operation, as a little carelessness can spoil all previous efforts.

Biscuit firing It is not unusual for most ceramic articles, whether functional or ornamental, to have several firings. The reason for these firings is to allow different changes to take place at certain temperatures.

Once the clay articles are dry, they are placed in the kiln to be biscuit fired. This process is to harden the clay so that it may be easily glazed. Normally the biscuit is fired to a temperature below that of the gloss. Bone china is an exception, receiving a higher biscuit than gloss usually around 2208°F–2264°F (1220°C–1240°C). Care must be taken at this stage because the water in the clay is being driven off by the heat. This generates steam which must have a means of escape, otherwise the work may explode. Shrinkage takes place during all periods of drying and firing.

In stacking a biscuit kiln, pieces of work can come into contact with each other without the danger of them sticking together. The aim, when packing a biscuit kiln, is to fill the kiln to the maximum capacity which will ensure an even firing. Ware can be stacked inside or upon one another. However, it is important to take care not to put too much strain on the bottom objects. Flat ware can be placed on small supports, while cups are placed with their rims together and lidded objects fired with lids in place.

Gloss firing In the second or gloss firing, great care must be taken to avoid ware touching each other, as they will stick together when the glaze melts. The foot rings or bases of pots should be totally clear of glaze, as should the kiln shelves or batts. The batts are best coated with a batt wash, which contains flint or alumina, to protect them from drips of glaze. Again an evenly packed kiln helps toward a better heat distribution. Care in placing batts and props is essential, placing props so that the weight is evenly distributed and warping prevented.

Biscuit firing
This is the first firing which dries and hardens the clay so that it can be glazed. For the biscuit firing, this three-phase electric kiln heats to a temperature of between 1140°F and 1160°F (610°C and 625°C). Pieces can come into contact with one another during the biscuit firing, as they will not stick together. As shown here, lidded pieces can be biscuit fired with the lids in place. However, it is important to give each object the support it requires. Here, the bottom pieces are stacked on small supports, while the extended leg of the figure, a vulnerable part of the piece, has its own support.

Gloss firing
The ware is stacked differently for the gloss firing. The temperature in the kiln is higher than for the biscuit firing. During this firing, it is vital that the pieces do not touch one another, otherwise they will stick together when the glaze melts. This ware is stacked on kiln shelves, which have been covered in batt wash. This helps to protect the shelves from drips of glaze. This picture shows the pieces after firing. For both firings, careful packing of the ware will help ensure that the heat is distributed evenly.

WAX

Below This is the wax model for *The Apple*, a life-size bronze cast by the British artist Sean Rice. The wax shows the texture which the final cast will retain. The finished sculpture is in patinated bronze on a slate base.

HISTORY

Wax has been used for modeling effigies for thousands of years and was certainly in use long before the advent of bronze. During the Italian Renaissance many sculptors made small wax maquettes as preliminary studies for larger works. Some wax maquettes by Pietro Bernini (1562–1629), Benvenuto Cellini (1500–1571) and Giambologna (1529–1608) still survive today. Wax modeling developed to a high level for miniature portraiture during the seventeenth century, and was an invaluable aid to anatomists in recording dissection. The anatomical waxes of the Italian sculptor Gaetano Giulio Zumbo at La Specola in Florence and later those of Joseph Towne (1808–1879) at Guy's Hospital in London were of particular interest, realizing a remarkable standard of natural interpretation. The development of pigmented wax brought new directions in wax modeling and inspired, among others, the Swiss

Marie Tussaud (1760–1850) to make wax likenesses of famous people; the museum she founded is still a popular attraction in London.

During the nineteenth century artificial wax fruit was made which reached disconcerting levels of naturalism. In the twentieth century, Roy Herbert, working in the department of botany at the National Museum of Wales in Cardiff has created some astonishing wax models of botanical specimens.

Artists have used this medium in a number of ways, sometimes mixing additives to it to soften it or make it more flexible. Sometimes they have added substances like animal fats, oils, tallow or gums, making the wax more malleable. Apart from being a modeling medium in its own right, wax for the past 4000 years has played a vital part in the process of casting metals, such as bronze. The wax model, inside a refractory mold, is fired out in a kiln at a high temperature. This leaves a void, which may be filled with molten metal. This is known as the *cire perdue* or lost wax process.

Above This is a rare example of a wax which has survived intact. By the sixteenth century Italian sculptor Giambologna, it shows Christ before Caiaphas. Although the wax is cracked in places, the great detail can still be seen on the surface.

Tools for modeling wax
The tools pictured here include all those that are necessary when working with wax: a surface of either glass or marble (**1**), a small wax scraper (**2**) or a large one (**3**)—depending on the size of the work to be done—nails (**4**), a craft knife (**5**), pencils (**6**), a scriber (**7**), and various dental instruments (**8**). These are used for working in detail.

Types of wax
Many different types and blends of wax are available for modeling and each is specially constituted to have particular properties and uses. They may be suitable for modeling only, or for casting techniques, some are hard and some soft. In addition there is a range of different

MATERIALS AND TOOLS

Until recently beeswax was used for modeling; however, this has now become very expensive and has largely been superseded by cheaper microcrystalline waxes. These new types of wax are by-products of the oil industry and are produced in various blends, providing the sculptor with hard, soft and ductile waxes for various types of modeling.

Few tools and equipment are needed for wax modeling. As with modeling in clay, the hands are the most important 'tool', especially when working in soft wax. However, steel rifflers and wooden or metal spatulas can also be useful. A spirit lamp or candle may also be needed for heating the blade of metal spatulas.

Polystyrene can be used for building up the initial masses for large works—thus cutting down on the amount of wax needed. Copper wire is important for making armatures. A soldering flashlight or low brazing flame can be used to 'weld' wax edges together. A saucepan for melting wax is a vital piece of equipment, as are brushes for applying molten wax and wax rods for use as runners and risers. Surforms or files are useful for finishing surfaces off. A runner cup or gate will be needed for pouring metal into the molds. The best shape for this is a cylinder with a curved base. This basic shape can be cut from polystyrene and smoothed with a surform or file; it should then be covered with soft wax and the surface worked to an even finish.

colors. Red modeling wax (**1**) is a hard wax, and, as it is particularly suitable for casting, it is usually modeled over an armature of core. A general purpose modeling wax (**2**) is used like clay, to build up a mass layer upon layer. It can also be used to form the original model in lost wax casting. The white wax (**3**) shown here is purely a modeling medium and is not suitable for casting processes. It is formulated to provide exceptionally fine detail and can be very accurately shaped. Beeswax (**4**) is a natural substance with a long history as a sculpture medium. It was traditionally used for models to be cast in bronze. The more recently developed micro-crystalline waxes are less expensive than beeswax and have largely superseded for general sculptural purposes.

ax modeling I. The first
ep in wax modeling is to
epare a sheet of wax. Begin
 spreading oil evenly over a
arble slab.

2. Heat the wax until it is
liquid, and scoop some out
with a ladle. Pour it quickly
and evenly over the oiled
marble surface.

3. The wax must be allowed
to cool slightly, but not too
much, so that it remains
malleable. Meanwhile, brush
oil over the palms of the
hands.

Lift the wax carefully with a
oad, flat knife, so that it lifts
 a whole skin from the
arble without cracking.

5. Turn the wax over with the
knife, so that the other side
cools flatly against the slab.
The wax should still be warm
and flexible.

6. Knead the wax into a
malleable ball. Work it
vigorously until it is the
correct texture.

The wax is ready for
odeling when it is in a pliable
mp with a texture similar to
ft candy. If it hardens too
uch, it will crack.

8. Begin to model the wax
into the basic shape required.
Gradually extend the
modeling process with hands
and tools.

9. Corrections or repairs can
be made to a wax model with
fresh wax. Mold the soft wax
on to the model with the
fingers.

. Tools for wax modeling
n be heated in a flame. It is
portant to check whether
e tool can be left in the
me or just passed through it
iefly.

II. The hot tool melts the
wax and gently molds the
forms together. First work up
the basic shape of the form ·
required.

12. Begin to describe details
of form and surface finish with
the heated tool. This type of
modeling is used for small
models.

MODELING IN WAX

Wax is used to model small scale sculptures directly, as well as to form an outer shell over a core or armature for a sculpture which is to be cast. Wax does not harden fully and is therefore a vulnerable and relatively impermanent medium. A solid wax sculpture must be treated with care and not subjected to excessive heat or placed in a position where it can be knocked or eroded.

However, modeling in wax can be very rewarding, both in the practice and the result. It is especially suitable for making small figurative sculptures.

In order to model with wax, it must be kneaded into a malleable mass. Some waxes are composed in such a way that they are constantly pliable, and the heat of the hands renders them more so. A mass of wax for modeling can also be made by pouring melted wax on to a flat, cold surface so that is solidifies into a sheet. The sheet is picked up and rolled and kneaded while still warm to form the solid ball. The form can then be manipulated with the hands and fingers and fine details added with heated modeling tools.

Modeling techniques are largely a matter of personal style and preference and are best developed in practice. No particular rules can be stipulated, as the essence of a successful modeled sculpture lies in the interaction of the sculptor's dexterity and the natural qualities of the material. Both for solid wax models and those with a core or armature, the wax can be added in small lumps or strips and coaxed into shape with fingers or tools. Wax can also be melted into the existing surface with heated metal spatulas.

The surface qualities of wax are its characteristic sheen, which can be enhanced by passing a flame over the surface, and a slight translucency. The outer form of the model can be smoothed to form a cohesive, unbroken surface, or left to show the activity of modeling, with craggy texture and half melted lumps of wax adding to the vitality of the form.

When the model is on a large scale especially for subsequent casting, it is easier to maintain the vigor of the surface texture than on a small scale, where too much detail may obscure the form. However, wax is a most responsive medium and on any scale encourages a full expression of the art of modeling.

If any corrections need to be made to a wax sculpture, such as when it becomes damaged or needs modifying, these can be carried out so long as the wax is still quite fresh and has not become too hard. To mend a broken piece of sculpture, melt down some new wax and gently mold it onto the model with your fingers.

ARMATURES FOR SMALL WORKS

Unless the projected model is a very simple one, then a wire support or armature will be needed on which to form the wax. Make this out of copper wire and braze the wires together where they intersect. Brazed copper wire will withstand the wax firing and is also the most readily absorbed metal when molten bronze is poured into the mold. Steel wire should not be used as it is a bad conductor of heat and will chill the molten bronze, causing bad misrunning. When misrunning occurs, the molten metal hardens too fast in places, and this results in slight fissures on the surface of the sculpture. These have to be repaired with a welding flashlight and bronze rod. Another reason for not using steel is that it rusts easily.

Soft and ductile modeling wax can be formed into its final shape entirely by hand. Harder waxes can be modeled and drawn together with steel rifflers or wooden modeling spatulas in a similar way to modeling clay surfaces. Metal spatulas can also be used, and a spirit lamp or candle may be used to heat the blade. The advantage of using a candle is that the black sooting that it leaves on the steel tool transfers during the modeling process and enriches the color of the wax. This also helps to reduce the natural translucency of many waxes, making it rather easier to develop the form. When working on a small scale, it is also possible, with care, to 'flame' the model. This can reveal the very fluid and plastic characteristics of the material.

ARMATURES FOR LARGER WORKS

For larger wax sculptures, a larger and stronger internal armature is needed which can, eventually, be removed during the molding process. As this armature will not be left inside the mold, it can be made of any suitable strong material. In order to economize on the amount of modeling wax needed, initial masses can be built-up with sections of polystyrene which are attached to the armature by brushing the surfaces with molten wax. When this preliminary build-up has reached a suitable size, it should be sealed with molten wax, forming a good basis on which to apply the final thickness of wax. Mold sections are taken from a finished wax model such as this.

Wax modeling on an armature 1. Use copper wire with brazed joints to form the armature. Set it into a wax base.

2. Press small pieces of wax onto the armature, modeling with your fingers to build a basic form.

3. Continue to add wax to the model, developing the volume and structure of the figure in a gradual process.

Left This bronze cast is typical of much of the work of the Swiss artist Alberto Giacometti. Emaciated figures cast in bronze from clay models with roughly textured surfaces are characteristic of much of Giacometti's work. This bronze statue, entitled *Man Pointing*, dates from 1947.

4. Apply tiny pieces of wax with a metal modeling tool to model surface detail and delicate forms.

5. Pass a candle flame lightly over the wax to weld and harden the surface. This also enriches and darkens the color.

HOLLOW BRONZE CASTING

In order to make a wax model for casting hollow bronze, it is important firstly to build a core which is the shape and likeness of the intended design; keep it slightly reduced in size. Ideally, it should be about ¼in (6mm) under the actual size. This can be done using a refractory compound—one which can withstand heat—either modeling direct onto a support armature, or modeling it in clay, producing a flexible mold, and casting a refractory core. The core should be left to cure and then dry before any wax is applied. Curing is the process in which the material dries. It goes through various stages in setting and needs to be left for at least 24 hours to mature completely.

It is easier to apply the initial coat in the form of liquid hot wax and, once this has set, to continue modeling the surface with a soft wax. The modeling is done in the same way as already described. If the final surface is gently flamed it will produce a harder and more resilient outer skin, making the wax less vulnerable to damage when it is handled later on.

THE LOST WAX OR CIRE PERDUE PROCESS

This process involves making a flexible or plaster mold from the original clay model, pouring wax into it, thus creating a wax casting. After preparing the wax cast, a second mold is formed around the wax in a refractory material to form an 'investment mold'. This mold is then baked to a high temperature in a kiln, to remove all traces of wax. The baked mold is referred to as a 'ludo mold'. Molten metal is then poured into the ludo mold to fill the void left by the wax, which was melted out during the earlier baking. This loss of wax during baking gives the process its name.

Making runners and risers Runners and risers must be made out of wax when using this method. Runners are channels in the mold through which the molten metal runs to fill the mold. Risers are also channels in the mold but their function is to allow air and gases to escape. The best way to make runners and risers is to use steel rods which will be covered by wax. The basic sizes of rod that will be needed are 30in (76cm) lengths in diameters of ⁵⁄₁₆ (8mm), ⅜in (10mm) and ½in (1.25cm). To make the wax runners and risers, cut two slabs of clay about 3in (7.5cm) by 1in (2.5cm) by 1in (2.5cm), and place them onto a clean, smooth surface, preferably metal. Embed the end of the steel rods into these at either end so that the clay blocks are supporting the steel rods approximately ½in (1.25cm) from the work sur-

Modeling on a core 1. Model or cast a core slightly under the size for the finished work. Make it from refractory cement.

2. The core should be quite dry before adding wax. Brush on a layer of melted wax to about ⅛in (3mm) thickness.

3. Build up the basic structure of the form with small pieces of wax modeled onto the waxed core.

4. Develop the surface of the model and add detail with more wax pieces, shaping them with fingers or modeling tools.

5. When flaming with a candle, keep the model moving so that the wax softens and seals, but does not melt out of shape.

6. In addition to coloring and finishing the model, the candle flaming strengthens it for subsequent casting work.

Coring a hollow wax 1. Support the wax on a soft cushion bed. Mix up cement coring material and drop it inside the wax.

2. Insert galvanized wire through the center of the core. This should have been previously measured and bent into shape.

3. Build up the core material above the top of the wax. This will increase its stability during the casting process.

4. Push long pins through the wax and into the core to hold it in place. Leave the pin heads standing above the wax surface.

face. Next, build shuttering around the outsid allowing at least ½in (1.25cm) gap all round. mold is made using a vinyl molding compoun This is made from PVC (polyvinyl chloride), strong, flexible substance which has supersed gelatin in mold making.

Pour the hot vinyl mold into the shuttered ar until the steel rods and the clay are covered by least ½in (1.25cm) of the molding compoun When cold, remove the shuttering and turn ov the mold, revealing an oblong mold with tv oblongs of clay set in it. Remove the clay so th the end of the steel rods show through. Usin very sharp knife and metal straightedge, cut alo the top of each steel rod with a single clean cu When this has been done, the steel rods and a residual pieces of clay can be removed. The be wax to use for rods is a flexible but strong ty which has a low melting point. The rods oft need to be bent, so brittle wax is not suitable as would make the rods snap.

Pouring the wax into the mold at a gentle slop which allows the wax to run more easily along t narrow channels in the vinyl mold. When nea all the wax has been poured into the mold, pla it on a flat surface to complete the pouring. Nev use very hot wax on a vinyl mold, as it w damage the mold. To complete the roddi system in the lost wax casting process, a runn cup—or gate as it is sometimes—called will needed. The size of the runner cup is depende upon the size of the wax to be cast. Note that aft the bronze has been poured into the mold, t running system often uses the runner cup as storage tank of molten metal. This helps eliminate shrinkage in the casting as the bulk the cup keeps some metal semi-molten for up 10 minutes after it has been poured. The bron has to be poured into the runner cup and, if t surface is rough, the bronze will break off sm pieces of the mold which will find their way in the casting. If this happens, pitted areas w occur, and there will be a lack of detail in the areas. As the bronze is poured into the mold fills the areas previously occupied by the wax.

Left *The Rape of the Sabines* by Giambologna is one of the great achievements of sixteenth century sculpture. It is a highly complex figure composition. This wax sketch model was one of the artist's preliminary versions. It shows the careful positioning of the figures and the attention paid to the exact placing of the limbs. Because wax is mainly used as a transitional medium, relatively few waxes have survived.

The runner cup is where the molten metal is poured into the mold.

The molten metal runs down the runners into the mold.

The air rises out of the risers as the mold is gradually filled with metal. By the end of the pour, the complete system should be filled with metal.

It is important that the system of runners and risers is arranged so that all parts of the mold are filled with metal, leaving no air holes.

In order to arrive at the final sculpture the runners and risers have to be removed and the surface worked to the desired surface.

Left These molds show a simple piece with the runners and risers in position. The wax at the top of the mold is the runner cup into which the molten metal is poured.

Above It is unusual for a cast to be preserved with the runners and risers intact. However, this bronze of a mounted figure by the seventeenth century Dutch sculptor Martin Desjardins still remains as it was immediately after being cast. The work is fairly small – about 22in (56cm) high. But it still requires a very complex network of runners and risers to ensure that no air pockets are trapped because of the complexities of the composition.

MAKING HOLLOW WAXES

A hollow wax can be produced using a flexible mold in two ways. For the first method, the mold is first tied up tightly and aligned internally. Wax is then melted in a pan over a low heat until it is liquid. Never leave a pan of wax which is being heated. If it heats too fast, it can explode. Leave the melted wax until a 'bloom' appears on the surface, it is then ready to be poured into the mold. A wax with a 'bloom' looks clouded and has lost its shine. A small quantity of the melted wax is poured into the mold, rolled around the inside and then poured out. This is left to cool until set and the process is repeated until the wax casting is about ¼in (6mm) thick. When the completed wax casting has cooled, a core of refractory cement, reinforced by some galvanized wire, can be poured in. When this has set, the cored wax can then be removed from the mold and left for 24 hours for the core to cure. The wax can then be worked on if necessary before being cast into metal.

In the second method, the mold is left open, the wax is melted in a pan over a low heat until liquid and brushed onto the mold surface. This is a delicate process which must be repeated. Care must be taken to brush all over the surface of the mold each time the wax is applied. When the pieces have reached the desired thickness, and the edges cleaned, the mold is carefully re-assembled and securely tied up. The seam inside can be sealed by brushing it with liquid wax if there is access; if not, wax can be poured in and rolled. When it is cold, the core can be poured. It is easy to see the build-up of wax using the brush method, and it is more easily controlled. However, the pour and roll method is faster, more efficient and does not leave any seams.

USING THIN SHEETS OF WAX

Drapery and abstract sections can be fabricated and modeled by using precast thin sheets of wax. These sheets may be smooth or can have texture cast into them when the wax is poured. When the sheets are set and firm they may be cut into the required shapes, curved or manipulated by hand and assembled by using a heated spatula to spot weld the edges. If great care is taken it is possible to use a soldering flashlight or low brazing flame to actually 'wax weld' edges together using wax rods as a form of filler rod for the seams. Once the model has developed some structural strength, it will then be possible to continue where appropriate with modeled inclusions.

Making a hollow wax by pouring and rolling 1. Pour a small quantity of melted wax into the assembled mold.

2. Roll the wax around the inside of the mold and pour it out. Repeat this process to build up an even layer.

3. This picture shows the completed hollow wax. It should be thick enough to stand up to subsequent work for casting.

Brushing a hollow wax cast Brush melted wax into both halves of a mold. Build up thickness with several layers of wax, covering the whole surface each time. To join the two pieces assemble the mold and seal the outer seams, then brush more wax into the inside seams. Let the wax set completely before opening the mold.

Pouring a wax sheet 1. A flat rubber mold should be made for this purpose. Heat the wax and pour some into the mold.

2. Tilt the mold gently to spread the wax across the flat surface. Allow it to set into a thin, malleable sheet.

3. Manipulate the wax sheet into the shape required. Weld it onto a wax model using the heated tip of a metal tool.

MAKING A SOLID WAX MODEL

solid wax can be taken from a flexible mold, by ply pouring the mold full of wax with a bloom the surface and leaving it to set. A wax casting be taken from a plaster mold if required. This often useful for simple relief casting where any dercuts are minimal. The plaster mold should left to soak in water for at least one hour or til it is thoroughly saturated. The molten wax then be brushed on in the same way as shing wax onto a flexible mold. When the wax about ¼in (6mm) thick, leave it to cool and rden. The whole mold should then be im-rsed in water and, with a little help, the ckened wax casting will float away from the ster. This process is unsuitable for detailed rk because the surface is not as crisp as a ber molded surface. Also, fractures in the ster mold surface can occur very easily if any x adheres to it.

sting a solid wax model
Assemble the vinyl molding npound in its plaster jacket.

Tie it with wire and prop it upright.

Melt a quantity of wax in a n, enough to fill the mold. r it smoothly into the ld.

3. Wait for the wax to set and then dismantle the mold. Ease the wax model out carefully, peeling back the rubber mold.

SAFETY

Clothing Always wear protective clothing. Asbestos or other types of heat-resistant gloves are vital. Cover your arms so that they do not get burnt by molten metal or wax and always wear stout shoes, ideally, steel-capped boots. Trouser legs should be tapered and not flared. When casting, wear a foundry mask to protect your eyes from the glare of the metal.

Fire Both vinyl molding compound and wax are potentially explosive, so melt them slowly and always keep an eye on them. Always have a fire extinguisher to hand and insure against fire. If possible, make sure that there are always two people in the working area when pouring metal, so in the event of a fire one of them can try and extinguish it.

Ventilation Good ventilation is essential in a studio, since the fumes from vinyl molding compound can be an irritant if inhaled too deeply in an unventilated space.
Tidiness A further precaution is always to keep the floor space clear to prevent tripping up when carrying molten substances.

Hair short or held back
Foundry mask or goggles
Roll neck sweater
Protective clothing for arms
Asbestos or heat resistant gloves
Leather apron
Leg covering not flared
Sturdy boots, preferably with steel-capped toes

MOLD-MAKING

Right The Swiss artist Alberto Giacometti developed a highly personal style which reflects his view of the vulnerability of man in the twentieth century. Most of his works, both sculptures and paintings, especially those executed during the 1940s and 1950s, portray emaciated, insubstantial figures. By the 1960s his figures had become rather more solid, as can be seen in *Bust of A Man* from 1961. This bronze cast clearly shows the rough working on the clay model.

PRINCIPLES

All types of mold-making always follow the same principle regardless of the type of mold used. Basically, the process involves taking a female mold or negative from an original and the casting a reproduction original from the negative mold. Until the development of synthetic vinyl molds in the 1950s, the materials and methods of mold-making had remained virtually unchanged for centuries.

Right This plaster model for a monument dates from the nineteenth century. The sculptor John Flaxman had a great reputation and worked in several media. He is known particularly for his monuments. The flowing lines of this example reflect his talent as a graphic artist as well as a sculptor.

Below These molds and bronze axe date from the third or fourth millenium BC. grasp of simple mold-making was necessary before molten metal could be used to create weapons or implements. From such simple beginnings as this axe shape, the complex molds needed for later sculpture developed. The basic principles of mold-making have remained virtually unchanged for centuries. The whole of the casting process, regardless of the media involved, is complex and it is important to remember the three main stages – modeling, mold-making and the casting itself.

TECHNIQUES

TOOLS AND MATERIALS

[In] making plaster molds of any type, the same [tool]s and materials are needed as for working [in] plaster (see pp 140–159). There are two [typ]es of flexible mold-making compounds – cold [and] hot melt. These are readily available from [scul]pture suppliers.

[M]aterials needed for mold-making include [bra]ss shim, hessian or sacking, brushes for paint[ing] on the mold-making compound and a vessel in [whi]ch to melt the flexible mold compound.

[S]IMPLE PLASTER CASTING

[A s]imple plaster cast can be made for a relief if it [has] few or no undercuts. Undercuts are, quite [natu]rally, areas of a sculpture or mold where the [ma]terial has been cut into horizontally, for ex[am]ple, on a female nude sculpture the area under [the] breasts is formed by an undercut. The finished [cla]y original should be walled around the edge [wit]h clay and the wall sealed into place. Next, a [coa]t of creamy plaster should be 'thrown' by hand [ov]er the surface, making sure no air is trapped [any]where. Throwing plaster involves mixing a [bow]l of plaster, and, when it thickens, throwing [han]dfuls of it onto the sculpture using an action [sim]ilar to sowing seed. When this layer of plaster [is] set, pour ½–1in (1.25–2.5cm) of plaster into [the] relief and add some form of reinforcement, [suc]h as iron rod or fire wood, to give added [str]ength. This simple mold can be used for wax [cas]ting, if it is soaked well with water before use. [T]he rest of the clay figure should then be [tre]ated in the same way as the main front section. [If t]he mold is to be filled with plaster, it is possible [to] make large back sections as the plaster can be [po]ured into the mold, but if the mold is to be used [for] glass fiber or reinforced ciment fondu, numer[ou]s sections must be made as the seams of the cast [wil]l need to be filled as the mold is built up during [th]e final casting.

[R]ealignment of the mold sections for final [cas]ting is important. This can be done easily by [ma]king a zigzag in the brass shim wall in simple [are]as of the seam, which will act as a key. A clay [wa]ll can be used instead of brass shim, but only [on]e piece of mold can be done at one time. The [cla]y wall should be removed and clay wash [app]lied to the seam before the next section is [do]ne. Locating keys can be cut in the seams on a [cla]y-walled mold as the molding process pro[gre]sses. These small conical holes form a crude [typ]e of male-female joint, which help join the [pa]rts of the mold correctly.

PLASTER WASTE MOLDING

A plaster waste mold can only be used when more than one cast is required from an origi[nal] clay model, because the mold is chipped aw[ay] when the cast is made. The cast can be made [of a] variety of materials ranging from plaster, g[lass] fiber with resin to ciment fondu and glass fi[ber] matt.

To make a plaster waste mold, first split [the] clay into 'piece' areas and build a wall out of [fine] gauge thin brass shim—a type of brass fo[il] along the seam lines chosen. There is usually o[ne] large section, for example, the complete front o[f a] figure, and depending on the choice of the f[inal] casting material, numerous back pieces. T[wo] simple pieces may suffice if a solid plaster cas[t is] going to be made from the mold.

When the brass shim dividing wall is in pla[ce,] 'throw' a coat of plaster at the largest section [of the] mold. This initial coat of plaster is often colo[red] with powder paint so that, when the mold [is] removed from the final cast, it is easy to tell [the] difference between the external plaster, the co[lor] coat and the cast inside the mold. Each time a [coat] of plaster is applied to the mold, the edges of [the] shim seam must be cleaned. A old spoon is id[eal] for this. Once about ¼in (6mm) of color coat [is]

Plaster waste mold 1.
Divide the model into sections for the mold. Place a wall of brass shim along the seam lines.

2. Set the shim so that each section of the mold will be easily detached. Pad out the back iron support with clay.

3. Make small zigzags in the shim at intervals, so that location keys are built in as the mold is constructed.

4. When mixing the first coat of plaster, add a little color by first dissolving pigment in the mixing water.

5. Throw a smooth coat of plaster over the whole model to ⅛in (3mm) depth, flicking it on with the back of your hand.

6. When the color coat is complete and no clay remains visible, clean the edges of the shim with a spoon.

7. Paint high and rough areas of plaster with clay wash, before continuing to make the mold.

8. Throw on a thick layer of plaster over the color coat and add to it until it is about 1½in (3.8cm) deep.

9. Build up a heavy layer o[f] plaster against the brass sh[im] but keep the seam edge cl[ean] as it must be clearly visible[.]

10. Bend reinforcing irons into shape to fit onto large sections of the mold. Make them continuous to support the weakest points.

11. Flick wet plaster onto the points of contact between iron and plaster.

12. Use scrim soaked in plaster to attach the irons, winding it round the iron and against the plaster surface.

13. Thicken plaster on the mold where necessary, and make sure the irons are firm. Leave the mold to dry for one hour.

14. Damp the seams and e[ase] in a chisel to separate the [] mold sections. Pull away o[ne] section of the mold.

een applied and allowed to set, then clay wash
e high points of the coated section. A clay wash
 made by filling a soft clay thumb-pot with
ater, this will produce a slip-like substance
hich can be applied by brush onto the coated
ctions. This clay wash allows for easy separation
hen chipping out the final cast from the mold, as
 separates the back-up plaster from the color
at.

   Next, back up the color coat with more plaster
ntil it is about 1–1½in (2.5–3.8cm) thick. To
rengthen the mold, apply section irons external-
, attaching them to the outer mold surface with
crim, a type of open-work sacking, and plaster,
king care not to cross any seam lines with the
crim or reinforcement. The strength given by the
ons reduces the need for excessive back-up
laster and prevents movement in the mold
ctions when left to dry in preparation for being
sed with glass fiber or other materials.

PIECE MOLDING

iece molding in plaster has now mainly been
perseded by rubber molding compounds. How-
ver, it is still practiced by some artists and is still
sed extensively in ceramic reproduction.

   To use this process, first bed the original into
ay up to the half way mark, this must be done

The thickness of the plaster mold can be seen. The first coat of plaster, which contains the color, is about ⅛in (3mm) deep. The second, white coat is about 1½in (3.8cm) thick.

Brass shim is placed along the seam lines. It enables the parts of the mold to be separated.

After each section of the mold is removed, the clay is hollowed out.

. As each part is removed,
ean out clay from the inside
d remove the brass shim.
assemble the mold.

Plaster piece mold This is different from the waste mold in that it is made in several sections. It is thus easily taken apart and reassembled and can be used to make a number of casts. The model is embedded in clay to half its depth and a clay wall constructed to mark out the first piece (**1**). This section is covered in plaster to a thickness of about 1in (2.5cm) and finished with a smooth surface (**2**). When this is dry, the clay wall is removed and a second plaster section is built up against the first, cleaned and smoothed to fit neatly (**3**). An outer jacket of plaster is made to fit over and hold together both pieces (**4**). This process is repeated for the other half of the model and a mold of the whole form is produced in several sections, with a two-piece outer jacket.

(**5**). The number of pieces which will form a mold and the division of the whole shape should be carefully thought out beforehand.

exactly as the piece sections have to pull off with ease and must have no undercuts. Next, build clay wall along the exact halfway mark of the section left above the clay bed. All of this work must be clean and accurate, as the efficiency of the piece mold depends upon it. Build up the first piece in plaster to a depth of about 1in (2.5cm) and finish it to give a smooth, clean exterior. A day later, when the plaster is cured, remove the clay wall, take off the piece, check it for ease of removal and replace it in exactly the same position. Then clay wash the seam, and build up the second piece in the same way as the first.

There are now two piece sections covering the original above the clay bed. Any roughness on the outer surface of these pieces should be smoothed down with sandpaper or a surform. After this clay wash the piece sections and build a one-piece exterior jacket over them using scrim and plaster. When this has cured, it can be removed, checked and replaced. The clay bed is removed and the original with its two piece sections and plaster jacket in place, turned over and the whole process repeated on the other side of the original. Always check that the seams and the exterior of the piece sections have been clay washed, as failure to do so will result in a useless mold. When the complete mold has cured, it can then be carefully opened. Remove the exterior jackets first and then the piece sections. The piece sections are chamfered or beveled along the outer seam edges so that a V-shaped seam is made, which provides a grip to pull on when the pieces are removed from the cast taken from the piece mold.

RUBBER MOLD-MAKING

Rubber molds can be made from cold cure or hot melt rubber molding compounds. The most popular cold cure compounds are latex and silicone rubber, both of which give excellent detail. However, hot melt rubber molding compounds are used most commonly. These provide a flexible, durable rubber mold that can be reused. They are economical, as after use they can be remelted and used again. Hot melt rubber comes in different hardnesses and different degrees of flexibility; this is denoted by different colorings. The most commonly used one is a red hot melt rubber molding compound, made from polyvinyl chloride.

SIMPLE RUBBER MOLDING

A simple rubber mold can be made from a small object using a clay wall instead of a plaster retaining jacket. The original should be placed on a clay bed. If it is porous, it should be sealed with

ellac or a suitable sealant. Shellac is a varnish
hich is made from the resinous secretion of an
sect, the lac. Build up a clay wall around it with
out ⅜–½in (1–1.25cm) gap between it and the
iginal, making the final height 1in (2.5cm)
gher than the highest point of the original.
heck that the wall is well supported and that it is
ell sealed at the base to the clay bed. Melt some
nyl mold in a pan and pour it in. Leave to set,
d, when cold, remove the clay wall. It may be
cessary to build a simple two-piece plaster
cket around the set vinyl mold. This can be
ne by placing a strong thread along the pro-
sed seam line, covering the whole mold with
e mix of plaster until it is about ½in (1.25cm)
ick. When the plaster starts to set, pull the
read from one side (putting your finger on the
her end) to the other side, and it will cut the
tting plaster.

The state of the plaster has to be just right for
is process. If it is too soft, the seam will rejoin,
it is too hard the thread will break. When the
aster jacket has cured, remove it from the
xible mold. Using a sharp knife, cut the mold
d remove the original. When cutting the mold
oose where you cut carefully, so that, if poss-
le, the mold is kept in one piece. Make as few
ts as possible. When the original has been
moved, clean the mold thoroughly and return it
the plaster jacket. It is now ready for use.

ONE-PIECE RUBBER MOLDING

rstly, secure the original in a safe position and,
porous, seal it well with shellac or some other
pe of sealant. Then cover it carefully with strips
wet newspaper. Extra care should be taken if a
ft clay original is being covered, as any damage
ne will have to be remodeled before the mold is
ured. Strips about 1in (2.5cm) wide and 4in
0cm) long are the most efficient as they can be
rapped around the forms. When this is finished,
ll out soft clay into sheets about 6in (15cm)
uare by ⅜in (1cm) thick. Cover the newspaper
ith the clay sheets until the whole model is
vered in a smooth clay skin about ½in (1.25cm)
ick. Draw a seam line on the surface of the clay
in, following the simplest, straightest areas, but
viding the clay skin in half. Check that the final
aster retaining jacket will pull away from the
nyl mold and will not trap itself on an undercut.
undercuts have been created in the clay skin,
en build up with more clay until the right form
achieved.

Next choose your running and rising points.
unners and risers are solid cylinders of clay;
nners are usually 1½in (3.8cm) in diameter and
sers ¾–1in (1.8–2.5cm). With the running point

One-piece rubber mold 1.
Place the original model on a clay bed and cover the whole surface with strips of wet newspaper.

2. Cover the model with sheets of clay about ½in (1.25cm) thick, pressing the clay firmly around the form.

3. Smooth out the surface of the clay jacket. The vinyl molding compound will later take the exact shape of this clay layer.

4. Draw a seam line along the center of the clay coat around the whole form, marking it out into two halves.

5. Set a thick roll of clay to stand vertically from the lowest point of the clay jacket. This will form the runner.

6. At the highest point set a thinner roll of clay to make a riser. Model it smoothly into the jacket at the base.

7. Extend the seam line up the sides of the runner and riser, and build a clay wall about 1in (2.5cm) deep along the line.

8. Mix a quantity of plaster to a creamy consistency and throw it onto one side of the form, covering the clay completely.

9. When the first thrown coat of plaster is complete and free of air bubbles, throw a second thicker coat over it.

10. Keep the top edge of the clay wall clean by scraping it down with a spatula.

11. Reinforce the jacket with scrim soaked in plaster. Do not let it cross the edge of the clay wall.

12. Build up the plaster·to form a thick, even coat. It must be particularly strong at the seams, against the clay wall.

13. When the plaster is dry, peel away the clay wall leaving the seam edge exposed.

14. With a spatula, gouge small holes in the plaster seam to provide location keys for when the jacket is later reassembled.

15. Make a small pinch pot of wet clay and fill it with water. Brush around inside, dissolving clay into the water.

16. Paint the clay wash over the whole plaster seam edge. This will seal it to separate the plaster jacket halves.

17. Build up the second half of the jacket in the same way as the first. Do not allow plaster to obscure the seam line.

18. When the plaster has dried, tap a chisel into the top seam and ease another into the side seams to separate the halves.

19. Pull the plaster jacket apart and clean out clay and newspaper from this and the original model.

20. Reposition the original and plaster jacket on the clay bed. Seal seams and base with clay and tie firmly with string.

21. Melt a sufficient quantity of vinyl molding compound and pour it into the jacket through the runner, filling it to the brim.

22. Tap the plaster with a wooden paddle to release air bubbles in the rubber. Leave the mold to cool completely.

23. When the rubber has set, untie the string and pull the plaster jacket apart to reveal the vinyl molding compound.

not allow the hot vinyl mold to pour onto the
[ori]ginal, as it will skin upon contact. Set the
[run]ner to the back or the side of the model or use
[an] exterior tube to pour down, which can be
[re]moved when the molding has been completed.
[Bu]ild the runner in clay so that it is approximately
[2in] (5cm) higher than the highest point of the clay
[ski]n. It is best to make it cylindrical in shape, as it
[ha]s to be removed from the plaster jacket, first in
[cla]y and then secondly in the flexible mold. Next
[ad]d the riser on the highest point of the clay skin.
[As] the name suggests, it makes the vinyl molding
[co]mpound rise by allowing the air to escape when
[th]e mold is poured into the plaster jacket through
[th]e runner. The riser should be the same height as
[th]e runner. Make sure that the runner and riser
[ar]e well joined to the clay skin and run smoothly
[int]o it. If they do not, build up with more soft clay
[un]til they blend in satisfactorily.

[B]uild the clay wall along the line which was
[or]iginally drawn, making it about 1in (2.5cm)
[de]ep. Mix the plaster to a creamy consistency and
[thr]ow the initial coat, making sure that a com-
[ple]te cover is achieved and that there are no air
[bu]bbles around the intersection of the seam and
[cla]y skin. Back up with jute scrim and plaster and
[int]roduce exterior irons if the jacket is more than
[18]in (45cm) high, to give it extra support. During
[thi]s process, keep the clay wall edge clean and do
[no]t cross it with scrim or irons.

[W]hen the half plaster jacket is cured, remove
[th]e clay wall and cut three or four conical key
[loc]ation points in the plaster jacket seam. Clay
[wa]sh the seam thoroughly. Build up the other half
[of] the plaster jacket in the same way as the first
[hal]f, again being careful not to cross the seam line
[wi]th plaster, scrim or irons. After each coat of
[pla]ster or plaster and scrim make sure that the
[se]ams are scraped down and well cleaned, so that
[ev]entually the sections of the plaster jacket can be
[ea]sily separated.

[A]fter the plaster jacket has cured, open it using
[bl]unt chisels and a mallet. Place the chisel blade

on the seam and tap lightly. Do not try to open it
in one go or from one side, but try gently from all
sides and from the top, so that the stress on the
plaster jacket is spread over the whole. The
jacket after a certain amount of light tapping will
split up the seam and can be removed easily. Take
care not to disturb the original, as the jacket will
need to be relocated later. The plaster jacket may
pull away some or all of the clay skin when it is
removed. Clean out all of the clay from the jacket
and off the original and clean off all the newspaper.

The original should now be clean, and, if it is
made of clay, mend any surface damage which
may have occurred. Check the plaster jacket and
if there are any small holes, fill them with clay.
Next reassemble the plaster jacket around the
original, making sure that it is replaced in exactly
the same position. If it is not put back together
correctly, the mold will be thick on one side and
very thin or non-existent on the other side. Tie
the plaster jacket together securely using string or
for even better results, wire. Also secure the mold
down so it cannot ride upwards. Bear in mind that
the case has to withstand the pressure of the
molten vinyl mold when it has been poured in.

Seal the seams around the base with soft clay.
The mold is now ready for the hot molding
compound to be poured in. When this has been
done, leave the mold until it is cold. Untie and
remove the plaster jacket. The runner and riser
may make this difficult, so use a sharp knife to cut
through these at their base, being careful not to
cut into the main rubber mold. Next cut the
rubber mold open with a sharp knife, always
remembering the shape of the original. Keep
away from detailed areas, keep the cut clean, it is
very easy to make a jagged cut in a rubber mold.
Try to keep the mold in one piece, if it has to be
split in two, make sure that both pieces are well
supported by the plaster jacket. When the original has been removed, reassemble the flexible
mold and plaster jacket. The mold is now ready.

26. Having released the original, reassemble the rubber mold in the plaster jacket ready for casting.

. Use a sharp knife to cut [the runner and riser just [ab]ove the outer surface of the [m]old.

25. Partly slit open the mold with a knife to release the original, but leaving the mold itself in one piece.

Latex rubber mold Latex is brushed onto the original in successive thin coats. Each layer should be allowed to dry out to a transparent film before the next is applied. Latex is very flexible so should be supported in a plaster jacket which is laid on before the mold is lifted from the original.

_ PIECE RUBBER MOLDING _

Piece rubber molding is similar to one-piece rubber molding as newspaper and clay skin, are both used in the same way. The seam line is drawn, but instead of just one line splitting the mold jacket in half, one side of the mold jacket is complete, but the other side is split into sections transversely. Check for any undercuts and build up with soft clay until each mold section will 'pull' cleanly. Build a runner and riser on either side of the main seam line and blend in. Next build the main clay wall about 1in (2.5cm) deep around the clay skin and plaster jacket on one complete side of the mold in the same way as for one-piece rubber molding. When this is finished remove the clay wall, cut location keys, clay wash the exposed seams and build the next clay wall across the remaining area to be covered. This area can be split into as many pieces as wanted, but the pieces should be kept simple.

As each plaster jacket piece cures, remove the clay wall, cut location keys, clay wash any exposed seams, and repeat the process until the clay is completely covered. When the final plaster

piece has cured, open the mold using a chisel a a mallet. Since only one side of the jacket nee to be removed, this is best done by two peop As soon as the seam shows signs of opening, o person should hold down the pieced side of t mold while the other removes the main piece mold. Clear all of the clay from this piece and ti up the remaining clay and newspaper, so that i flush with the jacket seam. Try to seal any sm points that might allow the hot rubber mold seep onto the other side.

Reassemble and tie together sealing all sea with soft clay. Next, pour the hot rubber moldi compound into the cleared side. Leave to co Remove all of the pieces on the other side, tr away any mold that has seeped through, clear of the clay and newspaper out and replace t bottom section. Tie together and pour hot vi mold carefully into the gap left up to the top the section. Leave this to cool until set. Rep until all of the sections have been filled.

When all the pieces have been poured and cold, remove the plaster jacket and open t mold. The rubber mold will peel apart reveali the original. The pieces of mold should be plac back on the plaster jacket pieces, so that they fully supported and retain their shape.

Melting hot rubber molding compound Hot m rubber is made from polyvinyl rubber. Wh melting it gives off toxic fumes that can harmful especially to smokers and should not inhaled. There are specially designed melters the market for rubber molding compounds, th are expensive but efficient. However, hot m rubber can be melted in a saucepan over a ring—but not an electric cooker. The rubb should be cut into 1in (2.5cm) cubes and a lit placed in a thick bottomed old saucepan. T should be put on an asbestos mat over a gas ri keeping the heat low. As the rubber melts ad little more, stirring continually to prevent sticki and burning. Continue this process until enou rubber has been melted for the mold. O enough rubber to make a small mold or a mu piece mold, where each section is poured indiv ually, can be melted by this process.

However, using a large specifically design melter, up to 5 gallons (23 liters) of the moldi compound can be melted and kept hot for po ing. A quick melt attachment will handle la chunks of rubber and it is a reasonably qu process requiring little attention except for charging the quick melt attachment with rubb The rubber mold should be poured when it liquid, do not attempt to pour a lumpy melt as t will result in a poor mold. Pour the rubber slov and evenly so that the level in the plaster jack rises steadily, avoiding trapping air or chilling a thus solidifying, during the pour.

Rubber piece mold This is a similar process to the one-piece rubber mold, but, instead of constructing the plaster jacket in two halves, it is made in several sections over the clay coat. The clay is removed from one section and the hot rubber poured in and left to set. A second piece of the jacket is then cleaned out and replaced, then filled with rubber. This is repeated until the mold is complete.

SILICONE RUBBER MOLDING

...licone rubber is a cold cure rubber molding ...mpound. It comes in two parts, a rubber ...lution and a catalyst. The catalyst is usually ...ted and the rubber base is white. The two parts ...e mixed together and then poured into the ...old. Silicone rubber is expensive and because of ...is can only be used economically for small ...olds.

The preparation for using silicone rubber is the ...me as that for vinyl mold, the only differences ...ing that the clay skin should be made no more ...an ¼–⅜in (6mm–1cm) thick, and the plaster ...se must be tied very tightly. Instead of claying ...e seam, it is better to seal it with thin plaster. ...licone rubber is extremely penetrating and ...aks, seeping through even the smallest hole in ...e jacket, but it also gives excellent fine detail. ...ecause it is a cold cure molding compound, it ...n be used on originals that will not withstand ...e heat of hot melt rubber compounds. Mix the ...o parts of the compound together well, making ...re that all of the rubber base is mixed in. Leave ... stand for 15 minutes so the air rises out of it ...d then pour slowly into the mold until it is full. ...ap the sides of the mold occasionally as the ...bber is poured, this releases any trapped air. ...eave it until set, between 24 and 36 hours, ...pending upon the atmospheric temperature. ...pen and treat in the same way as a rubber mold. ... silicone rubber mold can be used with a variety ... materials and will withstand the heat of molten ...ad.

LATEX RUBBER MOLDING

...atex rubber is a cold cure molding compound ...d can be used to make very flexible molds. It ...n be brushed onto the original or sprayed on, ...t this requires special equipment. Do not use ...tex on porous materials like wood and plaster, ...less they have been well sealed with shellac or ...other sealant first. When using latex always ...ntilate the room well.

First, secure the original in a safe position and ...st it in French chalk (talcum powder) or ...aphite powder also known as plumbago. Then ...ply the latex all over with a brush. Allow each ...at to dry thoroughly to a transparent film. ...atch out for white patches, especially in under-...ts, as these patches denote that the latex is not ...operly dry, and, if more latex is painted on, it ...ll never set. The number of coats required is ...lated to the shape of the original. If it is a simple ...ape, six coats will be ample, but if it has a lot of ...dercuts, up to 10 will be needed. Reinforce-

ment can be incorporated in the latex: cotton scrim is best and can be applied and brushed over with latex after the second brushed coat. This method of reinforcement requires no outer support, but is not as flexible as a pure latex mold with an outer jacket. A plaster jacket can be made for a latex mold in a similar way to a plaster jacket for a rubber mold. This should be done before the latex mold is peeled off the original, so that the case supports the latex in exactly the correct position. Often, latex molds are filled with sand when placed in storage, to prevent the latex drooping inside the plaster case and thus losing its original form.

Silicon mold The preparation for a silicon mold is the same as that for vinyl molding compound, but the clay coat over the original model is made only about ¼in (6mm) thick, this being the eventual thickness of the mold. Silicon is mixed and poured cold so it can be used to mold for instance, from a wax model, which would melt in the heat of liquid vinyl molding compound. However, it is expensive and only really suitable for small works.

Taking a mold from a hand 1. It is essential to grease the hand thoroughly before starting mold-making.

2. Place the hand on a clay bed and start to build clay around the contours.

3. Work the clay into the outline of the hand until it is embedded in clay to half its depth. Smooth down the surface.

4. Build a continuous clay wall around the clay bed and up over the wrist. Seal any gaps.

5. Mix a bowl of thin plaster, and drop it over the hand to form a smooth coating.

6. Build up with thickening plaster to fill the whole area inside the clay wall. Wait while the plaster sets.

7. Strip away the clay wall and check at this stage that the hand can be easily released from the mold.

8. Turn over the hand and mold. Rebuild the clay wall and cut location keys in the plaster. Clay wash the mold seam.

9. Build up the second half of the mold in the same way.

10. When the whole mold is dry, tap along the seam line with a chisel to separate the two halves.

11. The finished mold contains a highly detailed impression of the hand.

TAKING A MOLD FROM A LIFE FIGURE

is process is a particularly delicate one and ould not be attempted by anyone inexperied. Only simple molds should be made, like, example, a hand molded from life.

The hand and arm to be molded should be free m any cuts or scratches which could be irried by the plaster and finger nails should, ally, be short. Start by thoroughly greasing the nd and arm with petroleum jelly taking care to tten any hairs on the arm so that they will not come entangled in the plaster mold. Then place e hand and arm on a bed of clay and build up e clay to the halfway mark on the fingers, hand

and arm. Plaster or plaster bandage can then be applied to build up the mold, but take care to keep the edges of the mold neat. This needs to be done quickly as the plaster bandage is light and fast setting. If only plaster is used, build it up to 1in (2.5cm) thick to give the mold strength.

When the plaster has set, the mold, hand and arm should be turned over, the seam clay washed and location keys cut. The whole process should be repeated, taking care to keep the seam clean. When the second piece of mold has been made, it should be removed gently from the hand, so as to preserve detail. If this is not done gently, the mold will shatter or crack. This is because the plaster will not have set all the way through or achieved its full strength.

king a mold from life
se plaster hands and the
face were made from
ds of life figures. The
side of the mold which
de the hands is fiberglass
the inside is vinyl, a useful
terial because it reveals
y fine detail, such as
erprints, in the molded
ds. The mold is screwed
ether and plaster is poured
ough the bottom of it.
er about 20 minutes it can
unscrewed and the molded
ds are ready. The wax face
sk was produced through a
cess of covering the face
h petroleum jelly, followed
carefully placed plaster
dages. The wax mask is
n made from the plaster
ld. This can be extremely
gerous and should never
attempted without expert
ning or supervision.

CASTING METAL

HISTORY

Metal casting and in particular bronze casting has evolved over a period of about 4000 years and has remained virtually unchanged in its principles to this day. The lost wax method of casting in bronze was known to the Sumerians in the Indus Valley around 2000 BC. It continued to evolve in the Middle East and was used in China around 1500 BC. Two basic methods of bronze casting emerged in the Ancient World, the direct and the indirect methods.

The direct method meant that the sculpture had to be modeled as a solid form in wax, over which a refractory material was formed. The wax was subsequently melted away and molten bronze poured into the resultant void to make a solid casting. Similarly, wax was modeled over a shaped refractory form, which, in the process, became a core. The core was then held in place by metal pins pressed through the wax followed [by] the application of an external coating of refracto[ry] material. After the wax had been melted awa[y] then the resultant space between the core a[nd] mold could be filled with molten metal to produ[ce] a hollow section casting. This method in bo[th] instances results in the original modeled wo[rk] being destroyed during the process.

The indirect method, introduced by th[e] Greeks, required the production of a piece mo[ld] from the original model in order to produce a w[ax] casting which could, if necessary, be cored a[nd] could then follow the same process already d[e]scribed. The mold could then be used to repe[at] the process if necessary. Both these methods a[re] still used today. The lost wax technique is still th[e] most satisfactory method of producing cast scul[p]tures in bronze, although two important alterna[a]tive developments in metal casting emerged in th[e] eighteenth and nineteenth centuries—sand mol[d]ing and electrotyping.

Left This bronze of Alexander the Great is an example of the sculpture of the Greek Hellenistic period. It is difficult to link the names of over 500 known Greek sculptors with the work which survives, and equally difficult to date accurately any of the sculpture of this period. Here the thickness of the metal can be judged.

Far left Early Chinese bronzes, dating from the later part of the Shang dynasty (1300–1028 BC) could quite possibly have been made by the lost wax method, in use from about 1200 BC. Ceremonial vessels resembled their secular counterparts, in this case a *Ting* or type of cooker.

Below The bronze reliefs of Donatello (1386–1466) are renowned for their spatial complexity and dramatic effect, as exemplified by the *Miracle of the Birth* from the Basilica del Santo in Padua.

Sand molding was developed during the eig[h]teenth century. It involves finely graded sa[nd] either slightly dampened with water or moisten[ed] with an oil binder, being rammed firmly ove[r] sculptured form in a series of split sand moldi[ng] boxes. These boxes are 6in (15cm) deep and [are] made of cast iron; they are joined together b[y] sliding wedge. The boxes are separated and [the] original pattern removed to leave a perfect i[m]pression. Runners and gas vents are cut into [the] sand, the boxes reassembled and the me[tal] poured. The advantages of such a process a[re] mainly that it is cheaper than alternative metho[ds] and that the gases can escape very easily throu[gh] the sand. However, this is a process developed [in] industry, largely for commercial castings, mos[tly] in iron. It is best used for simpler lay for[ms] where the division of the sand mold is not [too] complicated and does not require unduly intric[ate] draw pieces to overcome undercuts. Nowada[ys] even industry has turned to injection wax patte[rns] for its complicated machine castings, us[ing] ceramic shell dip molding as a refractory inve[st]ment or mold.

Electrotyping, introduced in the ninetee[n]

Right Rodin (1840–1917)
was one of the most
celebrated French sculptors.
The craftsmanship of his
modeling and his preference
for depicting character and
movement are exemplified by
this study for *John the Baptist
Preaching*. He has had a
profound influence on many
future sculptors. **Far right**
Picasso's *Man with Sheep*
(1944) is a product of what
could be described as the new
iron age of the 1940s and
1950s, initiated by the open
form iron sculpture of Julio
Gonzalez. **Opposite left**
Cain is a fine example of a
modern bronze by Sean Rice.
Opposite right The
sculptures of Matisse were
first shown in 1905. His *Back
No 2* dates from 1913 and is
typical of the strong
simplification of planes which
characterizes his bronzes of
figures and portrait heads.

ntury, gives a mechanical reproduction of an
iginal model in bronze. An electric current is
ed to transfer particles of metal from a bar
spended in an electrolytic solution, to build up
deposit on the face of a mold until sufficient
ickness has been established. The 'castings' are
ually very thin and accurate, but tend to lack
e surface vitality and character of a poured
etal casting.

Many sculptors now form original patterns
om expanded polystyrene which has unique
operties at high temperatures. The polystyrene
ttern can be simply rammed up in a box or sand
t with slightly dampened sand. Then an appro-
iate pouring channel and rising vents must be
troduced. The molten metal can be poured
rect into the retained pattern, which burns away
stantaneously and allows for its replacement by
e metal. Again this is a method best suited to
latively simple and undetailed forms and, on
e whole, to solid castings. Hollowed sections of
olystyrene can be cast in the same way using a
pported core of rammed sand on the cavity
de. Large sections should not be more than 1in
.5cm) thick.

Aluminum Aluminum has the great advantages of being light, strong and relatively cheap. However, it does not weather well and cannot easily be colored. After polishing, the surface of the metal will become very shiny, but it requires lacquering to ensure it will keep its shine.

Lead Lead is an interesting metal when used on a small scale. Large pieces tend to distort as it is very soft. Lead also has a low melting point.

Iron Iron has been used by sculptors, especially for architectural works. However, it is rather brittle, and not very popular with sculptors today.

Bronze Bronze is probably the most popular metal for casting. It is very hard wearing, will take a variety of finishes and has a pleasing natural color.

MATERIALS AND TECHNIQUES

ALUMINUM

Aluminum is a strong light metal with a much lower melting point than bronze and is comparatively cheap. It achieves a high silver polish which can be temporarily retained with a good lacquer. However, it is apt to oxidize, particularly outside, weathers to a rather lifeless gray color and it is not readily responsive to color treatments.

LEAD

Lead has been used for many centuries, particularly for garden sculptures, fountains and architectural details. It also weathers to a dull gray, but seems to retain more surface vitality than aluminum. However, it is very soft and prone to damage, and it is obvious from surviving examples of eighteenth and nineteenth century work, that over very long periods large pieces eventually tend to distort and compress under their own weight. It is an attractive material for using on small simple castings and, as it has a low melting point, affords most students and enthusiasts the opportunity to try metal casting in their own home.

IRON

Iron has been used sculpturally for fountains lamp-standards and other architectural detailing since the development of sand casting for industrial purposes. However, it is rarely used by sculptors today.

BRONZE

Various metals have been used through the ages for the production of sculptured objects and its evident that certain metals are preferred both for aesthetic and practical reasons. Bronze is naturally the most popular alloy due to its durability, natural color and range of patination.

GOLD AND SILVER

Gold and silver are usually considered too expensive for most sculptural purposes and, although the lost wax method is usually employed, additional technical advances, such as vacuum assisted casting and centrifugal casting, have been introduced to achieve better mold penetration of the precious metal. This results in sharper definition

LOST WAX CASTING WITH BRONZE

The principles of casting bronze are broadly similar to those for other metals. There are two basic methods, direct and indirect, both solid and hollow. Solid castings are usually more limited in size due to the fact that a bronze casting should not be more than 1in (2.5cm) in thickness. Thicker sections will result in bad shrinkage, cracking and distortion, and cause difficulty in attempted repairs. Consequently, when considering casting a figure or figurine, the thickness limitations will prohibit a casting of much above 10–12in (25–30cm) in height and, if the figure is rotund, it may need to be even smaller.

For a small sculpture, take a rod of approximately ⅜in (10mm) diameter down its full length with connecting rod sections and place horizontally to strategic simple areas of the figure. The main rod will probably stand about 1in (2.5cm) from the wax sculpture to enable sufficient space for ease of sawing when removing the rods in bronze. One or two rods, about ¼in (6mm) in diameter should then be similarly attached to high points and extremities as risers or vents. These should be attached by rods sloping upwards from the model to the outer rod in order that air and gases can escape with the rising metal. The runner first mentioned should be attached to the bottom of a runner cup which should be made from wax coated polystyrene for lightness placed above the casting. The cup will vary in size depending upon the size of the model, but should always be large enough to give a good head of metal during casting and allow for continued feeding to the bronze during cooling.

All rod attachments should be sealed firmly with a heated steel spatula and should only be applied as far as possible to convex surfaces and not hollow sections. This will permit easy removal of the rods when in the bronze.

Founders usually have their own preference for particular refractory investments, which are the molding compounds applied to the wax and withstand the heat of prefiring and the thermal shock of the molten bronze. Most of these investment compounds have, traditionally, a plaster of Paris base binder, which has various grades of sand, fire-clay, brick dust and grog added in varying proportions. Molds made of this type of material are usually quite large and heavy in relation to the object being cast and are also extremely fragile after the wax has been fired out of the mold. To help strengthen the mold— or ludo mold, as it is called—some founders strengthen the investment with metal rods or mesh. Alternatively, a refractory cement can [be] used as the basis of the investment.

Mix the first coat of investment or 'fine coat' [—] ciment fondu with dry sieved sand and plaster [of] Paris—to accelerate setting—in the proportio[n] of one plaster, two ciment fondu and six sa[nd.] The second backing coat or coarse coat shou[ld] consist of a prepared, commercially availab[le] lightweight castable refractory cement. This ty[pe] of preparation not only has the advantage [of] comparative lightness to volume, but is also ve[ry] strong even when fired out, and seldom requi[res] additional reinforcement.

The fine coat should be sieved and mixed d[ry.] Then mix small quantities with water to form [a] creamy consistency and apply carefully with a s[oft] brush to the rodded wax until ¼in (6mm) thi[ck.] When the first coat has set, the second coarse co[at] of lightweight cement and plaster (in proportio[n] of 10 to one) can be built up to strengthen [the] mold. This should lead to a mold of a fairly sim[ple] shape extending to about 1in (2.5cm) outside [the] wax rodding. If suitable, the second coating m[ay] be poured to form a fully cylindrical mold [by] setting a former in some suitable material arou[nd] the finely invested model. A hollow wax with [a] core of the coarse investment is handled ve[ry] much in the same way as already described [for] solid casting. The essential difference is that st[eel] pins should be pushed through the wax model [to] touch the core and still allow sufficient len[gth] outside the wax to be held by the exter[nal] investment. These pins will keep the core ac[cu]rately suspended within the mold and preven[t it] from falling. In order to ensure that the bro[nze] will flow through the wall section of the holl[ow] casting, which is usually ⅛–¼in (3–6mm) thi[ck,] more rods (two or three runners) will be need[ed] and a more sophisticated network of feeders a[nd] vents will be necessary. The mold, when finish[ed,] should be left for about 48 hours in order to c[ure] fully after which it can be fired out.

FIRING OUT

The process of firing out and baking lost wax lu[do] molds is very important, and it must be stress[ed] that, if this is not done correctly, then [the] consequences when pouring hot metal can be[—] literally—explosive. Consider carefully the ty[pe] of kiln or furnace suitable for this proce[ss.] Remember that in the first instance the w[ax] contained in the mold will pour out and either [fill] the air with black smoke or ignite and burn [off] within the furnace. Some founders, particula[rly] when firing out a number of molds, find a suita[ble] place and build a temporary kiln out of fire bri[ck] and fireclay around the mold, producing a ma[de]-to-measure structure, as it were, and then int[...]

Below This picture shows the model with the runners, risers and runner cup in position. The arrangement of the runners and risers is very important, because it is vital that the bronze reaches all areas and details during pouring and that no air bubbles are trapped.

ce a gas or paraffin burner to supply the
cessary heat. The Benin in Nigeria still use
ushwood and timber stacked like a great
nfire around a heaped mound of their ludo
olds to get the necessary heat for a satisfactory
ing of these molds.

Try to find a means of firing which will allow
u to work within your existing studio without
e environment taking on too much of the
pearance and character of a battlefield or
ickyard. Important considerations are the
cessity to regulate the flame when firing differ-
t molds and the erratic and unpredictable
mensions of individual molds. The completed
d cured mold can be placed runner cup down-
rds in the kiln in such a way as not to be
ectly in line with the flame and so that they will
t fall over.

Firing should be slow to begin with to allow
ter vapor to escape and to prevent sudden
acking. However, ciment fondu based refrac-
ry molds can be fired more quickly than a
aster of Paris refractory mold. When the water
por has cleared and the wax has melted, the
olds can be heated quite rapidly to a bright
erry red heat right through without any fear of
uctural breakdown. It is very important that
e molds are seen to be red hot all the way
rough to guarantee that any last vestige of wax
removed.

When the furnace has cooled down, the sec-
ns can be removed to reveal the baked mold.
ese must be removed carefully as a ludo mold
fragile and susceptible to sudden shocks or
ocks. On turning the mold the right way up, the
nner cup uppermost, it will then be possible to
spect the mold to check whether it is satisfactor-
fired out. If the runner cup is clean and free
m signs of sooting, then the mold is safe to
ceive molten metal. If, on the other hand, there
the remotest sign of black sooting even around
e neck of the runner cup, or at the exits to the
ers, the mold must be considered as possibly
safe to pour. In this case there will at best be a
rbulence during the pouring, and surface de-
uction on the face of any casting may be caused
the evident small residue of wax remaining
thin the pores of the mold.

If in doubt, it is far better to re-fire the mold
ther than to risk a metal pouring. Assuming the
old is satisfactorily fired, it will now need to be
wered into a sand pit or suitable container and
mly rammed up with dampened sand, taking
re not to allow anything to fall into the runner
p or risers. A cup cover is a good idea. The
rpose of the compressed sand is to strengthen
e resistance to the bursting pressure within the
old during the pouring of the molten metal.
so, should the mold crack under stress the sand

**Lost wax casting with
bronze** This important
method of casting is very
complex and requires
specialist equipment. Start
with a wax model. Several
wax rods are needed to
prepare a model for casting
(**1**). These are made in a vinyl
molding compound, originally
formed around metal rods.
Runners through which the
hot bronze will pour are set
on the model first (**2**). Small
sections run out horizontally
from the model and attach to
vertical rods brought up from
the lower part of the model to
above the head (**3**). A runner
cup is formed from
polystyrene covered with wax
(**4**). This is lost in firing out the
model leaving a well in which
to pour the bronze. The
runner cup is attached to the
top of the runners (**5**). Risers,
which release air as the
bronze is poured, are set at an
upward angle from the model.
They branch into vertical rods
which stand to each side of
the runner cup (**6**). The fully
rodded model is then encased
in a refractory compound up
to the top edges of the runner
cup. The first coat is a thin,
smooth mixture of sand,
plaster and cement which is
brushed on and blown into
the detail (**7**, **8**). Two coarser
coats of cement are then
applied (**9**), building up a
smooth cylindrical shape
around the model (**10**). This is
referred to as a ludo mold.

11

12

13

Breaking the investment
After pouring, the mold should be allowed to cool slowly. Do not be tempted to remove the mold too quickly. If the mold is removed before it is properly cooled, fractures in the cast and severe shrinkage can result. Once cool, the mold can be lifted out of the pit (**1**) and broken open with hammers to reveal the bronze cast (**2**, **3**, **4**,). This should be done with great care. Before starting further work, the cast should be firmly fixed. A small model can be clamped in a vice (**5**). All traces of the investment should be thoroughly cleaned off (**6**).

The ludo molds are put in a burn-out kiln and fired to get rid of the wax. This process leaves a hollow impression of the rodded model inside the mold (**11**). The kiln is sealed up and gas heated under pressure to achieve the right temperature. The wax runs out of the mold and through a hole in the base of the kiln. The mold must be fully cleaned out, otherwise problems may occur when pouring the bronze. The molds are taken out and embedded in sand with the runner cup facing upwards. Sand must not fall into the mold. The bronze is melted down in a crucible and lifted out with lifting tongs (**12**). Asbestos gloves, goggles or a protective helmet and a thick leather apron are minimum safety requirements for the person handling the hot metal. The crucible is then placed into a metal pouring ring. Impurities are skimmed from the top with a ladle (**13**). The metal is lifted (**14**) and poured smoothly into the molds until they are quite full (**15**). Metal escapes from the risers at this point. A black powder thermal coating is thrown on the metal (**16**). This keeps the bronze molten in the runner cup so it will flow into all the details in the mold. Whenever molten metal is being used, it is extremely important to take great care over safety. Heavy duty shoes or boots should be worn to protect the feet from falling weights and heat. Asbestos or other fireproof gloves must be worn. In addition to thick pants and a sweater with long sleeves, a protective leather apron should be worn for further protection. Above all, you should never try to deal with molten metal — however small the quantities — by yourself. Always have another person present.

14

15
16

against the mold will immediately chill and arrest any escape of metal.

Crucibles for pouring molten metal come in various shapes and sizes. For pouring as a single operation, a crucible of up to 60lb (27kg) capacity must be considered a maximum. Around 40lb (18kg) of molten metal is about the most comfortable, bearing in mind the high temperature involved. A single pouring ring is recommended slightly tapered to fit snugly around the crucible. The ring should fit all the way round so as not to exert undue pressure at just one or two points only.

When pouring hot metal, it is best, if possible to have someone else at hand to help in case of mishaps. However, if working single-handed shortened crucible lifting tongs can be made to adapted to help lift the hot crucible out of the furnace.

The crucible can then be placed in the pouring ring and the metal skimmed in order to remove floating dross. The metal should be poured slowly and evenly so as not to cause turbulence or chilling during the pour. It is better to let the mold cool down slowly after pouring since over enthusiasm and impatience to get the casting out can result in fractures and severe shrinkage in the castings. Casting is one sculptural process where patience pays great dividends.

Chasing and fettling

Chasing and fettling are the terms used to describe the process of finishing a bronze or metal cast. The amount of finishing required depends firstly on the quality of the mold and the pour, and secondly on the artist's own wishes. Lost wax casting will generally produce a reasonably good finish. The initial finish will be improved if a good alloy of bronze is used and if the mold is of high quality. Chasing is the process of finishing or adding detail to the surface with tools. The first step is to cut the metal rods off the surface of the cast with a chisel (**1**, **2**) and hacksaw. (**3**). Finally, a file should be used (**4**).

FINISHING

Chasing and fettling When the casting has cooled, the mold may be broken away with a hammer and chisel followed by the careful removal of the bronze rods that comprise the running and rising system. Care should now be taken to file and grind away the rod marks and to remove any metal flashing or small defects with sharpened old chisels. Textured matting punches should be used to match up textured surfaces so that the casting is not covered in a rash of smooth filed patches. This process is known as chasing and fettling. The process of finishing a bronze cast takes both time and patience. It is worth devoting the necessary time to this, in order to achieve a good finished result.

Pin holes can be drilled out and tapped to take threaded bronze rod of the same color metal. If the casting comprises a number of sections, as in a larger work, then the finished pieces will need to be welded together and the seam weld will need chasing and fettling. The completed bronze may be polished and then waxed or lacquered. It may be preferable to patinate and color the surface with one of a number of chemical treatments to achieve a more subdued and subtler surface finish.

Tapping Holes in a bronze cast left by pins which held the core of the wax model must be filled to finish the surface. The holes are first drilled out (**1**) and tapped (**2**) to give them a thread. A bronze rod is also threaded and screwed into the hole (**3**). The rod is sawn off at the surface of the cast (**4**) and filed down to the correct finish (**5**). The process of finishing can be fairly extensive, depending on the type of finish the sculptor wishes.

RESINS AND GLASS FIBER REINFORCED PLASTICS

Resins and glass fiber reinforced plastics are relatively new materials, which were originally used in industry for constructing boat hulls, racing car bodies and other products where lightness and strength are prime considerations. They were not used by artists as a material for casting until the early 1950s.

There is, therefore, little history or tradition attached to these materials. However, the materials are relatively cheap and easy to obtain, and so may seem ideally suited to the beginning sculptor. However, the materials are potentially dangerous, and great care should always be taken when using them.

Although the use of resins and glass fiber reinforced plastics is still fairly new in sculpture, many young sculptors have used the materials in their works, and more established artists have experimented with the expressive potential of resins and glass fiber. Two important contemporary artists who have used resins and fiberglass are the American Robert Morris (born 1931) and the British sculptor Phillip King (born 1934). Morris has worked in a wide variety of media, ranging from molded fiberglass to rope, wood, aluminum and even—in a 1968 piece called *Earthwork*—peat, soil, grease and brick. One of his best known works using fiberglass is *Untitled* (1967), which is an arrangement of four pieces of fiber glass. Phillip King was one of the first British sculptors to use glass fiber. Broadly speaking, his approach is 'additive', in that he adds one part to another until the work is completed. Some of his works are painted, others left in the natural color f the original material. In addition, many ounger artists are using resins and glass fiber in ew and exciting ways, and new approaches to ne medium are still being developed.

MATERIALS

One of the main uses of resins and glass fiber is as quick and relatively easy way of casting from nolds, in comparison with casting in metal. Fiberglass, as its name implies, is composed of nin filaments of glass, which are assembled with a onding agent into various forms. The main orms of fiberglass are mats, which are flat pieces, apes or strips, and loosely bonded strings of glass ber, called rovings.

Resin itself is a by-product of oil. There are everal types designed for different uses. Resins elong to the thermosetting group of plastics. The erm 'thermosetting' means that the substances equire some form of heat to enable them to be haped or molded. Unlike the plastics in the hermoplastic group, however, thermosetting lastics cannot be remolded once they have set. The main resins used by sculptors are polyester esins and epoxy resins, the polyesters being the nore popular.

RESINS

olyester resin comes in a liquid form, which has ne consistency of treacle. This is changed to a olid form by a chemical reaction, which is riggered by adding two other elements to the olyester resin. The first is called an accelerator nd is usually the chemical cobalt napthanate.

The second is a hardener or catalyst, usually the chemical methyl ethyl keytone peroxide. Adding these two substances produces a chemical reaction, which, in about 30 minutes, changes the liquid into a gelatin-like substance. This period, during which the sculptor must work, is known as the gel-time. As the process continues, the material gradually becomes harder. Many factors control the setting time. These include the proportions of accelerator and catalyst, the bulk of resin involved and the amount of heat being chemically generated or applied. The change from liquid to solid is usually called 'curing'.

A wide range of polyester resins is available, but the most useful for sculpture are laminating and clear casting resins. Laminating resin is normally used in conjunction with glass fiber and built up in layers—laminated—to produce a shell-like cast. Clear casting resin, on the other hand, is usually poured into the mold to give a solid cast of resin without any laminated or layered reinforcement. Clear casting can be poured in bulk without the excessive heat build-up, cracking and discoloration which occur with laminating resin. This makes it more suitable for pouring into intricate molds than laminating resin. Also, because of its transparent nature, clear casting should be used for embedding objects or specimens. Both types of resin can be used with inert powder fillers and pigments to give color or texture. Powdered fillers tend to dissipate the heat, as well as strengthening the resin.

Cured resin is, by itself, rather brittle, but with the addition of glass fiber reinforcement, has a very good ratio of weight to strength. Its weathering properties are not, however, too good and so a filler, such as marble dust or slate dust, is

Above Robert Morris's *Untitled Work* in gray fiberglass made in 1965 has a diameter of 24in by 96in (60cm by 240cm). The clean lines of the molded glass fiber follow his style of using each sculpture to embody a single, relatively simple plastic idea and his concern with primary structures. This sculpture both occupies and encloses space.

Far left John de Andrea's life-size couple (1978) uses cast vinyl polychromed in oil to achieve this very realistic and startling life-like effect. The vinyl provides the medium for a very literal expression by the sculptor and the coloring and tone of skin is carefully worked at to sustain the illusion of real life.

Bottom left *Modern Sculpture of Genghis Khan* by Philip King demonstrates the flexibility that can be achieved by working in resin and fiberglass. The thin head piece is balanced precisely on the conical form. The base projection manages to give an impression of molten liquid frozen in a moment of time. The work is painted in the bright primary colors that King often uses in his sculptures.

Materials for resin casting
Resin casting is a quick and relatively simple way of casting from molds, but the attention to safety that must be exercised cannot be over-emphasized. When mixing resin solutions the manufacturers' directions must be followed exactly (**inset**). Failure to do so could be very dangerous. A wide range of the many materials necessary for the various stages of resin casting is displayed here: glass fiber mat (**1**), acetone (**2**), liquid hardener (**3**), transparent shellac (**4**), assorted metal fillers (**5**), parting agent (**6**), thixotropic paste (**7**), silicone mold rubber (**8**), wax parting agent (**9**), cleansing and barrier creams (**10**), curing agents (**11**), assorted powder fillers (**12**), tins of polyester resin (**13**), polishing compound (**14**), buffing compound (**15**), white wax (**16**), chopped glass fiber (**17**), polishing attachment (**18**).

normally added in order to provide a more resilient surface. Laminating resin is a greenish-gray color in its natural cured state, another form of protection is to apply paint to it, which solves weathering and color problems instantly.

Resin is resistant to most common solvents, but, before it is cured, it can be dissolved by acetone or hot water and detergent, although the latter demands vigorous rubbing. Once cured, resin stripper, which is a very strong, caustic-based, toxic substance, will dissolve it over a period of several hours. In general terms, resin and glass fiber are fairly permanent and resilient materials for sculpture.

Most resins are already pre-accelerated, and therefore require only the addition of the catalyst to begin the curing process. The easiest method of estimating the amount of catalyst to be added is by judging weight and percentage. For a slow mix, 1 per cent of catalyst should be added giving a pot life—the period in which the mixture can be worked—of about half an hour. For a fast mix, this ratio can be increased to 2 per cent. A proportion of 1 per cent of catalyst is equivalent to 10cc per kilogram of resin. A graduated catalyst bottle or measuring device and a weighing scale will enable any amount of resin to be

correctly catalyzed. These proportions apply at room temperature of 60°F (16°C). Changes from this temperature will slow or quicken the gel-time and pot life. The bulk of the resin involved also affects this, a thin layer will gel more slowly than a thick one.

The amount of resin needed for a particular cast can be estimated roughly. First, cut out glass fiber mat to cover the mold surface and weigh it. For the gel-coat, the weight of resin needed will be equivalent to one layer of 1½oz (42gm) glass fiber mat. For laminating, the amount needed will be twice the weight of the mat.

GLASS FIBER

Glass fiber is produced in a variety of types, weights and forms. Rope, rovings and tapes are normally used for joining and reinforcing, chopped strand mat and woven mat are used for laminating. Whilst woven mat is normally stronger, chopped strand is more versatile for oddly shaped molds. Different weights of chopped strand mat are available, the lightest being surface mat, used for ensuring that sharp angles and corners, as well as intricate detail, are

Tools for resin casting

Resin can be worked with a variety of tools, many of which are also used in other sculptural processes. Those pictured here are essential: surform (1), dreadnought files (flat and rounded) (2), hacksaw (3), scissors (4), craft knife (5), decorators' brushes (6), palette knife (7), spatula (8), tungsten carbide and wet-and-dry paper (9). Resin is easily removed from tools prior to gelation by washing in acetone. But once it has cured, a resin stripper must be used. Immerse tools in the stripper overnight and wash with water after the cured resin has dissolved. Resin stripper is caustic and toxic and so must be handled with extreme care. At the end of a casting session, wash out all brushes with hot water and detergent. A thin film of wax or oil applied to scissors, rollers and knives before use will help prevent seizure and clogging and make removal of resin easier. Clean casting surfaces daily and apply a thin film of wax to them. Dusting the interior of rubber gloves with French chalk will prevent them adhering to your hands.

...pregnated. As a general rule, the heavier the ...t, the more difficult it is to impregnate and the ...s flexible it is for bending around corners or ...er bumps. The mat is held together by a ...nding agent which dissolves during lamination, ...d most mats can be split to give thinner layers ...fore casting, if required.

TOOLS AND THEIR USES

...ost tools needed for resin work are common to ...her sculptural processes, however several ...ecialist tools may also be needed. A catalyst ...easuring bottle, made of plastic and calibrated, ...ovides a clean, efficient and safe vessel for ...talyzation and is relatively inexpensive. A cast-...g table with a glass, melamine or galvanized ...el top can be used for casting flat sheets or ...minating geometric solids direct. It also pro-...les a clean reuseable surface for general work. ...thin layer of wax on the surface will enable ...red resin to be cleaned off easily with a scraper. ...ecialist rollers can be purchased for laying up ...ge, smooth flat areas. These consist of a set of ...und, washer-like units on a spindle which ...shes the resin into the mat and forces out air

Because of its smooth hard surface, resin is particularly suitable for spray painting. However, spray guns and compressors are expensive and, although useful for applying fast drying coats of cellulose primer and obtaining high gloss finishes, it also requires a great deal of experience and ability to be able to use them well.

Cured resin can be worked with a variety of tools, such as files, surforms, saws and abrasive papers. It is, however, a hard material and so direct working can be time-consuming. A metal hacksaw can be used for cutting straight edges, whilst a coping saw may be handy for irregularly shaped cuts. To avoid splintering when cutting, apply pressure and direction from the gel-coat side. Dreadnought files, abrafiles, surforms and other files suitable for metal work are all satisfactory for trimming and shaping. Filing at a slight angle will eliminate juddering and subsequent splintering. For finer shaping, coarse preparation paper and a range of wet and dry papers, which can be used with wooden or rubber blocks, are best. A sanding disc attached to an electric drill will swiftly remove surplus resin, but, for safety reasons, this work should be done outside or in an isolated place. It is also important to wear a mask during all these operations.

Drilling can be done by hand or by power usi̶ bits suitable for metal. Solid resin may build heat during drilling. Applying water will preve̶ this. On smooth surfaces, use a punch or a strip̶ masking tape to stop the bit slipping.

It is often necessary to join cured, mold̶ sections either permanently or temporarily. W̶ a mold which has to be laid up in separa̶ sections, the following procedure should be a̶ hered to. Ensure that the seams of the cast a̶ level with the mold seams, and that no resin̶ other deposits will prevent mold sections fr̶ meeting. If the interior of the complete mold̶ accessible when assembled, tie sections togeth̶ and seal seams on outside with modeling clay. ̶ a brush to a stick of suitable length. Pour a sm̶ amount of catalyzed laminating resin into t̶ mold, and rotate it with the seam in a verti̶ plane. Apply pre-wetted pieces of glass fiber w̶ the extended brush in order to strengthen t̶ seam. If cast sections have to be removed fr̶ the mold, tape these together with masking ta̶ around the seam and continue as above.

With a blind mold, where the interior cannot̶ reached, two choices are available. With sm̶ compact molds, mix up an appropriate amount̶ laminating resin and pour into one section. ̶ onto the other portion of the mold, tie and se̶ quickly. Rotate the mold with the seam in t̶

Using a plaster waste mold 1. First protect hands with barrier cream. Work on both halves of the mold as follows.

2. Seal the inside of the mold with two or three coats of shellac, giving it a tough, shiny surface.

3. When the shellac is dry, brush a thin, even layer of wax over the whole mold. Take care not to fill in the texture.

4. Apply a coat of separating agent over the wax shellac. The mold is now prepared for casting.

5. Measure a suitable amount of resin gel into a waxed paper cup. Stir in pigment and mix with a wooden spatula.

6. The percentage of catalyst to be added to the gel must be carefully calculated. Weigh the amount of gel in the cup.

8. Apply gel coat all over the mold with a soft brush, making a thin, even layer. Leave for about half an hour to stiffen.

9. Apply fine surface matt̶ the gel coat while it is still tacky. Tamp the matt into a̶ the mold surfaces.

7. Measure catalyst in a marked bottle, 10cc per 2.2lb (1kg) of gel. Pour it into the gel and mix it in thoroughly.

11. Lay in a layer of coarse chopped strand matt and press it into place. Wet it out with resin.

12. Allow the resin to hard̶ slightly. With a sharp knife̶ trim off matt standing abov̶ the edge of the mold.

tical plane until the resin gels. To shorten the
-time, use double the amount of catalyst. With
ger blind molds, the seams may require
engthening with glass fiber. This is achieved by
tting a strip of glass fiber about 1½in (3.8cm)
de and tacking the strip around the seam of one
ction, ensuring that only half the width of the
ip is impregnated, while the other half stands
ove the seam. When the strip has adhered,
low the same procedure as for small blind
olds, ensuring that unimpregnated glass is
shed into the interior of assembled sections
fore they are tied and sealed. With more
mplex molds, a combination of the above
ocedures may be needed. Try to anticipate
ssible joining problems when making and de-
ning the mold.

Flat sections of resin can be joined by simply
ughening the two surfaces, applying a layer of
pregnated fiberglass and clamping them to-
ther until cured. With sections which join at a
nvex surface or where only a temporary joint is
quired, a bolting method should be devised.
lts and other fittings are best located during the
nination process but may be added later. Spe-
l bolts known as 'big heads' can be purchased,
ordinary bolts with large washers, which dis-
rse stress over as wide a surface as possible,
ould be used. Fix the bolts to the cured glass

fiber surface with several layers of fiberglass. A
smear of wax applied to the threads will ensure
that stray resin can be removed after curing.

Solid resin can be machined in much the same
way as metal, turning on a lathe being perhaps the
most common method. Excessive heat build-up
may be dispersed by water or cooling fluid.

TECHNIQUES
PREPARING MOLDS

Molds for casting resin can be made from a
variety of materials. The mold must be moisture
free, able to be sealed and prepared with separating agents, and capable of being removed from
the finished cast. Plaster, wood, metal, glass fiber,
cardboard, masonite, vinyl mold compounds,
glass and thermoplastics are all suitable materials.
The choice of mold material depends on the
nature of the mold required, and this, in turn,
depends on the nature and numbers of the casts
required to be made from the mold. Although
individual molds create individual problems,
there are several basic types which should cover
most eventualities.

Plaster Although plaster is convenient and quick,
it has a high moisture content, is subject to
warping, liable to breakage and very porous. The

Catalyze laminating resin
d brush it on, to wet out the
tt. Eliminate any air
bles in the resin.

Apply a strip of matt
und one mold section half
ve and half below the top
e. Wet out the bottom
.

15. Tape up the mold and seal
the seam. Revolve the mold
so the resin inside wets out
the remaining matt. Leave to
cure.

16. To release the cast from
the mold, use a hammer and
chisel to chip away the plaster.
Clean off the finished cast.

14. Pour a puddle of resin into
this half of the mold. Fit the
two halves together, tucking
the strip of matt inside.

Resin mold release procedure I. Resin can be cast inside a resin mold. Wax and separator are applied before casting.

2. To release the cast, first tap around the outside of the mold with a piece of wood to loosen the cast.

3. Slide a thin, flexible knife between cast and mold and work it around to free the edges.

4. Following this procedure, you can grasp the cast and slide it easily from the mold.

construction and preparation of the mold are, therefore, of paramount importance. The mold should be as thin as possible in order to speed up drying, to minimize the possibility of reabsorption of moisture and to minimize the chance of warping. After removing the mold from the original, reassemble the sections and tie them together. Dry the mold until all the moisture has evaporated. To test this, scratch the mold with a fingernail, and, if the mold is dry, this will produce a dry powder and an irritating noise. The mold surface should be sealed with several coats of shellac, until a shiny surface results. Avoid any build-up of shellac in hollows, and ensure that the seam is also sealed. When dry, a layer of wax should be applied with a clean, dry cloth. If the mold is heavily textured, apply the wax with a brush. A coat of PVA release agent should then be applied with a sponge or brush to complete preparation. The release agent is water based, and, when dry, forms a thin covering like a plastic bag on the mold surface. Carefully applied, the shellac, wax and release agent should not affect the surface quality, even retaining fingerprints from the original. Polyester resin is a very efficient adhesive and, for example, penetration of sealer and separators will impair the final result.

Wood and metal molds These are normally us to cast geometric shapes and are construct directly as molds. Care has to be taken that undercuts occur, and that the mold is reasonab rigid. Complex molds, which can be assembl and disassembled for access during laminati and for ease of removal of the finished cast, c be made using bolts. Any gaps should be fill with modeling clay. Wooden molds require t same preparation as plaster, using shellac, w and PVA. Molds constructed from metal do require sealing, and a layer of wax and PVA w effect a release. For larger molds, which are to used for repeated castings, it is best to constru compound molds, using wood with metal su faces.

Glass fiber and thermoplastics These require sealing, and a release can be effected just usi wax. However, if the casts are to be painted, layer of PVA should also be used, as traces of w on the finished cast create adhesion problems f most paints. Vacuum-formed thermoplastics us ally require support during casting. Wood cradles, to which the edge of the plastic can stapled, prevent distortion and provide a fi mold surface.

Flexible molds Any flexible molding material ca be used, providing it can withstand the he

CASTING PROBLEMS

Condition	Reason	Possible cure
Shellac or plaster adheres to surface	Badly sealed mold. Damp mold. Uneven separator.	Immerse in warm water. Denatured alcohol may dissolve shellac. Take dow to surface with wet-and-dry.
Paint will not adhere to surface	Separator or wax on surface. Cast not fully cured.	Wash with water or acetone wet and dry surface. Leave cast to cure further.
Surface wrinkles	Laminate applied too soon. Gel-coat too thin.	Apply filler and work down.
Surface tacky	Mold not properly sealed.	Apply heat or wash down with acetone
Surface blistered	Uneven setting of gel-coat due to uneven catalyst addition. Uneven wetting out of laminate, or damp brush.	Cut out affected areas, fill and work down.
Surface pin holes	Uneven or aerated gel-coat.	Fill and work down.
Surface cracks	Result of excess exotherm caused by over-catalyzation or too much resin.	Fill and work down.
Surface soft areas	Patches of dry laminate.	Cut out, fill and work down.
Surface color uneven	Uneven mix of pigment and gel. Uneven application of gel.	Apply coat of pigmented resin to back of cast or paint surface.

MOLD PROBLEMS

Condition	Reason	Possible cure
Gel-coat not setting	No catalyst. Low temperature or damp mold.	Heavily catalyze and mix laminating resin into gel-coat. Apply heat.
Laminate not setting	No catalyst. Low temperature.	Remove and apply fresh laminate. Apply heat.
Gel-coat only slightly set	Too little catalyst. Low temperature or damp mold.	Laminate carefully; the exotherm from lamination should send off the gel-coat. Apply heat.
Laminate set but remains tacky	Over-catalyzation or too much pigment in laminate.	Clean with acetone, or apply coat of laminating resin.
Mold will not separate	Faulty mold, undercuts etc. Uneven separator or mold damp.	No problem with waste mold, with others cut mold to effect release. Immerse in warm water to dissolve separator and release vacuum.

erated during the gel period. The mold should
encased in a rigid jacket to prevent distortion
ring casting. No sealing or wax is required, but
hin coat of PVA will help prevent tackiness on
cast surface. These molds are particularly
ful for repetition casting of objects which
olve complex undercuts or texture.

rdboard and paper Molds made from card-
ard and paper should be prepared in the same
y as plaster molds. However, the nature of the
terial obviously limits the size for which these
lds are suitable.

easing the mold Plaster waste molds are re-
sed in the usual manner, that is by breaking in
ne way. With plaster piece molds, seams
uld be gently and evenly prised apart. If
istance is encountered, soak in warm water to
solve the PVA. With wood, metal and fiber-
ss molds, tap the exterior of the mold with a
oden mallet or stick to release the suction.
aking in warm water may also help, as will a
n palette knife slipped between the cast and
ld and then flexed. Flexible, glass and vacuum-
med molds should present no problems.

CASTING WITH LAMINATING RESIN

fore starting to cast, cut the mat to shape with
ssors or a sharp knife, and place on one side.
e first stage of the casting process is to apply
gel-coat to the prepared mold. This initial
at will form the surface of the cast, so great care
st be taken. Estimate the amount of resin
eded to cover the cast surface, and add fillers or
ments as desired, stirring gently but firmly
til an even mix is achieved. Decant the amount
be used. Then estimate and add the appropri-
quantity of catalyst. Stir the catalyst gently
til it is thoroughly mixed. Violent agitation will
use the catalyst to splash and aerate the resin.
t the gel-coat stand for a minute to allow any
bubbles to disperse. Apply the gel-coat evenly
the surface of the mold with a brush, ensuring
at undercuts are covered and no air bubbles are
pped. Disperse any pools of gel-coat with a
ush, and leave to gel.
Wash brushes in acetone and dispose of excess
sin. Check the mold during the gel process. If
ols have reformed during gelation and heat
ild-up is occurring, a damp sponge on the area
ll help dissipate the heat, but remember to dry
any moisture before laminating starts. When
e gel has set, lay the precut sections of glass
er in place, overlapping the seam by around
inch (1.25cm). Estimate and catalyze the
ount of laminating resin, and apply with a
pling motion of the brush until the glass fiber

Laminating 1. Construct the frame to be laminated. Lay it on a waxed metal worktop and mark around the edge.

2. Mix up and catalyze resin gel. Brush the gel all over the marked area to form a thin layer. Leave it to harden.

3. Lay a sheet of chopped strand matt over the gel coat. Mix and catalyze resin and brush it into the matt.

4. Place the frame squarely on the resin area and press it down firmly.

5. Add a reinforcing layer of expanded paper honeycomb, cut to fit into the frame.

6. When the resin is partially cured, trim the shape with a sharp craftknife to make a neat, clean edge.

has become transparent. Ensure that no air
bubbles are trapped between the glass fiber and
gel-coat, and that the mat has adhered to the gel-
coat. If the mold has a heavy texture, small pieces
of mat should be pushed into those areas. If the
gel-coat has been left overnight, a thinly brushed
layer of catalyzed resin will help the glass fiber
adhere during impregnation. Successive layers of
fiberglass may be applied without waiting for
previous layers to cure, but care should be taken
not to disturb or raise the initial layer.

Before the cast has completely cured, the
excess glass fiber can be trimmed from the seam
edge with a sharp knife. Reinforcing should be
carried out at this stage using, for example, glass
fiber roving, paper rope, honeycombed cardboard or prepared metal or wood structures. The
cast should be left for as long as possible, but at
least until the laminate surface is tack free.
Premature removal will increase the possibility of
distortion and warping.

Casting problems Most problems result from
human error. Panics can be avoided by careful
preparation. Ensure that tools, materials and
solvents are assembled before casting is begun.
Cut the fiberglass to shape before mixing any
resin. Make sure that the casting area is clean,
organized and well ventilated. Check that separation has been correctly completed, and ensure
that the mold will not be stuck to the surface.

7. Leave resin to cure completely. When dry, slide a palette knife underneath to release it from the worktop.

8. A lamination of glass fiber resin is tough but lightweight and may be more suitable for smooth surface cover than wood.

Bolted resin mold If a resin mold is constructed with an outer seam line standing away from the mold surface, it can be joined with small bolts through the seam. This makes it easy to release from the cast.

SOLID CASTING

Solid casting is sometimes a very good method of casting resin, especially if the mold is too thin or intricate for laminating or if a clear transparent cast is required. A thin or intricate cast can be achieved by impregnating the resin heavily with a powder filler, in order to dissipate heat and add strength, and by spooning and squashing the material into the mold.

For clear casts and molds which require pouring, such as a waste mold of a quarter life-size figure for example, clear casting resin is preferable to standard laminating. The clear casting variety takes longer to gel and cure, and has been developed to produce less of an exotherm. This means that it can be used in quantities which with laminating resin would crack, smoke and discolor. The amount of catalyst added is, however, much more critical, and test pours should be tried first. The amount of catalyst can vary from 2 per cent for a peanut-sized object to 0.6 per cent for an object the size of a tennis ball. It should be possible to pour a resin block of about 22lbs (10kg) weight in one pour with the clear casting resins now on the market. Shrinkage of about 8 per cent in volume usually occurs, and exposed surfaces tend to remain tacky. This can be avoided by placing a melamine sheet over the surface after pouring.

Preparation of molds is the same as for laminating resin, as are removal procedures. Pigments and powders can be added before catalyzation required. Ensure that the prepared mold is level and firmly supported before starting to pour. Having poured the resin, agitate to help trapped air escape, and leave to cure. If excessive heat build-up is noticed after gelation, place the mold in water or in a fridge to reduce the heat.

With transparent casts, embedding objects, samples and so on, problems of cracks and discoloration may occur due to over-catalyzation or excessive volume. There is unfortunately no formula to guarantee perfect results, as each individual mold will present different problems. With larger volumes, pouring can take place over a period of time, allowing each layer to cure before the next is added, until the total mold capacity is reached. When cured, the resin can be treated in the same way as laminating resin, and transparent castings can be polished and buffed to give the same appearance as clear perspex.

BUILDING UP DIRECT

Although primarily a molding material, resin and glass fiber shapes can be built up direct, using an armature covered with chicken wire, units made of wood, cardboard, expanded polyurethane or papier-mâché. Working direct involves reversing the order of the casting process. The fiberglass is applied first, the shape defined and finally the surface is resolved and finished. This method is generally best reserved for shapes where surface definition is not critical, as fiberglass in its cured form can be difficult to work. Sheets of material, cloth or hessian can be impregnated with laminating resin and draped or hung until cured. With areas over 1 foot (30cm) square, a supporting layer of fiberglass may be needed to add rigidity.

FINISHING

There are two main categories of finish—those applied before curing and those applied after. The first requires a decision before the casting process begins and is always integral to the gel-coat. Powder fillers such as chalk, china clay and talc can be used to apply a heavy gel-coat, which can then be worked and sanded back after curing. Slate powder, marble dust and other hard powders will give the gel-coat better weathering properties. All powder fillers must be inert, and, as a rule, require extra catalyzation. Metallic filler powders, such as bronze or aluminum, which are

Reinforcing 1. Cut lengths of glass fiber roving and soak them in catalyzed resin.

2. Apply roving around the inner edges of a cast to add strength and rigidity. Use a brush to settle it in place.

3. Additional support can be made using rolls of newspaper. Cut a thin tube of paper to length and lay it into the cast.

4. Put small strips of chopped strand matt across the paper. Wet it all out with resin and leave it to cure.

Finishing 1. Pick up filler on a spatula and smooth it into a hole or dent in the surface of the cast.

2. Allow the filler to dry and rub it down with coarse tungsten carbide paper. Finish it with fine carborundum paper.

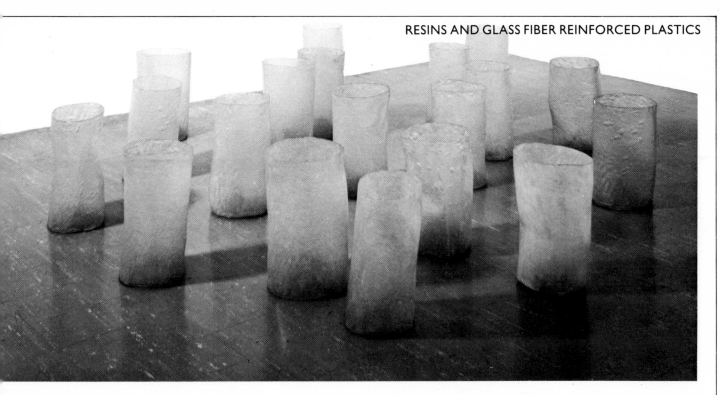

led to the gel-coat, give a metallic finish to the
al cast. The amount of powder in the gel-coat
l determine the degree of likeness to the real
stance, and, because of the resulting density of
gel-coat, you should make sure that it is
alyzed throughout.

After removing the cast from the mold, the
face should be rubbed over with wire wool and
n burnished to bring out the shine on the metal
gments suspended within the resin. Colored
tal flakes, available in a wide range and
nbination of colors, can be added to the gel-
t to produce a glittery surface on the final coat.
lored pigments, both opaque and translucent,
y be bought ready suspended in resin. These
be added to the gel-coat to give the cast
uilt color. This should be added to the resin in
roportion of 1:14 prior to catalyzation. Keep
nind some uncatalyzed gel-coat for repairs after
noving the cast from the mold. The cast can
n be polished with rubbing compounds, color-
toring car polishes and wax polish.

If a finish is to be applied after curing, the
lowing general preparations should be fol-
ved. Remove all traces of the release agent
h warm water and detergent, wash with clean
ter and allow to dry. Gaps and holes can now
filled with a plastic filling compound, and,
en set, worked down to the cast surface. To
sure that the cast has a key, rub with fine wet-
d-dry paper.

A vast range of paints is available, and most are
table for use on resin. The type of paint should
chosen to give the desired finish. Generally for
high gloss finish, synthetic enamels, poly-
ethane or acrylic lacquers and cellulose auto
int are the most common. For matt finishes
/A water-soluble paints, emulsions, matt cellu-
e or synthetic eggshell paints can be used.
oss finishes can be taken down to matt by
plying a matt polyurethane varnish. Having
cided on the type of paint, a suitable undercoat
1 be applied and smaller holes filled and

worked down. For high gloss finishes, a cellulose
primer can be applied with a spray gun, and
pinholes filled with cellulose putty, prior to
adding the top coat.

After the paint has set, the application of
rubbing compound, color restoring polish and
wax polish will give a high gloss surface as on an
automobile. For less high finishes, synthetic and
water-based paints may be applied with a brush.
The paint surface is only a thin skin and will
faithfully reflect the surface underneath. Therefore, for a high gloss finish, a smooth surface is
needed, usually achieved by working through
several grades of wet-and-dry paper.

Above Eva Hesse's
Repetition 19, III (1968) is a
collection of 19 tubular
fiberglass units. They are
between 19in (48cm) and 20in
(50cm) high by 11in (28cm) to
13in (33cm) in diameter.
Unlike many artists using resin
and fiberglass, she is aiming at
an organic effect, rather than
the clean-cut precise lines
often identified with this
medium.

SAFETY

Polyester resins and glass
fiber are not pleasant to use
and can, in some cases, be
harmful. It is essential,
therefore, that certain
precautions are observed.
Explosion Resin, catalyst and
acetone have low flash points
and so must never be
exposed to naked flames.
Catalyst and accelerator will
explode if they are mixed
together neat. Most resins are
now pre-accelerated, so that
only the catalyst has to be
added.
Fumes Fumes from resin
products, catalysts and
acetone are toxic and must be
used in a well ventilated area.
A fume mask should always be
worn. Smoking not only
increases the danger of fire,
but also means you are
inhaling toxic fumes deeply.
Skin irritation Resin and
glass fiber are irritants, so use
barrier cream or rubber
gloves when handling them.
Catalyst is a very efficient
oxidizing agent, so avoid any
skin contact. In cases of skin
contact, wash the skin
immediately and copiously

with cold water. If resin or
catalyst enters the eyes do
likewise, and always summon
medical help.
Dust When sanding or
working cured resin, wear a
dust mask, as the dust is
composed of glass and
insoluble resin particles. If
power sanding, use a mask,
goggles and protective
clothing.
Fire Resin left in bulk may
begin to smoke and even
ignite, so disperse unused
catalyzed resin over a large
surface area. If pots of resin
begin to smoke, douse them
in cold water and place
outside. Store resins, catalyst,
acetone and so on in a cool,
fireproof place. Fires should
be extinguished with carbon
dioxide or powder
appliances.

Face mask

Safety goggles

Protective gloves

WOOD

HISTORY

Accessible, light, easily worked and replaceab[le]
wood is an essential element of basic surviva[l],
the weapon, shelter, fuel. As a substance, woo[d]
part of man's history. With the discovery of m[etal]
and its subsequent development, tools for wo[rk]-
ing wood became more sophisticated. These to[ols]
widened the range of structural possibilit[y],
stronger boats, bigger roofs, spoked wheels. W[ith]
the availability of the material and the tools [for]
shaping and joining it, the circumstances w[ere]
ever present for their use in making images.

Wood and stone have always been the [tra]-
ditional materials of sculpture, owing to th[eir]
natural abundance all over the world. Since wo[od]
carving is a less daunting task than stone carvi[ng]
it has probably been more common, but [few]
examples survive from early civilizations, si[nce]
wood is not as durable as stone.

In areas where the climate is dry, wood ca[rv]-
ings have been preserved. Several small scu[lp]-
tures have been found from Egyptian tom[bs],
these either commemorate important people [or]

Left This figure of a woman
with a crown made of wood
and ivory is an example of an
early wooden sculpture which
has survived the ravages of
time. Wood is a much less
durable material than stone,
for example. Some of the
simple surface detail on the
face, crown and hair is still
visible.
Above The frozen tombs at
Pazyryk in the Soviet Union
have yielded many fascinating
objects which are extremely
well preserved. The tombs
gave a picture of the life of
nomadic peoples from the
third millenium on. This small
wooden table has roughly
carved legs with some surface
detail. It dates from the fifth
century BC.

Far right Wood carving i[s]
one of the world's oldest
sculptural practices. This
carved figure of the Buddh[ist]
'Saint' Lohan shows great
naturalism in the facial
features. The belt and rob[es]
are also fairly sophisticate[d]
their approach.
Right Tilman
Riemenschneider was an
acknowledged master of
wood carving in Germany
during the fifteenth centur[y].
This group of figures is
entitled *Three Helpers in
Need*. The relationships
between the figures, the m[any]
different surface textures [and]
the complex folds in the ro[bes]
show the artist's great skill[.]

pict on a small scale the day to day occupations ...he slaves of the dead person. The small carved ...res are brightly painted to make them more ...nplete and life-like. Their purpose was to ...ure that the master or mistress received the ...ie services in the after-life as he or she had ...n supplied with on earth.

Brightly painted wood sculptures are not a ...uliarity of early or primitive civilizations. ...til the Renaissance, it was customary to paint ...lpture, and many of the early European mas-...s of painting turned their hands to decorating a ...e variety of carvings.

...ome of the richest examples of wood sculpture ...ne from the tribal cultures of Africa, South and ...rth America, the Pacific Islands and Austral-...i, including various stylized carvings for use in ...gious rites and ceremonies. Masks, figures and ...ms exist from many historical periods, often ...vily decorated or bearing traces of their origi-...colors. The forms and design of the sculptures ...onged to traditions handed down through ...erations. In Nigeria, terracotta heads have ...n found of a design which suggests that the ...e originated in wood carving and was trans-

lated into another medium.

The craft of wood carving has been widely used in making furniture and in association with building and construction techniques in many different cultures. The Mayans decorated the wooden framework of their temple buildings with intricate relief patterns. Simple wooden boats were carved by the Romans and a tradition of carved decoration has lasted through many modifications of design and function. Furniture such as tables, chairs, beds and storage chests have been beautified with much imaginative imagery, from scenes and figures to simple engraved patterns. Particularly fine examples come from China, a country with a great heritage of art and craft. Wood carving has often been combined with gold or silver inlays for a luxurious effect.

The close connection between sculpture and religious architecture gave rise to a period of outstanding sculpture in wood in Northern Europe during the fifteenth and sixteenth centuries. The German artists Michael Pacher (active c1465–1498), Tilman Riemenschneider (died 1531) and Veit Stoss (c1450–1533) carved the most beautifully intricate altarpieces and relief

Above The statue of St Mary Magdalene by Donatello was one of the artist's latest works. It is very expressive, combining subject matter and technique. The folds of the robe contrast starkly with those of the Riemenschneider piece.

Above This medieval carving of St Thomas Aquinas shows the uses of wood and paint combined. In fact, this practice was the main convention in European wood carving until the time of the Germans Riemenschneider and Stoss in the fifteenth century.

Above right Another application of wood carving was in figureheads for ships. This practice offered carvers a wide scope in subject matter and technique. This American example is fairly simple, but many reveal a complex use of both carving and painting.

decoration for churches, as well as small figures of biblical characters. Some of these are extraordinarily complex compositions. Both Stoss and Riemenschneider eventually abandoned the tradition of painting wood and allowed the rich, natural qualities of the material to remain visible.

Without doubt, wood carving was widely practiced in Europe in the centuries following the Renaissance, although many of the major sculptors of this period are best known for work in stone, or modeled forms. Much excellent work was done in decoration for architecture and furniture. Grinling Gibbons (1648–1721) worked in many locations in England on decoration for churches and private houses, and much of his work can still be seen.

The twentieth century has seen a number of artists favor wood as a material, despite the range of new possibilities in technique which has appeared in plastics, resin and metal welding. Constantin Brancusi (1876–1957) refined his carved sculptures into abstract shapes seeking the essential form of human and animal subjects, later moving into pure abstraction. In addition to using wood as a material for finished sculpture, he often mounted stone sculptures on specially designed wooden bases, and made wood prototypes for sculptures finally made in stone or metal.

The British artists Henry Moore (born 1898) and Barbara Hepworth (1903–1975) have de-

veloped their monumental style of abstract sculpture in wood. Both artists have been occupied with the relation of space and mass, often on grand scale, carving large, curving sculptures with deep depressions and holes passing right through the form. The rich color and grain patterns of polished wood give each sculpture a unique surface quality.

Wood readily lends itself to construction techniques, whether pieces are simply glued together, jointed with the traditional techniques of carpentry, or bolted in large sections. Artists exploring Cubist principles of form, such as Picasso (1881–1973) and Frenchman Henri Laurens (1885–1954) made wooden reliefs and free-standing sculptures with jutting, angular planes, interpreting a new vision of volumetric description. Surrealist artist Hans Arp (1887–1966) made a series of painted reliefs in wood, simple forms in vivid colors, based on the organic shapes of natural objects. The American sculptor Louise Nevelson (born 1899) creates reliefs like huge modern altarpieces, often incorporating preformed wooden shapes, such as chair legs or banister rails. The simple idea of stacking wood, as in a builder's yard, forms the basis of large sculpture by the American artist Carl André (born 1935). Interlocking stacks of wooden beams form a satisfying, symmetrical form in which the true nature of the material is completely undisguised.

The strong imagery of primitive and folk arts had a great influence on many areas of sculpture and painting. The head of the leopard (**below**) comes from Cuzco in Peru. Cuzco was one of the main centers of the Inca civilization from the mid fifteenth century. The carved figure of the thunderbird (**left**) is a much later example, dating from the nineteenth century. The piece was made by Canadian Indians from the north west coastal region. Both the form and the decoration are highly stylized.

Left *Wood Quarry* by the contemporary British sculptor David Nash shows how wood sculpture can be created and positioned in a natural setting. Here the placing and combination of the pieces of wood are the main considerations. In recent years, many sculptors have become interested in wood as a medium for construction as well as for carving.

Above *Head of a Woman* by Pablo Picasso is an example of late work by the artist. There are clear resemblances between this piece and the Peruvian and Indian works. This emerges in the stylization of approach and the use of color. Picasso's great talents enabled him to use a wide variety of styles and approaches.

99

MATERIALS
THE TREE

Before describing the ways and means of shaping wood, it is important to give an account of its origin—the tree. Each tree is peculiar to its particular species and location. Every year a tree covers its entire surface area with a new layer of fiber. The material for this fiber is produced by the paper thin cambium layer on the underside of the bark. The fiber gives wood its tensile strength and conveys water and nutrient from the earth to the leaves for photosynthesis and returns them as food to the cambium layer.

Trees growing on their own tend to spiral their fiber more than trees growing together where they develop a group strength against the wind. The timberman will watch for factors such as soil type and land drainage when selecting trees to fell and process.

Living wood is full of moisture. Once the tree is down and ceases to function as a living entity it begins to lose this moisture and shrinks. The extremely important process of controlling this drying out is called seasoning.

SEASONING

The purpose of seasoning wood is to produce timber of uniform and stable moisture content which will 'move' (crack or warp) as little as possible. Cracking, which is also—picturesquely—called heartshake, occurs along the grain of fiber when moisture is not leaving the wood evenly, but this cracking does not weaken the timber as it is 'with' the grain.

Other than pulping for paper, most wood destined for the building and furniture trade accordingly is sawn along the grain into planks of various thickness. Air dried or kiln dried, the timber is stacked with chocks separating each plank to allow air to circulate evenly. The stacks are sometimes weighted on top to prevent warping. When seasoning wood, which is planked or in the round (unplanked), allow a year for each inch (2.5cm) of thickness.

Air dried means that the wood should be stacked outside under a simple roof—a piece of corrugated iron supported on legs would do—somewhere where air circulates. When the wood is seasoned, store it inside an unheated shed. As a general rule, the bark should be removed, as bugs and fungus like to thrive in the damp area between the wood and the bark.

Even when seasoned, wood retains a certain amount of moisture and remains sensitive to its environment. Even centuries-old wood will open up in central heating. The cracks usually close again in normal humidity. If kept in a moderate environment, wood will stabilize to that environment. Natural wood is not an inert substance and this must be accepted before using it in any way as a sculpture medium.

Right A tree grows thicker gradually by an annual process in which a new layer of fiber is laid down beneath the bark. Cells on the underside of the bark, known as the cambium layer, produce the new fibers. As the subsequent layers grow, the innermost section of the tree is subject to chemical changes, which may also change its color, and forms the heartwood. The living wood, or sapwood, which is the most recently formed part of the tree, provides vitality by conducting moisture and nutrients through the fibers to the leaves and acts as food storage for the cambium layer. If the growth of the tree is uninterrupted, the process is hardly visible in the section of the wood. But if the tree is inhibited by unfavorable climatic conditions, in winter for example, growth rings appear which indicate the pattern of the successive layers of new fiber.

Sapwood

Cambium layer

Bark

Outer bark

Heartwood

Bark is sometimes enclosed between two limbs of a tree (**2**) which become merged as the new wood grows. In this close up picture (**3**) a dead section of bark is wholly encased in the more recent growth.

When a branch is pruned, it should be cut off close to the base. The small area of dead wood is covered by new growth in the fibers (**7,8**) and although this may form a bulge, the new wood is quite sound.

Crystalline deposits may occur in wood fibers (**6**). These are formed by the precipitation of mineral salts drawn up from the soil through the roots and fibers of the tree. The deposits are usually microscopic, but if enlarged, they can be a hazard when wood is sawn.

Growth of wood The fibers of wood tend to grow straight, in line with the vertical axis of the tree, and this forms the grain pattern. However, spiral grain (**1**) is found in many species. The twisting of the fibers causes the timber to split down the grain.

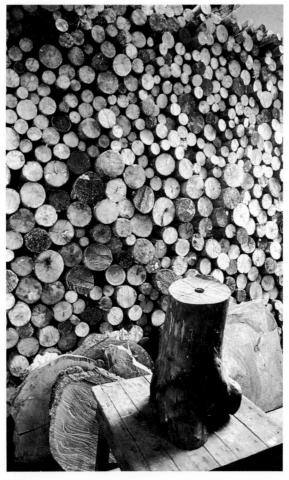

Knots form in timber at the base of a branch. The branch develops naturally from the wood fibers (**4**), distorting the grain. When a branch dies, the knot of dead fibers becomes loosely encased in the living wood (**5**), and may fall out when the timber is cut and dried.

SOURCES OF WOOD

[Fo]raging in demolition sites, old houses, barns, [and] factories can provide you with heavy beams, [floo]r boards, or banister ends. Furniture restorers [oft]en have good pieces in their junk heaps. Even [the] wood stacks yield the odd piece of oak, cherry [or] pear.

Forage for unseasoned wood as well. If you see [a f]allen hardwood tree in a field, find out whose it [is a]nd ask for a piece of it. Tree surgeons who lop [urb]an trees and local park departments are good [sou]rces. People handling and clearing such wood [are] usually sympathetic to the idea that it will be [use]d creatively. Build up a stock, stack it so air [can] circulate around it and forget about it. It will [sea]son in time, and you can keep adding to the [sto]ck whenever you come across likely pieces.

[B]uying is another obvious way to obtain wood. [Blo]ckboard, plywood, hardboard and masonite [are] made to be inert and consistent. Manufac-[tur]ed generally in standard sizes, these boards can [be] bought from timber merchants. 1in (2.5cm) to [½i]n (1.25cm) thicknesses make a rigid, flat plane. [Thi]n ply and masonite are good for a cladded, [cur]ved surface and for laminating a bend.

[O]ak, lime, beech and foreign hardwoods can [be] bought in the round from some timber mer-[cha]nts. Always try to talk to the foreman and say [exa]ctly what it is for, to ensure that you get a [sui]table piece. Building timber such as pine is [wid]ely available.

Left If the space is available, a stock of wood can be stored in the studio as it is acquired, giving greater scope for sculpture than ready-cut timber or boards. Lengths of wood should be stacked horizontally and not subjected to excessive heat or dampness.

Cherry

Cedar

Ash

Holly

Pine

Beech

Pear

Birch (Canadian)

Boxwood

TYPES OF WOOD

CONIFEROUS

Cedar This close grained wood is light and easily worked, but is durable for outdoor sculpture.
Columbian larch, pine, spruce (deal) These are soft woods with a pronounced grain. In general use in the building trade, they are useful for construction work, but not suitable for carving, having a tendency to split easily. Yellow pine is an exception, and is a good carving wood.

FRUIT WOODS

Apple A close-grained hard wood, apple is white when fresh, but dries to a reddish color. It is easily workable in carving.
Cherry Cherry is a traditional carving wood, used particularly for relief work. It has a lovely, red-brown color.
Holly This is a smooth, hard white wood with a fine grain, suitable for carving. It has a curious smell when cut.
Pear Pear wood has a range of colors from light red to strong yellow. It is even-textured, close grained and moderately hard.
Plum The grain of plum wood is quite distinct and the colors range from pink to dark red. It is hard, but not difficult to work. All fruit woods are good for carving, but, since the trees are relatively small, they cannot be used for large-scale work in one piece.

DECIDUOUS SOFTWOODS

Alder The alder is a small tree and the wood is light and easily carved. It has a reddish color and indistinct grain, but, because of its composition, is not suitable for splitting along the grain. It is used for making clogs.
Birch The bark must be removed when seasoning birch. It is a white wood with a soft, indistinct grain, and rots quickly outside.
Hazel The hazel is a small tree, and the wood is very pliable when it is green.

HARDWOODS

Ash Ash is a white wood which seasons very hard an is resilient in its length. It is easy to split when green an being durable outdoors, it i excellent for constructions which take stress. It is also used for the handles of met tools.
Beech This wood is soft when green and splits easily but is quite hard when seasoned. It has a light brow color. Beech, which is often

Chestnut

Mahogany

Sycamore (Plane)

Ebony

Maple (Bird's Eye)

Walnut

Elm

Oak

Yew

ed to make mallet heads, is
t suitable for outdoor
ulpture.
oxwood This is excellent
r small, delicate works as it
very hard and dense with an
distinct grain. Boxwood is
so the best choice for a
isel handle.
hestnut A durable wood
hich splits well whether
een or seasoned, chestnut is
rong in the length but has a
ndency to split. It is mid-
own, with distinct grain and
kes a finish well.
bony Ebony is a very hard
ood, black and dense,

suitable for small-scale work.
It is hard to come by and the
splinters can be poisonous, so
it is not a good choice for a
beginner.
Elm Elm is a dark reddish-
brown wood with an
interweaving grain. It resists
splitting but tends to warp
during seasoning. It is long
lasting outdoors if wet—
Roman drainage pipes of
elmwood are still found intact
and functioning.
Greenheart This wood is so
dense it will not float and is
used in the construction of
dock piers. It is difficult to

work for the sculptor, but is
very durable.
Lime (basswood) This is a
very suitable wood for
carving. It seasons well and
has an indistinct grain and light
yellowish color. It is a
particularly good choice for
relief carving but is not tough
enough for outdoor display.
Mahogany This wood has a
low moisture content when
seasoned and tends to splinter
if carved across the grain.
However, it is suitable for
carving, if the tools are kept
very sharp. It has a rich,
reddish-brown color.

Maple All maple wood is
close-grained but the texture
varies. The range of color,
from light to red-brown, gives
a good finish.
Oak The heart wood of oak
is durable in all conditions,
seasoning hard and continuing
to harden in time. The sap
wood is usually removed
before carving and must not
be used in construction as it
has no strength under stress.
The sap wood is easily
distinguishable from the
heartwood as a yellow layer.
The heartwood is suitable for
both construction and carving.

Sycamore (plane)
Sycamore is white and
moderately hard. It resists
splitting but rots quickly
outside. It can be difficult to
work but is obtainable in large
pieces.
Walnut This is an excellent
carving wood, dark brown in
color. It has a rich grain and is
much sought after as a veneer,
so it is expensive and difficult
to obtain.
Yew Yew is hard and durable
with a distinct grain. The
colors vary from light yellow
to strong reddish-brown. In
carving, it gives a good finish.

TOOLS AND EQUIPMENT
CUTTING AND CARVING TOOLS

Tools for shaping wood are designed and used, observing the linear structure of the grain. Each has a particular function related to its shape, size and weight.

Wedge The wedge has a tapered edge and is designed for splitting lengths of wood along the grain. A heavy metal hammer (sledge or lump hammer) is used to drive in a metal wedge and a wooden maul or beetle for wooden wedges. Most unseasoned wood will split easily, but elm, sycamore and knotty pine are rather resistant. Oak, ash, beech and chestnut split readily.

Wedges should not be too sharp, they part the fibers rather than cut them. Wood shaping tools are all a development of the wedge.

Axe The axe is simply a sharp wedge with a handle. The weight applied is the weight of the tool itself multiplied by the length of the handle. The difference from the wedge is that the axe will cut across the fiber. The first cut is made diagonally down the grain, subsequent cuts are made sharply across.

There are different sizes, weights and styles of axe head and different lengths of handle. It is important to be comfortable with the tool and to be able to use it without tiring. Big felling axes are too heavy: it is better to use a trimming axe with a 3½lb (1.5kg) head and a 30in (75cm) handle, and a 2lb (1kg) hand axe with a 12in (30cm) handle.

Adze The adze is an axe with the cutting edge on a different plane. It was originally designed for boat building, shaping curved beams and boards. The craftsman stood astride the wood, skillfully shaving it to the required thickness. Do not attempt to use the heavy long-handled adze. Without proper apprenticeship, it is all too easy for a glancing blow to chop into your foot. The smaller short-handled adze, similar in size and weight to a hatchet, is very useful and much safer. It is a form of crude chisel striking into and shaving the wood. Gouge blades can be used. African sculptors use the adze almost exclusively.

Chisel The chisel is the most versatile and precise wood shaping tool. Carpenters' flat chisels are the most useful for general work, with cutting edges ranging from 2in (5cm) to ⅛in (3mm). The flat chisel is designed both to cut across and shave along the grain.

Do not attempt to remove too much wood with each chisel cut. The chisel can behave like its ancestor, the wedge, and split along the grain,

Gouge The gouge chisel has a curved blade a can do the jobs a flat chisel cannot, such carving a concave surface or cutting a shall surface line. For engraving a surface a V-shap chisel is used.

Gouges come in a variety of curves and widt with straight or curved shafts. Curved shafts useful in cutting awkward surfaces round a through a hollow.

Plane The plane is a wide chisel blade held a particular constant angle for shaving a flat s face, useful for construction work and for prep ing pieces to be joined flush.

Draw knife This is a long, sharp cutting edge w a handle at right-angles to the blade at each e The weight applied is the sculptor's own wei by drawing the tool toward the body. This is l dangerous than it might appear because the ar cannot pull back far enough to allow the blade reach the body. The draw knife is for shaping, shaving along the grain, and is especially use for green wood.

Spokeshave A small version of the draw knife, spokeshave is useful for cleaning and smooth the surface of wood, as well as shaping it. It quite a small tool and can be used on a flat curved surface.

Files A file is a bar of metal with a roughen surface, attached into a smooth handle at o end. It is flat on one side and curved on the oth It is a heavy abrasive tool for evening a rounding the surface of the wood. A complet round file is designed for work on awkward partially enclosed surfaces.

Rifflers Rifflers are essentially small files on lo narrow shafts. They are shaped for work delicate or complex forms. Rifflers are availa in a wide range of sizes.

Sandpaper Abrasive papers come in vari grades, from very rough to very fine, and are us to achieve a perfectly smooth finish.

Handles Metal tools have wooden handles several reasons. As opposed to metal, wood more comfortable, light and warm to hold. A and hickory are good for axe, adze, hammer a mallet handles, being resilient in the leng Beech and boxwood make good chisel handle To give chisel handles a longer life put a me ring round the wood, just below the end, so t mallet hits wood and not metal. A piece narrow copper piping or a length of wire wrapp round and twisted tight will keep the grain of t handle together.

SAWS

The most effective way to cut across wood grain with a saw. This effectively consists of a row tiny chisels set at the edge of a plane of steel. T

Using a large crosscut saw
1. Raise the wood on blocks and fit wedge-shaped chocks to hold it in place.

2. Draw the saw evenly through the wood, cutting across the grain. The wedges hold it rigid against the moving saw.

…ing the bow saw Cut …oss the grain of a large …ce of wood with a bow …. Support the wood in a … horse.

set in a wooden handle, for manual use, or …tached to a motor for extra power.

…ng saw A saw with a long blade (5ft/1.5m) and … handle at each end is pulled, never pushed …rough the wood, and is used on heavy timber.

…wsaw This is particularly useful for rough cuts. …ard-tipped replaceable blades are very sharp …d give good service. Throw the blade away …en it becomes blunt. The bowsaw is designed … unseasoned wood but cuts seasoned timber …st as well.

…rosscut A seven-point crosscut saw in invalu-…le. A seven-point saw has seven teeth per inch …5cm). Buy a good one and it will last a lifetime. … crosscut is less effective on unseasoned wood, …t is excellent for general construction work. …e teeth are set and angled to cut across the …od grain.

Ripsaw The teeth of a ripsaw are set differently from those of a crosscut, as the ripsaw is designed for cutting down the grain.

Tenon saw This is a fine-toothed saw, 12 points to the inch (2.5cm), with a thick metal support along the top edge of the blade. The tenon saw has precision in cutting either across or down the grain.

Fretsaw The fretsaw is for cutting out curved or angular shapes from board. It has a narrow blade, set in a metal frame, and is easily maneuvered through the wood.

Bandsaw This is a narrow, power-driven blade, fixed into a heavy, stable support. The bandsaw is able to cut through hardwood boards up to 4in (10cm) thick.

Jigsaw This is another power tool with a narrow blade fixed into a machine casing. The radius of

Saws The best way to cut wood across the grain is with saw. A useful selection for many different tasks would include a chainsaw (**1**), bow saw (**2**), ripsaw (**3**), crosscut saw (**4**) and a tenon saw (**5**). The teeth on saw blades are set for specific functions. This picture shows the teeth on a tenon saw (**6**), crosscut saw (**7**) and ripsaw (**8**).

Tools for wood

There are literally thousands of tools which can be used when working with wood. Their functions are always related to their weights, shapes and sizes. Modern power tools which made work much easier include the electric drill (**1**) and the electric jigsaw (**2**). Surforms (**3**), various files (**4**) and rifflers (**5**) are all used for smoothing surfaces. For combining materials, socket spanner sets (**6**), screwdrivers (**7**), wrenches (**8**), coach bolts (**9**), studding (**10**), screws (**11**) and coach screws (**12**) are often used. Wire nails (**13**) and oval nails (**14**), pincers (**15**), the ordinary hammer (**16**), the ball hammer (**17**), pliers (**18**) and claw hammers (**19**) are also used for this purpose. Construction work often involves the use of polyvinyl acetate adhesive (**20**), dowels soaked in linseed oil for outdoor work (**21**), natural dowels (**22**), a template for making dowels (**23**), and augers (**24**)—with handles fitted (**25**) or with a brace (**26**).

cut is not restricted by a supporting pillar as is that of the bandsaw.

Electric chainsaw The chainsaw is useful in the studio as it is relatively small, light and quiet. It must be used thoughtfully and carefully as a power-driven blade is always dangerous. It is used to remove large areas of wood quickly. The speed can lead to over-zealous cutting and disrespect for the wood.

A petrol-driven chainsaw is used for cutting sections from a tree where it lies, in a field or wood. It can make certain cuts, such as boring through the wood, that other saws cannot, but it is noisy and dangerous, and gives off unpleasant fumes.

Bench circular saw A circular saw is power driven, and used for ripsawing along the grain. is no use in carving, but helpful in constructi work where wood is often used in its length rath than mass. It is set in a robust frame and l adjustable guides for angled cuts. Again, it potentially very dangerous and should be us with care and respect. Attachments to conver hand-held power drill to make a circular saw sufficient for the home craftsperson, but substitute for the fixed machine in the studio.

MALLET, MAUL AND BEETL

These are important carving tools which will so become close friends. Lignum vitae makes best mallet, being a heavy oily wood with a clo

The most versatile wood carving tool, the chisel, comes in an enormous range of variations; the most useful have cutting edges which are flat, U-shaped or V-shaped (**27**). The shape and size of the cutting edges vary according to the purpose of the tool. Mallets, also available in a wide range (**28**), are also vital for carving work. Mallets are usually made from the very hard wood lignum vitae. A maul (**29**) is made from a single piece of wood. Planes and squares come in many types. Pictured here are squares (**30**), a plane (**31**), an adjustable square for setting angles (**32**) and a marking gauge (**33**). Axes are available in different sizes and weights, with various handle lengths and head shapes. Pictured here are a felling axe (**34**), a trimming axe (**35**), a hatchet (**36**) and a draw knife (**37**), used for shaping by shaving along the grain. It is certainly not advisable for the amateur woodworker to invest in the complete range of tools available. It is of much greater use to obtain a few tools of good quality. Pre-planning will help you to purchase those you are most likely to need for the type of work you are undertaking.

erwoven grain. Beech is the next best, but it dually erodes with use.

A maul is made from a single piece of wood, m the base and root of a young tree. The otty tangle of fibers in the root base make a ilient club. The beetle is a big wooden sledge mmer for driving wooden wedges. A steel ring und the handle gives it more weight and a ger life.

DRILLS

ger This is a form of turning chisel for boring a e across or down the grain. It has two cutting es on either side at the end of a spiral shaft, ich winds out the shavings, and an eye at the

top to hold a wooden handle. When the auger is turned, the leading screw winds the tool into the wood. The turning blades shave the wood as they are pulled in by the screw thread.

The auger can make a long hole, much longer than the electric drill, hand drill or brace and bit, and wider, up to 2in (5cm) in diameter. The spiral can clear some shavings but after a few inches it may clog and jam the shaft. To avoid this take out the auger occasionally and remove the shavings. The auger is used in doweling or bolting big timbers together. For smaller holes use a brace and bit, or hand or electric drill.

Electric drill This is very useful for making preliminary holes for screws and dowels especially when there are a lot to do.

Wedges

Bench vice

Har

G

Sash

Tool

Wooden

Bench s

Storage

Above A steady, solid work bench of comfortable height is a vital piece of equipment. The bench should be fitted with a vice and a bench screw, so wood can be held fast as it is sawn, drilled or carved. A low platform underneath the bench provides a handy area of storage space for materials or work in progress. To keep tools tidy and accessible, a tool board should be fitted to a wall close to the bench, on which clamps, hammers, and cutting tools can be hung.

HOLDING WOOD

To enable the sculptor to work comfortably and efficiently, the wood must be held steady. This is achieved largely by common sense. A steady, robust bench is an important tool providing a comfortable working height and a base for a vice and bench screw (holdfast). Large pieces of wood can be laid on the bench or leant against it for for carving, held steady by clamps, or chocks nailed to the bench or floor. Very large pieces can lie on the floor and need only chocks to stop them rolling. To move big pieces use levers and rollers. Any stout length will work as a lever and sawn lengths of scaffolding pipe make good rollers.

For lifting and suspending, use a block a tackle on a gantry—a beam supported by tripods or on very sturdy tressels. For this, ide an H-beam of steel should be set across the stu and into the walls.

Vice A strong vice attached to a solid workber is an invaluable tool in all wood sculpture te niques. The vice should have short ½in (1.25c wood planks screwed inside the jaws, to giv better grip and prevent chisels from striking metal.

Clamps G-clamps and sash clamps are vita construction work, for temporary joining wt the form is worked out, and for holding secti in place.

SHARPENING TOOLS

is is an essential activity, calming in its method, d it puts you in touch with the all important lge'. Sharpening your tools can be good prepation for your work.

The purpose is to give the cutting edge a well pported 'keenness'. A sound edge will last for me time and can be kept by the occasional run an oilstone. Too fine an edge will break and kes a lot of work to restore.

When sharpening a flat chisel, what is impornt is the angle, correctly termed the 'ground gle', of taper from the main body of the shaft ward the tip. It should be neither too steep, ich would clog in the grain, nor too shallow, ich would weaken the cutting edge. The ound angle is best at 25° and the cutting edge ned angle' is best at 30°. Both angles should be t and not curved.

For the ground angle use a grindstone. A 6in 5cm) diameter wheel, ¾in (18mm) thick will e good general service, either electric or hand ven. For the honed angle, use a flat carborunm oilstone.

Be careful not to allow the tool to overheat on wheel as this will damage the resilience of the tal. The edge turns blue when overheated. If it es overheat, grind it off and start again. Have small container of water by the wheel and casionally cool the edge.

Hold the chisel at the required 30° angle and sh it along the oilstone. To stop the stone pping about, put it against a batten nailed to a nch. A burr will form on the edge of the chisel, is breaking off this burr that creates the sharp tting edge. To do this turn the chisel over and ve it once up the stone, holding it flat down on stone. Then continue as before, alternating se procedures until the burr breaks off. Work over the stone to avoid wearing a groove in the ddle.

The gouge chisel appears more difficult to arpen, but, once the rhythm of a figure of eight ovement is mastered, it is as simple as the flat isel. In this motion, rock the gouge edge from e to side as you move it over the stone. move the burr with a curved slipstone. Sharn a V-shaped chisel like a flat chisel, removing burr with an angled slipstone. It is as well to ve one oilstone for flat chisels and another for uges.

For sharpening an axe, use a file on the oulders' and a stone for the edge. Secure the e head in a vice and move the stone against the de. The same procedure is used for sharpening draw knife.

Saws need to be sharpened and 'set' to obtain the slight angle of each alternate tooth to the plane of the blade. This makes the cut slightly wider than the blade. If the saw is stiff in the cut, then it is not sufficiently 'set'. The setting is done with a saw setting gauge, the sharpening with a triangular file.

Put two strips of wood down either side of the saw edge and clamp it in a vice. The wood supports the thin plane of metal. Sharpen each tooth angled away from where you stand. Push the file evenly two or three times through each alternate valley. The file must be held horizontal. On a crosscut saw, where the blade is slightly angled from the handle, push gently against the cutting edge nearer the handle in each valley. On a ripsaw, file at right-angles to the blade. Start near the handle and work along to the end, then turn the saw round and do the same again. Both sides must be sharpened evenly or the saw will cut on a curve.

Sharpening tools It is vital to keep tools sharp, as blunt tools will not achieve the effects you desire. Useful tools for sharpening include a grind wheel (**1**), a file for saw teeth (**2**), a saw set (**3**), oilstone (**4**), slipstone (**5**) and oil (**6**).

Sharpening carving tools
1. Lubricate an oilstone with a thin trail of oil.

2. Hold a flat chisel with the honed angle of the blade flat on the oilstone. Push it up and down on the stone surface.

3. Sharpen a gouge by working in a figure eight motion on the stone, rocking the blade from side to side around the curves.

4. Finish the gouge by removing the burr from inside the blade with a slipstone.

Removing waste wood 1.
Mark a shape on the wood with chalk. Clamp it in a vice and make vertical cuts along the width with a bow saw, down to the level of the chalk mark.

2. Use a chisel to remove the waste wood between the saw cuts, following the chalk line.

3. Hold the chisel with the flat side up, so the angled edge of the blade follows the curve without digging into the wood.

4. Smooth down the cut surface with a rasp. Use the flat side of the rasp on conv curves.

5. Turn the rasp and use the rounded side for working into concave surfaces.

6. When one side of the shaping is completed, turn the wood in the vice and repeat the process on the other edge.

7. Smooth down the secor curve with the rasp as befo The shape is now cleanly formed.

Splitting wood 1. Hold a metal wedge to the sawn end of a length of wood and drive it in with a mallet.

2. Place a second wedge in the top of the wood, aligned to the first along the length.

3. Drive both wedges in further to split the wood open. The first wedge is loosened as the second is fully embedded.

4. Take out the first wedge and place it behind the second. Hammer it in, to lengthen the split.

5. Repeat the process until the length of wood is split right along into two pieces Cut any holding fibers with hatchet.

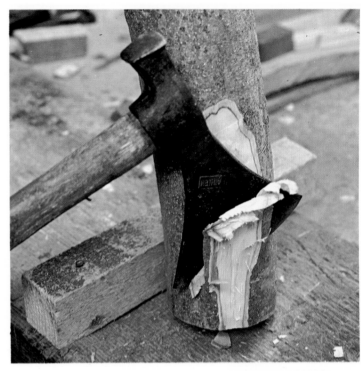

Using an axe Hold the top
of the wood and steady the
bottom against a bench chock.
Chip away the wood gradually
to form an angled cut,
working with the grain.

Using a drawtool Grasp the
handles of the tool at either
end and draw it along the
wood to strip away the bark.

Using a tenon saw The
tenon saw may be used on
small pieces of wood for
accuracy in cutting across or
down the grain.

TECHNIQUES
CARVING

Carving refers to methods of removing wood
from a mass to achieve an image. It is important
that the idea is appropriate to the material and
that the behavior of wood is considered. Use the
linear structure to your advantage. Wood is
stronger along its grain than across it. Mark out
the first areas to remove with chalk: When
possible use a saw to cut across the grain and
chisel wood away toward the saw cut. Keep the
wood well supported and cut toward the support.
Mark it with the chalk at each stage, have plenty
at hand. Keep turning the wood to approach the
form from all sides. Start with the heavier tools—
axe, saw, broad chisels and gouges—then work
with more precise tools to shave and file until the
related forms, planes and surfaces work together
to make an image.

Wood can sustain many degrees of surface, and
it is a mistake to assume that a smooth polished
surface is automatically the surface that is required. All tools leave their own specific mark on
the wood and these should not be disregarded.

Above This still-life by Fred Watson was carved in ash. The work is virtually life-size and was carved in different pieces which were then fitted together. The piece gives an impression of calmness, one of the effects the artist wished to achieve.

Roughing out 1. Make a drawing of the basic shapes required as a rough guide to carving. Mark up the block with chalk.

2. Drill into the block where it is to be deeply carved. This breaks the rigidity and forms a stop if the wood begins to split.

RELIEF CARVING

Light is the most important factor in relief wor and assuming the relief carving will be presente vertical on the wall then light will fall across t surface at an angle of 60° from above. The carvir modulates this fall of light. The more refined too are used for relief carving; engraver's tools, sma V-shaped chisels, gouges and rifflers. Working an angled bench is more comfortable than flat a bench and the light articulation is also mo accurate. Hardwoods, being close grained, a good for relief carving. Lime, cherry and waln are particularly useful.

CONSTRUCTION

Wood is traditionally a material for constru tion—of roofs, furniture, barns and houses. linear nature is perfect for this practice. There a countless books describing basic carpentry but not be conditioned by the traditions of joiner Observe them and use them as expedient. Ba cally, for sculpture, you need only observe t linear structure of wood and use it to yo advantage.

One of the contemporary concerns of sculptu is the way an object engages space. Constructio

3. Keep the block firmly clamped in a vice while carving. Use wedges to support an irregularly shaped block.

4. Cut along outlines with a flat chisel, making vertical cuts down into the wood.

5. Start to clear broad areas of wood with the chisel. Work along the grain toward the outline of each shape.

6. Use a gouge to give a clean, deep cut along outlines. Shave off the wood a little at a time.

7. The gouge is also used to cut across the grain. Avoid cutting too deeply in one stroke or the gouge may jam or split the wood.

8. Continue to work with flat chisels and large gouges, starting to define the shapes and planes within the block.

9. Roughing out gives the general form of the sculpture. It is then ready to be developed in detail with smaller chisels.

y involve space as much as material. It is worth
king large constructions in such a way that they
be dismantled into smaller units. This is
sible for storing and transport.

Clamps are invaluable, as well as offcuts and
ten lengths to prop and hold pieces in position
ile you try out angles and heights. Once the
itions are certain, the methods of jointing can
decided, with consideration of the weight and
ss involved. For permanent joins, a lap joint,
t joint, or mortise and tenon can be glued,
veled, nailed or screwed.

f dismantling will be necessary, use coach bolts
screws, or pegs rubbed with soap which can be
cked out. If the presence of a bolt head or nut
istracting, it can be countersunk to disguise it,
nut being tightened by a box or socket
nner. There are many ways of joining wood,
rt from traditional joinery, such as binding,
pping, stacking, leaning, and plaiting.

Large shapes can be made by building a
oden frame and covering it with panels of
nposite wood which is flexible, such as maso-
e or thin plywood. This is called cladding.

A mass can be built up by lamination. A bend is
de in thin composition board, ply or masonite,
with thinly sawn planks of wood. The pieces
bent and glued together, and held in position
il set.

Relief carving 1. Fix the block in a vice. Draw up the design in pencil and start by lightly graving lines with a V-tool.

2. Guide the V-gouge carefully around the pencil lines, tapping it gently with a mallet.

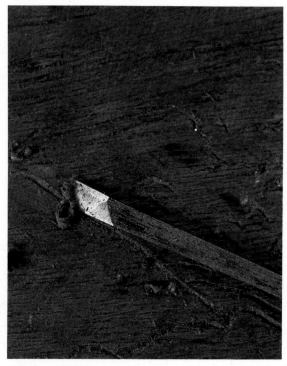

3. Use a chisel with an angled tip to shave away and shape the surface. Push it with your hand, not with a mallet.

ers 1. Rifflers are small
s with a filing head which
e in a variety of shapes
with straight or curved
ts.

se rifflers for delicate
ing and refining the
ace. Guide the head into
es with the forefinger.

Left *Curtain Blowing* by Claire Langdown is a modern relief carving. The artist has chosen a simple, everyday image and created it effectively in her chosen wood, obeche. The folds of the curtain help convey the feeling of movement as the curtain blows in the wind.

Bolting two blocks together 1. Set the blocks in position, raised from the floor and held firmly together with G-clamps.

2. Position the auger and turn the handle until the cutting end bores right through the wood. Keep the shaft vertical.

3. The bolts may be disguised by countersinking. Mark the circumference of the bolt washer around the drilled hole.

4. Using a small gouge, make vertical cuts around the marked circle to the depth required.

5. Clear away surplus wood inside the circle with a large gouge to form a small recess in the block.

6. Push the bolt up through the drilled hole and fit the washer and nut.

7. Tighten the nut with a socket spanner, screwing it down into the recess.

Squaring off a block 1. Clamp the block in a bench vice and use a square to mark the right-angle at one end.

2. Steady the blade of a crosscut saw along the thumb of your free hand. Draw the whole length of the saw through the wood.

Seasoned wood can be made pliable by l[...] containment with steam, in a process called ste[...] bending. The wood is bent to shape while plia[...] and sets in that shape as it dries.

Constructing a mass to carve involves dowel[...] pieces together to gain a bulk. For consistency[...] mass, the timber sections should be of the sa[...] species and if possible the same age, and [...] dowels too. But interesting results can [...] achieved by mixing wood types. Construct[...] with wood is an interesting technique, which [...] be of particular relevance to the beginner, wh[...] trying to develop sculptural skills.

Pegging wood with dowels 1. Make dowels by cutting small lengths of wood and rounding them off by hammering them through circular holes in a metal template.

2. Apply glue to the pieces of wood to be assembled and clamp them firmly together to form the construction.

3. Drill through the joints to make holes for the dowels. The dowels should be made of the same wood as the construction.

4. It is essential that the drilled holes pass through both pieces of wood at the joint. Pour in wood glue.

Left *Running Animals/ Reindeer* by the American artist Robert Stackhouse is a vast construction measuring about 12 feet by 6 feet by 66 feet (about 4 meters by 2 meters by 20 meters). The play of light and shadow through the slatted wood helps convey the impression of movement which the artist is trying to create. This shows how, in sculpture, light is often an important element in a work which is constructed from another medium.

Above This 1966 wood sculpture by the French artist Pol Bury shows an approach which contrasts with that of Robert Stackhouse. The combination of cubes and spheres makes a very restful work in which the viewer can compare shape and texture of the different types of wood. Many of Bury's works are mobiles or kinetic works in which the movement may be so slow as to be almost imperceptible.

5. Hammer in the dowels as far as they will go, to pass through the seam of the joint.

6. Use a tenon saw to cut off the dowels at the surface of the wood.

ADHESIVES

here are several types of glue which can be used construction work, some stronger than others. o glue is effective on damp or unseasoned ood. Many adhesives will fill a gap in a joint, but e bigger the gap, the weaker the bond. The llowing are effective in general use.

A good type is glue derived from animal or fish ins, bones and sinews. It comes in solid bars or anules and must be warmed, but never boiled, efore use. It is a basic, cheap glue for inside ork but does not resist heat, damp or humidity.

Joints must be clamped while the glue is drying. Casein comes in powder form and is mixed with water. It will set at a low temperature, resists heat and humidity, weakens when wet but hardens again as it dries. It is good for joints which take stress. PVA glue is suitable for general woodwork inside. It sets in 20 minutes and dries hard in 2 hours. It is adequate for general use but not very strong under stress.

Epoxy glues are very versatile for indoor and outdoor work. They resist wet weather elements and hold firm under stress. Although more expensive than other glues, epoxies are more reliable.

7. Work over the surface with a plane to take off any surplus dowel, leaving it flush with the outer surface.

Cutting down the grain
Clamp the wood and mark it
down the length. Use a ripsaw
to cut when working with the
grain.

Cladding Thin plywood or
masonite may be used to
cover a wooden framework
and can be bent around
curving forms. Put glue on the
frame and fit the board.
Secure it by hammering thin
tacks.

Right These two works
demonstrate very varied
approaches to wood carving.
The late seventeenth century
limewood carving of a cravat
by the English artist Grinling
Gibbons (**top**) shows the
great intricacy and detail for
which his works are
renowned. Constantin
Brancusi was one of the great
innovators of twentieth
century sculpture. These
versions of the *Endless
Column* (**bottom**) show
some of his many approaches
to this subject.

Shaping 1. Particular care
must be taken in shaping
fragile or unsupported wood
sections. A riffler is suitable
for this task.

2. A fine chisel may also be
used, pushed only with the
hand as the force of a mallet
blow may break the wood.

Spokeshave Use a
spokeshave to clean and
smooth down wood. When
drawn across the surface, it
should not drag or stick.

Rubbing in linseed oil
Apply linseed oil with a rag
act as stain and preservative
always affects the color, and
mixture of turpentine and
wax may be better for light
wood.

Contact glue is useful for joining perfectly flu
surfaces. A contact glue is usually applied to ea
surface and left to go slightly tacky before t
joint is made.

SURFACE TREATMENTS

A wood sculpture kept inside untreated or u
painted will gradually darken in color and
richness will dull. The dry fibers will absorb an
or polish which will keep the surface alive. Eve
form of surface treatment darkens the wood
application but in some cases the original col
will be restored as it soaks in. Raw linseed
mixed with rubbing alcohol can be brushed o
Polish A polish can be made of a mixture
beeswax and turpentine. Rub the mixture into t
surface of the wood, which will gradua ly abso
the polish.
Painting Wood can be stained or painted. F
painting proceed as you would when painting t
woodwork of a house. Fill in any cracks, a
paint in primer undercoat before the topcoat,
use gesso as a base for color.
Gesso A mixture of rabbit skin glue, whiting a
water, warmed but not boiled, gesso needs
'key' so the wood surface should not be t
smooth. A surface filed or rubbed over w
rough sandpaper is good. The gesso is brushed

rm. Load the brush and apply it in rapid single
okes. Gesso fills in cracks and gives an excel-
t surface for paint, particularly water based.
e paint should be applied in one fluid stroke,
t worked over as with household paint. Col-
ed inks give translucent hues on a gesso ground.
esso is not durable outside.

PRESERVATIVES

tside, wood weathers to silver gray over a
riod of time. This depends on the amount of
llution there is in the air. The natural elements
rk at the wood; the ever changing humidity
d temperature, fungus attack and wood-
vouring insects all take their toll on the wood,
stroying its structure. This natural process can
slowed down with wood preservatives.
Regular doses of tar-based creosote can keep a
od resilient and intact for a long time. It
rkens the wood considerably when first
plied, but weathers to gray in a few months.
There are many chemical preservatives on the
rket, some of them colorless. Soak the wood in
eservative many times to saturate the fiber. It
ll not penetrate unseasoned damp wood. The
od will need an annual coat of preservative
lowed a month later by an application of
seed oil. Finally, to help give a wood sculpture
onger life outside, shape it so that rain water
ll run off the sculpture and away from its base.

Above *Hyphen*, created in
1980 and 1981 by the artist
Paul Neagu, shows the use of
wood as a medium for shaping
and construction. For this
work, ash beams were bent
and bolted onto elm bases.

SAFETY

All wood working tools are
sharp and must be used with
great care. The sooner this
becomes an automatic habit
the better.
Support The wood that is
being worked should be
steady and well supported.
Cutting Just as you would
when sharpening a pencil,
cut away from your body.
The only exceptions are the
draw knife and spokeshave.
Using power tools All
motorized tools are
especially dangerous as the
motion of cutting is
accelerated, so injuries can
be much worse. Always
switch off the power as soon
as the work is finished. For
example, never leave any

power tool plugged in when
not in use. With power
tools, always follow
manufacturer's instructions.
The circular saw is
dangerous and liberties
should never be taken.
Always switch it off before
changing the depth of cut or
miter width. Have someone
to help you with long
lengths, and with large
sheets of composition board
or anything that is awkward.
Use lengths of wood to
guide small pieces through
the saw.
Using the bandsaw
Intricate cuts on the
bandsaw can so absorb the
mind that the presence of
the blade can be forgotten
and an accident occurs. The
jigsaw can cut through its

own live cable. Check the
cable and plugs of all electric
tools.
Using the bowsaw The
bowsaw tends to bounce on
the first cut if used too
vigorously and can bounce
into the hand.
Care with tools Blunt
tools are as dangerous as
sharp ones. The irritation
they cause makes for an
irrational use of the tool. Be
very careful with the axe
and hatchet, a blow that
does not bite can glance off.
Think about where you
stand in relation to the cut.
Common sense Common
sense is an important guide
in safety matters.
Clothing Wear sensible,
robust clothes and
footwear. Use safety
goggles when splinters are
liable to fly about.

Portable circular saw – all
power tools must be used
with great care.

STONE

HISTORY

The history of sculpture in stone is closely connected with early architectural traditions, where many discoveries about the use of the material were made. Local geological conditions clearly influenced the way stone could be used, particularly the distinction between hard stones such as granite, and softer stones such as limestone.

EARLY TRADITIONS

Prehistoric uses of stone still interest sculptors today. There are three structural types of prehistoric stone sculpture—rock-cut, simple buildings and standing stones. Rock-cut forms imitate caves, carved out from bed rock. These occur more usually in soft stone areas, often as tombs, but occasionally as dwelling areas, which are created entirely by the removal of material. These interior forms were often very refined though simple. Good examples can be seen in Sardinia, and similar principles of rock-cut tombs and dwellings are seen throughout the prehistoric world. The tradition continued and flourished in historical times.

Early Indian architecture achieved sophistication in the carving of great temples from natural rock strata, while the early Christian church in Ethiopia produced masterpieces of controlled mass and space. In such cases, the whole building could be seen in sculptural terms. More traditionally, the facades of these buildings are identified as sculpture. Famous examples such as the giant cliff-cut figures of Rameses II at Abu Simbel demonstrate the possibility of *in situ* carving. The facades at the city of Petra in southern Jordan demonstrate how the tradition of bed-rock carving became overlaid by detailing derived from a building tradition where columns and capitals are elements essential to support the structure.

Simple stone structures may have developed from the rock-cut tradition. The notion of cutting a chamber down into the rock, then roofing the cavity with giant flat boulders is probably a structural ancestor of the simple henge monuments, where two or more vertical stones are spanned by a heavy stone lintel. Stonehenge in southern England, the most famous of these, shows great refinement in the ball and cup method of joining post and lintel. Many henge monuments or dolmens, as they are also known, have a balance and poise which show a great sensitivity to the selection and placing of the massive boulders from which they are constructed.

Cairn-like structures, where smaller boulders are overlapped to enclose a roughly domed space, were common in the prehistoric world. The 'corbelled' arches spanned huts and passageways before the true arch was devised. This method survived much longer in Mayan architecture as an important way of making doorways.

The third type of prehistoric structure, the many and varied standing stones, have a more obvious association with sculpture. The alignments of Northern Europe, particularly in Brittany and Scandinavia, have attracted great attention in recent years, but their true origin and purpose remains speculative. Although many are of local stone, their natural forms were often modified by carving. Examples include 'menhirs' in Brittany, many of which are made of granite. Sometimes the stones were transported great distances, where it was considered essential to site special stones in particular places.

While the traditions of carving are more clearly related to the practice of the Egyptians and subsequent great civilizations, the structures of prehistory established principles of essential form making by reduction, simple structural building and essential landscape placement, all issues which concern sculptors now.

Egypt still has a plentiful supply of good building stone of different types. For the ancient Egyptians, limestone and sandstone provided basic material, while harder stones such as granite, basalts and quartzites were also quarried and carved for special parts of the work. The hieratic society of ancient Egypt, with its preoccupation with the after-life, meant that durable materials were directed to projects concerned with the permanence of the nobility. A high degree of organization and centuries of unchanging conventions led to highly sophisticated quarrying and masonry practices, as well as a refined tradition of carving, particularly in hard stone. Just as the society was strictly formalized, so carving played a constant role in relation to architecture, and the carved sculpture had a clear relationship with the cubic block from which it was reduced.

As in present-day masonry, Egyptian carving procedures depended on the known values of the front and sides of the block. However, this was due not simply to stylistic reasons, but also from conventions of Egyptian society, and to the structure of the material, which was quarried in cubic form following the parallel natural splits in the stone.

In ancient Mexico, a strong tradition of carved architectural sculpture developed, where, as in Egypt, the underlying form of the block was retained in the sculpture, although here the way of suggesting the figure or animal in the block was

Right One of the earliest types of stone sculpture was the formation of simple stone structures. Many of these reveal a great sensitivity in the positioning and balance of the stones. Carving featured in some prehistoric sculpture, including, for example, some menhirs in Brittany and Scandinavia. However, the practice of carving was more readily associated with Egypt. This carved statue (**inset top**) dates from *c* 2600–2500 BC . It shows the figures of King Mycerinus and his Queen. The surface is highly polished and the figures, particularly their hands, feet and faces, show the stylization characteristic of Egyptian art. The giant figure columns at Tula in Mexico (**inset left**) are an excellent example of pre-Columbian stone carving. Dating from around the eleventh century, these huge works are about 15 feet (4.5 meters) tall. An earlier example of carving comes from Nineveh (**inset right**). Dating from the seventh century BC, this is part of a limestone relief sculpture of deer hunting.

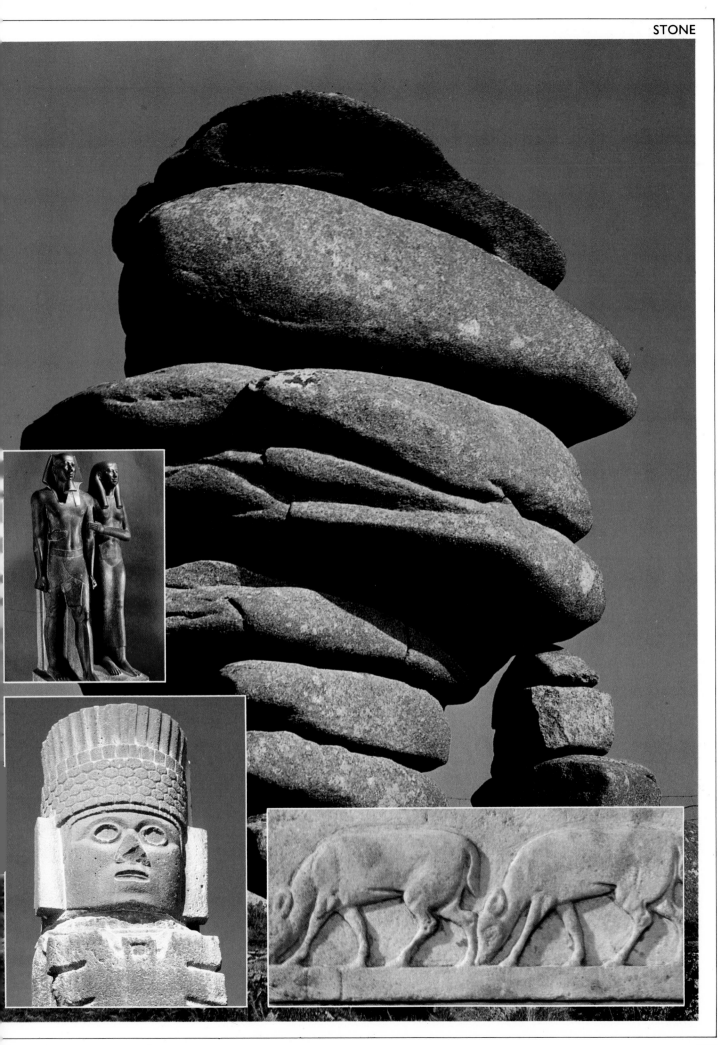

generally more abstract than in other traditions. Early figures, particularly the Toltec carvings at Tula, relate closely to elements of the building, suggesting a figure while hardly changing the form of a column. The extraordinary giant Omec heads from the Gulf coastal area seem to suggest that a giant boulder, rather than regular quarried block, was the original material.

The abundance of marble in the Mediterranean area strongly influenced the carving traditions of the ancient Greeks and centuries later provided the basic stone for the Renaissance masters. Unlike granite, which was so intractable in the face of ancient tools and methods, marble could be worked more freely. As attitudes toward the portrayal of the human form developed, forms became more extended, with holes being drilled through the material to free arms and legs in positions implying movement. The translucency of the material provided a close metaphor for the qualities of the figure and delicacy of draperies.

Although bricks and tiles were commonplace in Roman building, the use of marble for sculpture continued directly from the Greeks, and a highly organized industry quarried and masoned the marble dressings for the great Imperial buildings. Since the Romans could command the engineering skills that built the great aqueducts and roads of the Empire, it is ironic to see that structures such as the triumphal gates of Pompeii were built in brick and then disguised. The marble cladding formed a thin veneer, in much the same way as stone is finely laminated onto a concrete backing in many contemporary buildings, to provide a surface which no longer describes the underlying building structure.

Below Michelangelo's *Battle of the Centaurs* is an example of an early, although uncompleted, work in marble. Work on the sculpture probably ceased around 1492 when Michelangelo's patron Lorenzo de' Medici died. The general forms of the figures are well developed, showing the muscles and solidity of the forms, but the surrounding area reveals the marks of the tools and is still in an unfinished state.

MIDDLE AGES AND AFTE[R]

The great period of structural innovation in sto[ne] was undoubtedly the Middle Ages, when [the] great Romanesque and Gothic cathedrals re[p]resented the most advanced raising of stone t[hat] had ever been known. Workshops were set [up] near the cathedrals, to which quarried stone w[as] brought and worked by teams of masons, carv[ers] and sculptors. This system of on-site work co[n]tinued into industrial times, until eventually, w[ith] the arrival of heavy saws and other machinery[,] became more economical for masons to wo[rk] away from the site and nearer the quarries.

As far as possible, local stone was used, [but] sometimes supply was scarce or a particular sto[ne] was selected for detailed work. In these cases, [the] material was transported from afar by land [or] even by sea. For example, French stone is to [be] found in the southern English cathedrals, and [the] island of Portland in Dorset received a Ro[yal] Charter as early as 1078, when its famous lim[e]stone quarries were providing material for [the] Tower of London.

Apart from outstanding examples such as [the] twelfth century Giselbertus of Autun, most of [the] great medieval stone sculptors remain ano[ny]mous. However, the Italian Renaissance, wh[ich] saw the emergence of marble sculpture indep[en]dent of an architectural context, also gave rise [to] known individual masters. Pisano, Donate[llo,] Michelangelo and Bernini each stand out in th[eir] own right as artists. The famous marble quarri[es,] particularly those in the mountains near Carr[ara] in Tuscany, had been founded by the Roma[ns.] During the rise of the Medicis, they became [a] plentiful source of marble for the Italian c[ity] states. The material was quarried high in [the] mountains, as it is today. The white marble us[ed] by Michelangelo (1475–1564) came from [the] mountain of Altissimo at the summit of the ran[ge,] where zigzag tracks led upwards, and the blo[cks] were lowered directly down the mountainsi[de.] The retaining ropes were wound around woo[den] pegs driven into the cliff. This acted as a bra[ke.] These precarious methods which took ma[ny] human lives are now relieved by mechani[zed] transport and lifting equipment.

Michelangelo used his technical mastery a[nd] his insights into figure and group composition [to] develop his powerful and expressive sculptu[re.] He was capable of the finest, most sensitiv[ely] finished surface, but, when his intentions we[re] better conveyed by broad, rough shaping, [the] carving was left at an earlier stage. His wo[rk] contains an intimate record of his procedures a[nd] techniques—from punching away the rough sto[ne] through claw chiseling to fine honing.

His successors were faced with the almost impossible task of taking these insights further. Inevitably, the most successful developments lay in other directions. The Italian sculptor Gianlorenzo Bernini (1598–1680) aimed at a different kind of rhythm and movement in his sculpture, using marble almost like a fluid material, achieving improbable transformations, as in *Daphne and Apollo*, where the rock first becomes a figure in flight and then changes through Daphne's fingertips into foliage.

Many Baroque sculptors produced carvings for the great gardens of Italy and France in particular. Much of the work is interesting when seen as part of the organization of these formal landscapes, but the purpose of sculpture in such a context seems less important than that of the Romanesque and Gothic periods.

The Neoclassical movement of the eighteenth century, especially in France, turned from the vigor of the Baroque back to a concern for harmony of form, proportion and simplicity. These values were nonetheless approached by sophisticated means. For instance, the calm figures of the Italian Canova (1759–1822) are refined with precision and sensuality. He delighted in the different treatment of skin, silk and soft materials, but kept the quality in keeping with the overall context of the sculpture.

Marble came to be seen as the basic material for carving, and, by the nineteenth century, the practice of reproducing a plaster original in marble had become commonplace. Whereas in bronze casting foundrymen reproduced the actual marks of the sculptor during casting, in marble pointing, the skilled carvers in sculpture factories remade the sculptor's forms, and the original artist was not necessarily involved in the quality of the final surface. Meanwhile the introduction of mechanized methods gave a new facility to these craftsmen. Although technical accomplishment was highly advanced, sculptural sense came second to showing skill and dexterity.

At the turn of the twentieth century, the pioneers of modern sculpture attempted to find new equivalents for volume and mass, and the Salon traditions of the nineteenth century were avoided in favor of new forms. For example, Constantin Brancusi (1876–1957) brought a sense of the simplified forms of ancient and folk carving to his highly sophisticated work. Sculptors such as Frenchmen Henri Laurens (1885–1954) and Jacques Lipchitz (1891–1973) and Russian Ossip Zadkine (1890–1967), introduced fragmented planes which seem to question the solidity of their stone blocks. The Russian-born American Naum Gabo (1890–1977), although primarily a constructor, also found in small-scale carving a way of developing his abstract notions. The British artist Barbara Hepworth (1903–1975) worked primarily as a carver (of both wood and stone), and sometimes allowed bronze casts to be made from her carvings. Both French artist Henri Gaudier-Brzeska (1891–1915) and Briton Jacob Epstein (1880–1959) produced major modern works in stone, with a strong sense of the primitive and distant past.

All these artists preferred working directly into the stone—perhaps after some preliminary studies—rather than reproducing in stone, forms conceived by modeling and casting. Further examples include the British artist Eric Gill (1882–1940), who drew from the procedures of the medieval master carvers for his direct carving, and Henry Moore (born 1898), who, particularly in his earlier carvings, devised forms analogous to those of nature, which were suggested by the quality of his organic material. Swiss artist Max Bill (born 1908) carved geometric forms in granite, while the recent work of American Isamu Noguchi (born 1904), who worked for Brancusi, leaves a sense of scarcely touched nature, relating to the Japanese sensibilities behind the placing of stones in a contemplative garden.

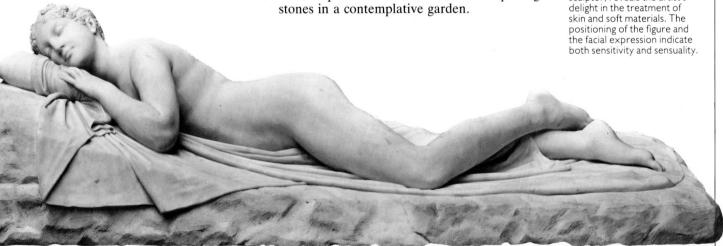

Below *Sleeping Nymph* by Antonio Canova, the eighteenth century Italian sculptor, reveals the artist's delight in the treatment of skin and soft materials. The positioning of the figure and the facial expression indicate both sensitivity and sensuality.

Igneous rocks The best known type of igneous rock is granite. Igneous rocks are the most weather-resistant, durable types of stone. All granites are very hard and will thus take a very fine polish. These rocks are extremely old and are formed by the solidification of molten material.

Sedimentary rocks The two principal types of sedimentary rock are sandstone and limestone. They are more porous than igneous rocks, and tend to give a textured finish. They are much easier to carve. Sedimentary rocks are produced by particles which have settled and become bonded by natural adhesives. They usually contain bone remains.

Metamorphic rocks are transformed igneous or sedimentary rocks. Pressure, great heat or chemical reactions in the earth's crust usually causes this transformation. Marble and slate are the metamorphic stones most frequently used in sculpture. But soapstone and alabaster are also stones which can be classified as metamorphic.

Cornish granite

Karin granite

Sandstone

Limestone

Marble

Slate

MATERIALS

There are three main types of stone—igneous sedimentary and metamorphic—each resulting from a different geological process.

IGNEOUS ROCKS

Igneous rock is formed by the solidification of molten material. The best known type of igneous rock is granite, which is composed of crystals created during the cooling process. There are many granites, of all colors, which come from a diverse locations as Scandinavia, South Africa, Brazil, North America and Britain. All granites extremely hard and will take a fine polish.

SEDIMENTARY ROCKS

Sedimentary rocks are formed by the settling of particles of material which become bonded by natural adhesives. The two principal types of sedimentary rock are sandstone and limestone.
Sandstone Sandstone consists of grit particles largely composed of silica, which adhere to one another. The particles are extremely durable, having been formed from other crystalline rock. When the bonding agent is tough, an extremely intransigent material results. Sandstone is widely distributed throughout the world.

The main colors tend to be the earth colors—ranging from red through to ocher, with some gray and blue-gray. The stone looks very porous and normally does not take a polish. The dust very dangerous.
Limestone Limestone is formed from the settling of calcareous or chalky material, such a fragments of shell or the tiny skeletons of countless marine organisms. There are many types of limestone, which vary considerably because of the different possible components and how they were formed. Many organisms began on the sea-bed and so limestone may even contain identifiable pieces of shell and fossil.

Although amalgamated into homogeneous stone, the different layers or strata—the grain of the rock—are still evident in many limestone Limestone contains distinct horizontal division which define the 'bed' height. This is the height of stone available before a natural break. This restricts the size of limestone for sculpture.

There are many limestones which are suitable for carving, as they are relatively easy to cut and their weathering properties are reasonable for soft type of stone. In fact, limestones 'case harden'. This means that the natural moisture-

quarry sap—found in most newly quarried
[ston]e gradually moves to the surface of the carved
[for]m, eventually making a harder shell which will
[pro]tect the rest of the stone. If this surface is
[sub]sequently broken, erosion of the softer in-
[teri]or can be rapid and harmful. Hence, reworked
[lim]estone weathers less well than does the freshly
[wor]ked stone.

[M]ost limestones range in color from creamy
[whi]te to brown. The main factor in determining
[col]or is the presence or absence of iron. Most
[cou]ntries have their own deposits of limestone.
[For] example, Portland and Bath stones are im-
[por]tant British limestones, while Alabama and
[Ind]iana are major types from the United States.
[C]halk is found naturally in rough pieces and
[can] be worked easily. Quite large lumps are
[pos]sible, but the stone will gradually break down
[if e]xposed to the weather.

METAMORPHIC ROCK

[Me]tamorphic rock is formed through the effects
[of p]ressure, great heat or chemical action. These
[pro]cesses transform the basic structure of igneous
[or] sedimentary stones. The best known types of
[me]tamorphic rock are marble and slate.

[Ma]rble Basically calcium carbonate, marble is
[for]med in a vast range of colors and consistencies,
[ran]ging from the pure white marble of Carrara in
[Ita]ly and the Pentelic marbles from Greece, to
[exo]tic veined marbles from Portugal, red traver-
[tin]e marbles from Iran and dense black marble
[fro]m Belgium. Pakistan produces green marble,
[and] Italy a wide variety of figured and plain
[ma]rbles.

[G]enerally, sculptors find the simpler types of
[ma]rble most suitable, particularly the Carrara
[ma]rble from Tuscany which comes in a range of
[wh]ites and grays. Textured travertine marble is
[als]o popular. It is usually cream in color and
[com]es from near Rome. Different types of
[ma]rble weather very differently, particularly in a
[cor]rosive atmosphere. One of the most reliable is
['or]dinario di Carrara'. It is a cold gray-blue
[col]or, tending to white.

[Ala]baster Italian alabaster is considered a type
[of] marble. It is translucent. However, most
[ala]basters are strictly speaking not marble, but
[rel]ate more closely to gypsum. They are soft and
[eas]ily carved.

[Sla]te This type of rock is formed by the
[me]tamorphosis of clay-like shale. The most sig-
[nif]icant characteristics are the strata, which make
[it e]asy to split the rock in one direction. Chunks
[of] slate can be quarried, but generally this stone is
[mo]st useful to the sculptor in slab form. It is
[ext]remely close grained and is often used for

letter cutting. Colors range through gray-blue and
green. Recently, sculptors have begun to use slate
as a material for construction.

Soft stone For those beginning to work in stone,
soft stones are normally preferred. However, it
can sometimes be more difficult to make a form in
very soft stone than in a stone with a little more
resistance. Popular stones of this type are alabaster, soapstone, porphyry and some of the softer
limestones, such as Bath stone.

Below *Red Stone Dancer* by
the French artist Henri
Gaudier-Brzeska was
completed in 1914. It is an
example of his individual late
style of carving in its energy
and primitivism. Gaudier-
Brzeska died in 1915 at the
age of 24. His artistic career
was brief but wide ranging.

TOOLS AND TECHNIQUES

Stone carving tools The varied point widths of the marble punches (**1**) are used in the different stages of roughing out the marble (broader points) and the removal of smaller masses and more delicate work (finer points). Round-ended chisels (**2**), known as bullnoses, are used for making channels in hard stone, while the scriber (**3**) is a fine metal tool which can be used for very detailed surface work. The hard lignum vitae mallet (**4**) can be used with any of these mallet-headed tools. The broad boaster (**8**) and wide spaced claw (**9**) are used at first to give a general form to the stone and are followed up by the forged flat chisel (**5**), the narrow tungsten flat chisel (**6**), the narrow spaced claw (**7**), and narrow tungsten tool (**10**) for definition work.

Stone rasps and files are abrasive metal tools used for finishing and fining down stone surfaces. Their surfaces have sharp projections or teeth which are formed by indentations in the metal while they are being made. The dreadnought file (**12**) is initially used for clarifying form, followed by a stone rasp (**13**), and the very small and delicate rasps (**11**), also known as rifflers. These are used for achieving a clear surface and with detailed work.

Stone carving hammers are made of untempered tool steel, and they usually vary in weight depending on their size. A small lump hammer (**16**), a small lead dummy hammer (**14**) and a slightly larger dummy hammer (**15**) are used to good effect with a range of fine claw chisels (**17**) and flat chisels (**18**). The pitching tool (**20**) is of value in removing large fragments during the early stages of blocking out the initial forms. When the heavy hammer (**19**) is used with the pitching tool and applied with force, the blows can remove considerable amounts of stone.

In order to reproduce a form according to its original dimensions the carver uses the method of 'pointing' using a compass (**22**). This is where, given two known points on the stone, a third can be found by using the distances from each of these points. Curved calipers (**21**) are used for accuracy of measurement when reproducing a shape in stone.

Long Portland punches (**23**) vary in length from 18in (45cm) down to thick waisted granite punches of about 4½in (11cm). Note the different lengths of the forged points. They are more drawn out for softer stone and stubbier for granite. They can be used with a long-headed hammer (**24**). A Lewis bolt (**25**), which is an expanding bolt, is inserted into particularly heavy stones prior to lifting them.

A revolving wooden bench or banker (**26**) provides a sturdy waist-high surface to work a stone on. Note that the two tops are both made of a double layer of planks glued together in opposite directions, so as to absorb the stress from hammer blows to the stone. The triangular frame delineates a rough enclosing border for the stone. This hammer can deliver a heavy blow and is used with granite (**27**). Note that the hammer head has a slightly curved top and ends angled downwards, the wood narrowing into the metal. Granite hammers have very delicate hafts with heads almost oval in shape. The hammer is held at the bottom to avoid vibration and jarring being transmitted to the hand. The stone carver who is beginning to work with different stones does not need to acquire all the tools shown on these two pages, but instead should concentrate on obtaining a few high quality tools from a reputable supplier.

This sequence of photographs shows some of the different stages in making a sculpture. The work, entitled *Expanded Column*, is shown while still in progress. The piece is by the British sculptor John Maine, who worked on the piece in Italy. The artist began working from a model made of Portland stone (**1**). The model should never be a prescription for work, but rather a starting point and guide for working with the stone. It is very important that, as the work progresses, the artist responds to the material, rather than simply trying to impose his or her ideas on it. In many cases, the work may change radically from the model, although, in this instance, the overall idea was, broadly, maintained as the work proceeded. Having selected the block of stone for the work, the next step was to position the stone so that work could begin (**2**). For heavy blocks of stone, lifting equipment and even cranes may be necessary. Before work starts on the stone, it is important to position the stone at the correct height. The most convenient height for a stone is probably about waist-high, but it should not be lower than knee-high. The properly supported stone must also be placed so that it is not liable to topple over or move when work is in progress. The stone chosen by the artist was a block of Italian Trani marble (**3**). Once in position, it was then sawn into the basic cuboid shape from which the artist worked (**4**). When the initial material was removed, the angles in the work began to emerge (**5**). Power tools are a good way of removing large amounts of stone quickly. The chips of stone on the ground can be seen around the base of the work. Creating a stone sculpture involves a number of gradual processes which smooth away the excess stone until the desired surface is reached. These operations remain basically the same whether the sculptor uses power or hand tools. Power tools are more suitable for large-scale work, as they take much of the effort out of the basic shaping. However, they need to be used with great care and due attention to safety precautions. The next stage in the work was to remove more stone and produce the first outline of the final shape. Here a diamond disc saw is being used, and the operator is wearing safety goggles (**6**). The general view after the first shaping (**7**) shows the marking out on the surface of the stone. Marking out provides an outline for the shape. The first shaping establishes the overall angles of the final shape. Here the upper surface of the angle is much smoother than the lower. Further shaping then follows. The stone is gradually being worked away down toward the marks (**8**). The saw cuts are clearly visible, showing that vertical cuts were made into the stone to enable the sculptor to smooth the surplus stone away more easily. Once the marking out indications had been reached, the planes of the sculpture were defined more clearly (**9**). Finally, rounding out of the forms began (**10**).

This series of pictures shows the processes involved in working on one small part of a larger work. The same processes must be repeated for the other parts of the sculpture, before any final finishing can start. In this instance the sculptor was able to work in the open air. This is advantageous because it lessens problems of dust and ventilation which can present difficulties if working inside. *Expanded Column* is a fairly large-scale work, so it is obvious that work on the piece will take a long time, even if the sculptor has help from assistants. One of the great fascinations of sculpture with stone is how the final shape gradually emerges from the roughly hewn block of stone.

QUARRYING

Most stones used by the sculptor will have been quarried, so it is useful, even for the beginner, to understand the general principles involved in obtaining stone from the earth. Stone is quarried in various ways, depending on the nature of the material and where it is found. Certain principles apply to the removal of blocks, particularly the use of natural divisions in the bed rock. These arise from geological pressures causing cracks, or in the strata created when the rock was formed. These are then augmented by man-made divisions, such as sawing or splitting. Sawing applies generally to softer stones and marble, whereas splitting has been used for thousands of years for all types of stone and still prevails today. Most stone is obtained through open-cast quarrying, whenever possible using natural advantages, such as an outcrop of rock, cliff edge, or even a mountain top. Sometimes stone is mined, where good material lies deep below an overburden which cannot be removed economically.

Massive chain saws are used to remove soft limestone, while, at Carrara in Tuscany, a network of wires runs throughout the mountain quarries, guided by a pulley system which directs the wire to the rock face. The principle of cutting by wire in quarries is the same as that in stoneyards where abrasive powder and water assist the process. In granite quarrying, a thermal lance is now used to cut the stone. This consists of a jet of flame, generally paraffin, boosted by compressed air, which forms a cut by melting the rock and blowing away the molten material.

Stone, while having great strength under compression, has comparatively little tensile strength. Very hard stones can split simply, as the hardness of the material assists the splitting action. Wedges force the rock apart by directing pressure from a line on the surface deep into the stone. The division is helped by drill holes which can sink down to a level of 3 or 4 feet (about 1 meter) in certain stones. Granite usually requires shallower holes. Nowadays drilling is mechanical; 'feathers' or split sleeves of iron are set in the holes, and wedges are driven between them in a rhythmic sequence. If the stone is sound, and the wedges are carefully aligned, a clean break can be made.

Lifting plays an essential part in quarry work, and, although the tackle is heavier than most masonry kit, the techniques have much in common. Wire hawsers and chains of appropriate caliber are used according to the weights and materials. For limestone, grips called 'nips' and 'pincers' are still used, following centuries of tradition. A fixed crane is normally on hand to lift the blocks and swing them out to be trimmed and then numbered for the stockpile. Mobile crane are also used.

HANDLING

When organizing masonry or carving, the firs consideration is to be able to move and turn th stone, and to set it in a convenient position fo work. The general principle is always to let th weight of the stone assist rather than counter th move.

Small stones up to roughly 1 cubic foot (0.0 cubic meters) can be lifted carefully by hand, bu keep your back as straight as possible. There little point in straining to lift a stone when the jo can be comfortably done with an assistant. Seve al techniques have been developed to manhandl heavier stones. Iron levers are commonly used t move large stones short distances. A woode block can be placed between stone and iron t prevent crushing. Rollers, made of wood or iro and sometimes clad in rubber, are a great hel Small trolleys or waggons make good, simpl transporters.

Medium sized stones can be lifted several fe by cantilevering onto support stones, which ar graduated in height up to the the final platform Where stones of more than about 300lb (136 k are regularly being moved, a hoist is indispen able. A block and tackle capable of lifting muc heavier weights is useful, but must be supporte in various ways above the work area. Commo supports are shear legs and gantries.

Nylon straps, 2½in (6.25cm) broad, suppo the stone. In special cases, an expanding bol known as a Lewis bolt, can be inserted into th block. This technique is traditionally used fo altar stones and foundation stones of buildings.

CHOOSING STONE

The sculptor's choice from the vast range stones with different qualities of hardness, co sistency and color is guided by many person preferences. Other basic concerns which must considered are the soundness of the block, th possible size of the block in a given material, th durability of the stone, its relationship to the si and the type of working methods available to preferred by the sculptor. There are many facto which make a particular stone more suited some forms than others. Some stones are brittl others erode quickly. Distinctive veins or graini may work with or contradict the sense of th sculptural form. Availability and cost are al important considerations.

SETTING UP A STONE

...tone is most conveniently worked at waist or ...ow height and should certainly not be at knee ...ght or lower. This usually means a stout ...oden bench, known as a 'banker', or some-...es another substantial stone is necessary as ...port. It is essential to place soft material ...lerneath the stone, since the blows of the ...sel on the top of the stone reverberate against ... base. Sacking or soft boarding are useful. ...aw is also a good material, but not if water is ...ng used.

...mall stones can be worked on a container of ... sand, or sometimes a very small stone is fixed ... base by plaster of Paris. Such stones can also ... clamped into a vice with softening over the ...s, but, as with the plaster method, any carving ... only be delicate. Heavy blows can fracture ...stone.

Preparation for stone work Before beginning work on stone, it is important to set the stone up correctly and to be aware of the correct posture and clothing. Some points to be remembered are listed (**below**). Similarly, the hammer and chisel should be held correctly (**left**).

Place the chisel against the stone at the appropriate angle, depending on the type of cut desired.

Hold the hammer firmly but not too tightly.

For the best results, the hammer should strike the head of the chisel at 90°.

If working in an enclosed area or whenever dust is liable to be a problem, a face mask should be worn. This is less necessary when working outside.

Wedges, often called 'plugs and feathers', are used for splitting the stone. Placed at intervals, they are worked into the stone, until it splits off.

Place the stone at the correct height using either a banker (a sturdy wooden bench) or another stone as support. The stone should be securely fixed before work begins.

An apron helps to protect clothing from dust and chips of stone.

Make sure the block of stone is well supported. Soft material should always be placed under the stone to cushion it against jarring.

Make sure that you stand with your feet firmly placed and slightly apart to ensure good balance.

Heavy duty shoes or boots with steel caps should be worn to protect the feet.

SAWING

There are many kinds of saws for stone, ranging from industrial plant to simple handsaws. It is useful for the sculptor to know about the larger saws, but, in practice, the smaller disc saws and tenon types are more likely to be used. In industry, traditional wire saws are still used for primary cutting. The wire is drawn across the block by distant pulleys, while water and abrasive dust (formerly sand, but now carborundum grit) is directed into the cut. Lateral saws like giant hacksaws are also used. These too originally used sand as a cutting agent, but now the blades are tipped with industrial diamonds, set in tungsten. Multiple blades of this type are used to cut several slabs at once, rather like producing a sliced loaf of ordinary bread.

Large disc saws, higher than a man, are known in industry, but usually about 3 feet (around 1 meter) radius is the maximum. Monumental masons often have a disc which can cut up to 5in (12.5cm). Most of these saws are diamond tipped and used with water to carry off the waste material or slurry. Hand-held disc saws can be used by experts, but these are extremely dangerous.

Tenon and cross-cut saws are traditionally used in shaping soft stones such as some limestones. Tungsten-tipped saws are now available, although formerly steel and forged iron proved very successful with such soft stones. 'Drags' with saw teeth are commonly used to smooth the surface of softer stones such as limestone.

Right Huge machines are needed for cutting stone commercially. Here a guillotine is being set up ready to cut through some stone. As in all aspects of stone working, safety is of prime importance.

_ SPLITTING AND COPING _

The simplest way to remove large pieces of stone is to split them off. This is generally cheaper than sawing, as less energy and time is used. The disadvantages are that the surface may need dressing after the split, and, of course, it is not possible to make a partial split into a block. Masons use the plugs and feathers employed in quarries, but also may use a simple method, known as coping, for removing small amounts. No drilling is needed. A series of small, sharp punches, 'coping punches', are used as primitive wedges. They are nested into holes cut out by punch or fine chisel, and then treated like 'plugs', being hit in a rhythmic sequence, until a crack appears between them, and a lump is split away.

Far left Stones are stored commercially in a stockpile. The quarried blocks may be split into smaller pieces. These slabs of granite have been made into slabs using a multiple-blade saw.
Left The wedges in this stone are the 'plugs and feathers' used to split stones. Although this is a good method of splitting off large pieces of stone, it cannot be used for smaller pieces. In addition, the surface may need dressing after the stone has been split.

Center left A hand-held diamond disc saw is an extremely efficient way of cutting through stone. However, it is very dangerous and should only be used under strict supervision. When using any power tools, always wear safety clothing – goggles, a mask (especially if working inside), stout shoes and a protective apron.
Left These saw cuts have been made by a power saw. The depth of the indentations makes it easier to smooth out the surface of the stone.

Pitching 1. The tools needed for pitching are the pitcher and a mason's hammer.

2. Gradually work along the edge of the stone with the pitcher. Start from one end and work to the middle.

3. Work in a similar way from the other end.

4. The purpose of pitching is to remove excess stone so that the more detailed work can begin. Like many carving processes, it involves gradually reducing the size of the stone block so that the broad outlines of the work emerge.

5. The amount of stone which is removed can be varied by altering the angle of the pitching tool. After pitching, chips of stone can be removed with a stiff brush.

ROUGHING OUT

The basic tools for roughing out are the pitchi tool and the punch, both normally hit by suitab hammers. The job of the hammer is to deliv energy to the tool with a minimum of jarring the wrist and arm of the mason or carver. T shape of the hammer head varies greatly. Simp cubic heads ranging from ½lb (0.25kg) to (1.5kg) or 4lb (2kg) deliver a deadened localiz blow and are used in marble work. The smal lump hammers of this type are common for lett cutting, where the weight of the head is firmly at the top of the straight, simple shaft. The blow directional but very controlled. The 'dummy' round-headed hammer which is normally used very close work. The head can be iron or ev brass or lead. This type of hammer is not dir tional and delivers a very specific local tap.

For stones such as limestone or sandsto requiring a heavy blow which follows through, hammer head can be as much as 6in (15cm) lo with a slightly carved top and ends angled dow ward. The haft bulges slightly below the hea and the wood narrows into the metal. Gran hammers have very delicate hafts with hea almost oval in shape. Here the springing qual of the haft absorbs the jarring of the hamm head against intransigent stone. A series of ligh blows achieves more than one great swipe.

Pitching The function of the various stone to is to convert the energy delivered by the hamm into specific forms for different jobs. The pitchi tool is shaped to strike a shock wave into t stone in order to make a localized split. It is r literally a cutting tool. One side of the tool virtually straight, and the blow is directed do this line. The other side is shaped toward t striking edge. The tool is most effective worki from a smooth surface. A succession of blows si by side can multiply the shock wave and spli stone in two. Large corner pieces can be stru off by pitching, while smaller blows directed i the mass can help to prepare stone for punchir

Punching The punch is the simplest yet m widely used tool for broad work. Basically pointed or near pointed implement, its len varies from long Portland punches which measure 18in (45cm) down to thick waist granite punches about 4½in (11cm) in leng Most punches have forged points. They are m drawn out for softer stone and stubbier granite. Nowadays, tungsten-tipped punches also available.

The punch should be held fairly loosely and at an angle to the stone. The most effective wa to follow blows along a series of parallel paths, that each strike reinforces the next. It is count

...roductive to try to hit individual blows too deep, ... the punch burrows into the stone and stops ...moving material.

With marble and granite, great care should be ...ken to stop punching just above the finished ...rface, since the blows make stun marks deeper ...an the actual cut, and these appear as whitish ...eas on a hard stone surface. A general rule in ...unching and most chisel work is to avoid hitting ...way from the central mass of the stone, es-...ecially at a corner, where it is a good idea to stop ...out 2in (5cm) short and then work inward from ...e edge in the opposite direction. Following ...ese instructions, work over the surface several ...mes, gradually reducing the amount of stone.

Punching The punch is a traditional stone carving tool, it was much used by Michelangelo. It is a long pointed tool which makes a series of parallel strokes along the stone. Do not hit too deeply, as the punch will simply penetrate the stone and not remove any material. Do not work right to the edge of the stone. Stop the punch about 2in (5cm) above the edge and work back from the other side.

Left Stone carving is a process of gradually working away excess stone to achieve the general shape of the work, and then refining and smoothing the surface. Different tools—the pitcher, punch and also power tools— create very varied surfaces. This picture shows one surface of the sculpture after initial roughing out. The different stages can be seen clearly.

Stone carving 1. First clear away broad areas of stone to rough out the shape. Tap down the stone with a pitching tool.

2. The initial taps weaken the stone. Hit the pitching tool hard with the hammer to split and break off sections of stone.

3. Continue roughing out with a punch. Holding it at a shallow angle against the stone, make parallel cuts down the surface.

4. Use a scribe to mark out a sharp edge for cutting. Guide the scribe along a metal ruler or square held on the stone.

5. Cut a draft along the scribe mark with a flat tungsten chisel. Define the edge sharply and smooth down the plane.

6. Shape the stone with a claw chisel, hit with a lignum vitae mallet. The claw leaves hatched marks on the surface.

7. Work down to the final shape with a flat chisel. Do not dig right into the block, push the chisel through the surface.

8. The flat chisel is used to remove claw marks and define the finished form of the carving.

9. Use a rasp to file down remaining chisel marks. On soft stone, the rasp can be used as a shaping tool.

Boasting a surface Hold a wide-tipped chisel at an angle to the stone surface and apply rapid taps of the mallet to push it along, forming a series of shallow, ridged marks.

CHISEL WORK

After roughing out, the stone is worked with chisels and mallets. This stage may be repeated many times with different sizes or combinations of chisels until the desired surface is achieved.

Mallets Round wooden mallets provide a more muffled blow than a hammer, and are gentler to use. The most common wood is beech, although heavier mallets are made of the extremely hard wood lignum vitae, which has to be treated carefully to avoid undue surface splitting of the wood. Mallets have a 'beat' which is determined by the grain. In practice, carvers tend to rotate a mallet in use to avoid undue wear on one part.

Chisels There are many varieties of chisel, but the main groups are hammer-head types which have a small hitting end, and mallet-head which have a broadened, rounded hitting end. The cutting ends may be tempered steel or tungsten. Between the punch and the normal chisel is a type of chisel known as a 'claw', which consists of a row of fine punches combined into one tool. Claw chisels are made in different widths and can be found with detachable claw heads which wedge into a patent claw holder. Although a little heavier to use, these are very practical, since the teeth of the claw wear out and need replacing.

The flat chisel is very commonly used for defining and finishing a surface. In practice, a 1in (2.5cm) chisel may be found much more useful than bigger chisels, even for large, flat areas, and a ½in (1.25cm) chisel is a convenient size for the early defining of form. Letter cutters use very fine chisels which can sometimes be very useful to carvers. It is usual for masons to follow regular punch work with claw treatment to establish a surface ⅛in (3mm) proud, and then remove the final stone with steady chisel blows in controlled sequence. However, carvers may tend to work in a freer, more random way, where they are finding a form by eye rather than working to a previously calculated shape. Here, the claw is most useful, as it can work around a form without giving the emphasis of a series of flat planes. Round-ended chisels are made for special jobs, but both these and gouge-shaped chisels are uncommon in stonework.

Right Chisel attachments are available for use with pneumatic tools. A power tool can deliver more rapid and consistent force than can be delivered with a hand-held mallet but the sculptor has less sensitive control of the cutting edge. Flat chisels (**1**, **4**, **5**) of various weights can be used to shape the stone. The claw chisel (**2**) is also a shaping tool, but leaves striated marks on the stone, owing to the toothed blade. A boucharde (**3**) is a heavy tool which bruises and wears away the stone. Power-driven chisels may be used where they will suit the quality and resistance of the stone, but the rapid action should not obscure the gradual development of form.

Pneumatic tools Industrial procedures led to the introduction of a range of tools powered by compressed air. Drills with hammer and twist action are widely used, and there are several systems of air hammers, which can be used to drive both punches and chisels. The Italians have developed a sophisticated range of cylinder-shaped hammer appliances which are standard industrial equipment for working marble and granite. Pistol-type air hammers are used on limestone with much longer chisels. The great advantage of air tools is the series of rapidly delivered hammer blows which are very suitable for trimming surfaces. The disadvantages are noise and possible vibration hazards, and, for some sculptors, the fact that the action of the chisel can become too insensitive. They are also more suitable for a stoneworker with some experience than for the beginner. Nonetheless, it is always essential to find procedures which are at one with the sculptor's intentions.

Power tools Power tools can be of great service to the stone sculptor. However, they should, like all electrical equipment, be used with great care. Power tools are not really suitable for the beginner; they are better for the sculptor with a little more experience. Among the advantages of power tools are that they work much quicker. Because they work by delivering a series of rapid hammer blows, they are especially good for trimming surfaces. There are several types of power tools. Of especial use to the sculptor are the power hammer and power chisel. The amount of stone removed varies according to the type and size of the tool being used.

Safety goggles

Marks of regular hammer blows

Power chisel

The main problems with using power tools are noise and vibration. If working indoors, it is wise to wear ear muffs to ensure that your ears are not damaged. Whether working inside or out, safety goggles should be worn to protect the eyes from the chips of stone which using power tools inevitably creates.

Power hammer

RUBBING AND POLISHING

There are craftsmen whose sole activity is rubbing or polishing, and for them the monotony of this stage of the work is lost in the recognition of how important a specific surface can be. Pacing the work is essential. It cannot be hurried, even when power tools are used. The basic materials are abrasive stones, usually carborundum grit in a range of thicknesses, bonded in shellac. The procedure is to work from coarse to fine, either dry, which is more laborious but more controlled, or, usually, with water to aid the cutting by removing the eroded stone. Silicon carbide paper, commonly called 'wet-and-dry', can also be used especially at the later stages.

Electric disc sanders are common in the trade, but, when used dry, they create a lot of dust, and, when water is used, there is a problem of keeping the water away from the power supply. Dust extraction should be considered when stones with a high silica content are being ground. One solution may be to work in the open wearing a face mask.

Finishing 1. Fine chisels may be used for delicate work in final shaping and trimming of the stone, and sharpening angles.

2. To avoid the risk of cutting into stone at the final stages use a riffler to file down and work into the detail.

3. Finish the surface by rubbing with abrasive stones. This work may be done wet or dry.

4. Finally, use wet-and-dry carborundum paper to achieve the final smooth surface.

Above Abrasive stones come in various grades of hardness. Work with the stones, which consist of carborundum grit bonded with shellac, begins with the coarse stone (**top**), continues with the medium grade (**center**), and the smoothest grade (**bottom**) is used for the final smoothing.

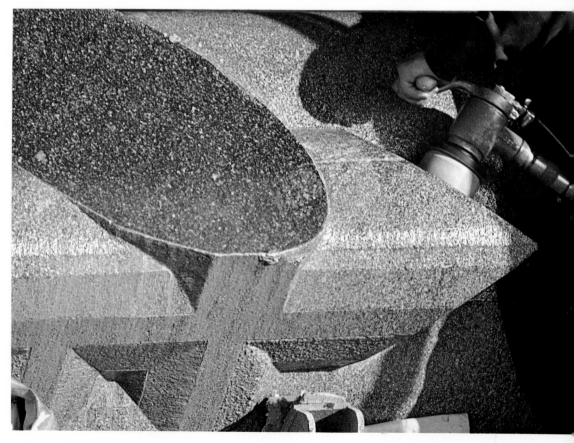

Right Power tools take much of the heavy work out of working with stone. Here a compressed air abrasive wheel is being used on granite. The shine which is produced during finishing can be seen. The work in progress is *Prism* by John Maine.

FIXING

possible, stones are best fixed when dry, hough the way separate stones sit next to each er should take potential frost damage into nsideration. Drilling and pinning is a standard y of joining stone. There are electric drills ecially designed for stone, some even have a mmer-drill action. Pins must be of non-ferrous tal, since iron rusts and will eventually burst e stone. Epoxy adhesives specially made for ne are usually used in a two-part mix. They are her white or 'transparent' and can be colored powder paint. These are usually very quick ing, and are best used out of direct sunlight. nite cement is sometimes used with stone, but rtar is preferable.

Left This shows the completed sculpture, *Pyramid* in its final site in a park. It is made from Portland stone, weighs about 20 tons and consists of 28 interlocking pieces. The work was assembled on site. The final surface texture is shown on the insert.

Above This studio shows work in progress on *Pyramid* by John Maine. The work took two years, from 1978 to 1980. Several of the pieces were worked on at the same time.

CONSTRUCTIONS

In recent years, many younger sculptors have become interested in using stone in conjunction with other media. Raw blocks of stone or slabs of slate, for example, may be stacked or set out in particular relationships. To overcome the gravity force in stone, the material has been used in conjunction with steel or wood in assemblages. which seem like reorganized nature or primitive structures. The implications from the range of different approaches to the medium is that stone is seen with new vitality as a material with many qualities that can be developed for a broad range of sculptural expression.

POINTING AND SCALING UP

These are methods of reproducing a given form stone, either as a facsimile, or larger in str proportion. First, the form is made in a conv nient material (often plaster of Paris).

'Pointing' is virtually a three-dimensio method, using the principles of triangulation, th is to say, given two known points, a third can found by using the distances from each of the basic points. In 'pointing', these positions a established in space, using an apparatus called pointing machine, which has adjustable arms th can be set to given points on the original mod When the machine is removed and then set around the stone block, these arms can be push against the surface of the stone. As the stone punched away, the arm is set deeper until event ally the prescribed point is established.

'Scaling up' can be achieved by the use of scaling board, which simply converts lengt taken from the model according to the ratio increase required. The scale on the board shou be established first.

These are traditional procedures, still wide understood and used in Italy. Reproduction this way is felt by many sculptors to overlo aspects of interpretation which should accompa the transfer of a form to a different materi However, methods themselves cannot be right wrong, but should be used with imagination.

Starting with the simple devices of a compass right-angled iron and a straightedge, masons ha developed a way of understanding very compl volumes. The skill has developed over centuri and is passed on to apprentices through sim procedures, which become second nature just li the practical use of the masons' tools. In so ways, the process is like 'pointing', in that there a logical development from known to unknow in order to make a specific volume. The ma differences are that usually no model exists copy, and, secondly, planes rather than points used to establish the volume. Special measuri tools—'shift stock' for angles, and 'sinki square' for depths—are more robust versions similar tools used in carpentry. These tools m also be useful to certain carvers.

Traditionally, masons are seen as craftsmen a succession from quarrymen through to carv in a stoneworking hierarchy. But for the sculpt each stage of handling stone presents its uniq problems, and may have a direct bearing on t sculptor's approach. It is no longer adequate separate preparatory work from the finishi touches. All stages are sculptor's preserve.

DIRECT CARVING

y method which does not use a model of the
oposed form is called direct carving. However,
s title was devised to describe a kind of carving
ere the form of the block or boulder gave rise
ideas about the form of the sculpture. The
ver changes the form somewhat, and, then,
ponding to the way the stone is going, he or
developes the idea further. This is perhaps the
st prescriptive method of carving.

SAFETY

The main danger areas in stone sculpture are hazards associated with weight, dust, eye protection and noise.

Lifting Lifting is very much a question of common sense, but certain rules apply to tackle. Never stand beneath a block, however confident you may be in the straps or chains. Particular caution with Lewis bolt lifting is advisable. Always allow for a stone to fall and roll, and especially take account of the possibility of a chain breaking and spinning away from the block. Steel-capped shoes are advisable.

Dust Any dust is an irritant to the respiratory system, but dusts with high silica content, such as granite and especially sandstone, are highly dangerous. A safety mask should be worn, and good ventilation is essential. Vacuum systems are helpful in conjunction with power tools. Goggles with safety glass should be worn when punching hard stones, and always when grinding. Remember the abrasive grit can scar the eye even when grinding soft stone.

Noise The worst noise hazards are associated with certain pneumatic tools and industrial saws. Take sensible account of noise levels and wear ear protectors when extreme conditions prevail. Remember that constant exposure to comparatively medium levels of noise can damage your hearing after a long period.

Quarry work In quarries and on site it may be appropriate to wear protective headgear. Procedures for blasting are normally clear, but a degree of unfamiliarity with the rules or simply being preoccupied create extra danger.

General However, with reasonable experience and awareness stoneworking can be perfectly safe. Problems usually only occur through being overtired or taking undue risks.

Left The statue of *St Matthew* by Michelangelo was begun in 1506. From the unfinished work, it is easy to see how the figure is emerging from the block of stone. It is interesting that this piece seems to show that Michelangelo worked from one face of the sculpture, rather than in the round. Those parts of the figure which jut out most are almost complete, while the virtually raw stone block is still visible around the outline of the figure.

PLASTER

Right Auguste Rodin was one of the major figures in sculpture at the turn of the century. In 1880 he was commissioned by the Museum of Decorative Arts in Paris to create a doorway for them. This virtually open ended commission was still unfinished on Rodin's death 37 years later. Work on the project was nevertheless important because of the creative freedom it offered Rodin. This plaster model of the *Gates of Hell* shows many unfinished areas. Some of the figures were developed into separate works.

HISTORY

...aster was used by the ancient Greeks to make ...sts from statues. The early Greek sculptor ...sistratos is credited with developing the process ...the fourth century BC. However, it is now ...own that the Egyptians used plaster for making ...ath masks and casting from parts of the human ...dy as early as 2400 BC.

...Despite its use by the great classical civiliza...ns, plaster seems to have fallen into disuse as a ...edium for sculpture after the decline of the ...oman Empire. It was not revived until the ...enaissance. The first main Renaissance expo...nt of plaster sculpture was the Italian Andrea ...rrocchio (c 1435–1488). He frequently used ...aster for making casts from life. Verrocchio's ...chniques were vividly described by his contem...orary Vasari in his influential work *Lives of the ...rtists*. This provides a fascinating glimpse into ...e practice of sculpture with plaster, which, ...cause of the nature of the medium, has changed ...tle over the years. Vasari wrote: 'Andrea was ...ry fond of making plaster casts, for which he ...ed a soft stone quarried in the districts of ...olterra and Siena and in many other parts of ...aly. When the stone is baked in a fire and then ...ushed and made into a paste with tepid water, it ...comes so soft that it can be fashioned into ...hatever shape is wanted, and, then, when it has ...ied out, it sets so hard that whole figures can be ...st from it. In the molds he has made from this ...one, Andrea used to cast various natural forms, ...ch as knees, legs, arms and torsos, which he ...pt by him for copying purposes. Then during ...ndrea's lifetime the custom started of doing ...expensive casts of heads of those who died, and ... one can see in every house in Florence, over ...e chimney-pieces, doors, windows and cornices, ...dless examples of such portraits, so well made ...d natural that they seem alive. This practice has ...ntinued until the present day and has proved ...tremely useful in making available to us the ...ortraits of many of those who appear in the ...enes painted in Duke Cosimo's palace. For this ...e are indebted to the talents of Andrea who was ...e of the first to make such casts.'

...This description illustrates much that is rele...nt for plaster sculpture today. The medium is ...eap, readily available and relatively easy to use. ...asari praises Verocchio's practice of casting ...om life because of the naturalness which he ...hieves in his work.

...The pursuit of naturalness at the expense of ...her sculptural values led to a relative decline in ...e art of sculpture which continued until the time ...Rodin. The Frenchman Auguste Rodin (1840–...17) surrounded himself with plaster casts of his sculptures or parts of them. Using these casts, he could assemble figures from the fragments and thus achieve the freedom with anatomical form which is characteristic of his work.

When Rodin exhibited his first major work, *The Age of Bronze* in 1878, first in Belgium and then in Paris, he was accused of casting it from life. These allegations were disproved, but they did bring to light that casting from life was a frequent practice among sculptors, and one which had, over the years, reduced the vitality of sculpture as an art form.

Since the days of the ancient Greeks, the main use of plaster has been as a transitory medium for finalizing a shape, before it is cast into a more permanent material such as bronze. This tradition has continued in the twentieth century. However, in recent years, sculptors such as the Americans George Segal (born 1924) and Claes Oldenburg (born 1929) have produced permanent figurative works in plaster. Plaster has also recently been used as part of a mixed media approach to sculpture. Its main use, however, remains that of a transitory material.

Below This picture shows an exhibition of work by the young British artist John Davies. Plaster plays an important role in his works, although they also include other materials. The figures are life-size. The figure in the foreground is called *Old Enemy* and was made between 1973 and 1975.

TECHNIQUES

Hydrated calcium sulphate $CaSO_4 2H_2O$ (gypsum), when heated to 350°F (117°C), loses 75 per cent of its water to form $CaSO_4 \frac{1}{2}H_2O$, which is known as plaster of Paris. It is named after the Paris region in France, which has an abundance of gypsum. Commercially, the plaster is more often called dental or superfine casting plaster and this is the grade most often used by sculptors.

Bought plaster comes in the form of a white powder which, when mixed with water, recovers the water it had prior to being treated by heat, and sets to a uniform mass with the same composition as the original gypsum.

Gypsum is found in a variety of forms, alabaster being one which is well known to sculptors as a soft and easily carved stone. Most of the gypsum deposits which occur widely are believed to have been formed by the slow evaporation of sea water, resulting in a mineral concentration which formed the gypsum.

PREPARATION AND TOOL

Work surfaces and the areas around them shou be as simple as possible, so that cleaning do can be relatively easy. Plastic sheeting can used to cover or surround the work space, plaster easily cracks off plastic once it has set. T sink used for cleaning bowls and tools should equipped with a plaster trap to prevent dra from being blocked.

Even allowing for an adequate draina system, surplus plaster should be scraped int trashcan, and the bowls and tools wiped cle with old newspapers, before being washed at sink. Plastic bowls are excellent for mixing plas in, as dried plaster can, if necessary, be eas cracked away from the surface by flexing bowl. However, it is preferable not to have resort to this practice too often or the bowl will weakened. Sharp or metal instruments should be used for cleaning bowls as the scratches t cause will tend to form a key for future plas

Below *Balustrade* by Barry Midgley is a mixed media work featuring plaster for the balustrades. The small trees visible above the landscape are made of lichen. Many artists have worked with plaster either as a transitional medium or as a component in a mixed media work.

xes, making cleaning the bowl progressively
re difficult.

f no plaster trap is fitted, a tin bath or large bin
be used to clean bowls and tools while work is
progress. When the work is complete, the
ster should be allowed to settle, the water
ured away and the sludge that has settled at the
ttom of the container disposed of.

Apart from mixing bowls, other items that
uld be available in the work area include paint
apers, old or cheap wood chisels for carving or
sing open molds, wooden wedges for splitting
lds or tightening ropes holding mold sections
gether, a tyre inner tube cut into rings for
lding smaller molds together, surforms, rifflers,
ster rasps and perhaps an old cheese grater for
ugh forming work. Finally, a mallet, hammer,
r of pliers, general purpose saw, junior hack-
w and a pair of scissors are useful. Experience
d the type of work being undertaken will
pand this list.

STORAGE AND CARE OF TOOLS

ster is usually bought in 1cwt (51kg) paper
cks which should be stored in a dry area and
sed from the floor on a wooden pallet to avoid
ntact with moisture. It is best to use fresh
ster when possible, but, if it has to be ordered
bulk and stored for a time, the paper sacks
ould be placed in large plastic bags and made
rtight. This will keep the plaster in good con-
tion for long periods.

Mixing bowls and tools should be cleaned
ring and after use, and metal tools rubbed with
oily rag to prevent rusting. Wooden formers
n be scraped down with a paint scraper and
rforms should never be left clogged with damp
ster. Although most tools used in working
ster are relatively cheap to purchase, they
ould, nevertheless, be treated with respect.

MIXING PLASTER

clean plastic or enamel bowl should be used for
ixing plaster. Clean, cold water is added to the
wl first, and plaster is sifted through the fingers
to the water. Any lumps which are found in the
y plaster should be removed. The plaster is
rinkled into the water until it begins to stand
ove the surface of the water, forming a 'desert
and', while the water soaks up through it. Once
the plaster is wet, tap the bowl to dislodge any
y plaster sticking to the sides of the bowl, and
w mix it thoroughly. The mixing should not be
rried out until this stage. Mixing is best done by
acing an outspread hand into the bottom of the

TOOLS

Tools for plaster
The great variety of tools used for working with plaster are usually not very expensive, but should still be treated with care, as clean tools are important for good results. The tools pictured here are for carving and shaping, and the same tools can be used whether the plaster is being worked for casting or being used in its own right. A few of the tools which are available for plaster work include: a float (**1**), pointing trowel (**2**), parting knife (**3**),

assorted modeling tools (**4**), scraper (**5**), spatula (**6**), wire brush (**7**), plaster rasps (**8**), assorted larger scrapers (**9**), flat chisels (**10**), claw chisels (**11**), hammer (**12**), dummy (**13**), knife (**14**), surforms (**15**), plaster rasps (**16**), scraper made from a broken hacksaw blade (**17**), wire brush (**18**), and a general purpose saw with an adjustable blade (**19**). Other useful items would be rifflers, wooden wedges, an old cheese grater for creating rough work, a mallet, pliers, a pair of

scissors and plastic bowls. Plastic bowls are the best possible containers for mixing plaster. Metal tools should never be used for cleaning these bowls, because they will leave scratch marks which will eventually make the bowl impossible to clean thoroughly. After metal tools are cleaned they should be rubbed with an oily rag to prevent rusting. Remember that surforms must never be left clogged with damp plaster.

Mixing plaster I. Fill a plastic bowl with clean water. With dry hands, sprinkle plaster evenly around the bowl.

2. Continue sprinkling plaster until it stands in small islands above the surface of the water.

3. Place your hand flat in the bowl and move it briskly from side to side to mix the plaster and water to a cream.

bowl and shaking the mix from side to side. T result should resemble thin cream and be o uniform consistency. If care is taken in followi these procedures, fresh plaster in good conditi should give about 15 to 20 minutes working ti before the chemical reaction which is taking pla makes it too thick to use. Old plaster will tend thicken quickly, and, if it is too old or has been stored properly, it will set but not harde

To test plaster, pinch some dry plaster betwe your fingers. If it retains its shape, it is usa but, if the shape disintegrates, the plaster is old has been exposed to damp.

When making a plaster mold to be used for s casting or press-molding, it is advisable to m sure the water and plaster, so that the parts of mold absorb moisture from the clay at the sa rate and thus do not cause distortion in molded item. The measurements for this equal volumes of water and plaster or appro mately 2¾lb (1.25kg) of plaster to 2 pints (liters) of water.

ACCELERATING AND RETARDING PLASTER

The setting of plaster rarely needs to be speed up, as its normal time of 15 to 20 minutes usually fast enough. However, when it is thoug necessary to accelerate a mix, it is proba simplest to use warm water. Alternative means acceleration include the addition of salt, appro mately ½oz (12g) to about 2 pints (1.1 liters) water. Increasing the amount of plaster in the n and vigorously agitating the plaster also accel ate setting, although this would be unsuitable fine work, as the agitation would trap air bubb in the mix and cause pinholes in the final surfa of the set plaster.

Retarding setting is more often desirable, p ticularly when working on large sculptures when modeling complex works, as the extra ti allows the surface to be more carefully controlle The addition of glue size to the mixing water the best retardant and also increases the streng of the plaster. Mix the glue size as normal and a a 1oz (25g) to every 2 pints (1.1 liters) of mixi water. To lengthen the setting time, increase t amount of glue size. The addition of acetic ac approximately 5 per cent, to the mixing water w also retard a mix. A further method is to a plaster to the water as normal but, instead mixing, leave the plaster and water to stand for minutes. The mix will thicken and remain plas for longer than a normal mix, but it will also weaker in strength. This method of retarding however, particularly useful when modeli direct with plaster or when doing final work su as filling surface blemishes.

Plaster trap This diagram shows a sink fitted with a plaster trap. One of the problems of working with plaster is that it inevitably creates a certain amount of mess. As plaster is relatively quick drying, frequent washing of tools, bowls and hands is necessary to prevent equipment becoming clogged, and dried plaster mixing with fresh. However, this vigorous activity can cause blockages in the sink pipes or drains, so, if you intend to use plaster often, or over a long period of time, it is well worth fitting a plaster trap to the sink. This is a second sink underneath the main basin, into which the water flows. The flow is interrupted and passes through a second outlet pipe which is a filter. The water runs through freely into the main drainage system, but small bits and pieces of plaster cannot enter the filter pipe and they gradually collect in the trap, forming a thick sludge which can be scooped out and disposed of elsewhere.

SEPARATORS

hen using plaster for mold-making or casting, it necessary to use a separating agent between the rts of a mold, between the mold and the aterial from which it is being taken, or even tween a plaster mold and the material being st from the mold.

p A thin clay slip, made by mixing clay and ter to a thin creamy consistency, is a simple parating agent, which is suitable for use on ld walls or to separate plaster from a wood sting box or baseboard. It would not be suitable r use as a barrier between a mold face and a st, as it would tend to fill in fine detail. To oduce a barrier between a plaster cast and a ster mold, brush soft soap vigorously onto the mp mold surface until a foam appears, dab off cess soap and repeat the process until a sheen pears. This separator allows very fine detail to reproduced.

Another separating agent that can be used on nple geometric forms is thin oil. When making mold from a hand or when life casting, pet- leum jelly should be used to allow release and event the skin being dried out by the plaster.

ARMATURES

hen modeling with plaster, it is necessary to ild an armature onto which the plaster can be plied. As when modeling clay, care should be ken when designing the armature to ensure that s the correct size and proportion and that it is id enough to support the weight of plaster to be plied and to withstand the handling and model- . For small-scale works, square-section minum wire may be adequate, whereas, for ger work, mild steel rod or tubes welded or lted together may be necessary to support the rk. Experience will help in the choice of nature.

el If mild steel is used to make an armature, it uld be painted with either shellac or metal mer to prevent rust marks staining the surface the plaster. Galvanized binding wire should n be bound around the main tubes to help the ster key onto the armature.

ood Wood is generally not very suitable for natures, particularly for complex forms, as it ll soak up water from the plaster, causing it to ell and crack the sculpture unless it has been ll sealed with shellac. Also, if it is necessary to er the armature after work has started, it is ier to bend a steel rod into the new position n to reorganize a wooden support.

re netting For a large volume model, wire tting is often used to help reduce the amount of

plaster needed. After building an armature in wood or steel, wire netting is wrapped around it and attached with galvanized binding wire. The netting should be shaped as far as possible to the profile of the sculpture being made and supported internally with crumpled newspapers, cardboard or polystyrene chips. Onto this framework layers of scrim—an open weave fabric—soaked in plaster are built up to the final shape, and a layer of neat plaster used to make a 'skin' for the form. This allows surface detail to be worked with a chisel, file or spatula.

Polystyrene For very large work, a more flexible working method is necessary. A block or blocks of polystyrene are stacked to the required height and then carved with saws, hot wire cutters or rasps to the required profile. This is then covered with a layer of plaster and scrim in the usual manner. The advantage of this working method is that it gives infinite room for changes of design, is light, strong and a rapid building method. The finished work can then, if necessary, be cut into manageable sections for casting or transporting.

Below In *Lovers* by George Segal, no attempt has been made to smooth away the modeled texture of the plaster. The theme of two figures touching is emphasized in the tactile quality of the actual material.

Above Using plaster, Brancusi achieved the clean lines and simple definition of form in *The Tortoise*.

MODELING

Having built an armature, the choice of plast modeling technique is very much a personal on However, some rules must be observed if t sculpture is to be successful.

When adding more plaster to plaster that h already set, it is essential that the latter saturated with water to prevent it from sucki water from the new mix and, in so doir affecting its strength. Failure to do this will ca the new plaster to crack away from the old plaster and prevent a proper bond. Until the fir surface is reached, keep the layers of plast roughened where possible, so as to form a k onto which additional plaster can be placed.

Organize the work so that the build-up plaster is as continuous a process as possibl without long periods when the work is left to d out. Should this happen, then the work alrea carried out must be saturated with water befo any more plaster is added.

If it becomes necessary to cut the surface ba and scrim appears on the surface of the work, it usually better either to cut it out or to knock t supporting wire netting in with a hammer a plaster over the hole rather than attempt just hide the scrim with a thin layer of plaster. If t latter course of action is taken, the scrim inva ably makes a reappearance at a later stage.

Modeling tools Tools used for modeling or sha ing plaster include metal modeling tools, plast rasps, surforms, paint scrapers, rifflers (for d plaster only), old wood saws or general purpo saws with replaceable blades, and broken hac saw blades.

Modeling with plaster 1. Make a suitably shaped armature with square-section aluminum and chicken wire.

2. Pad out the armature with rolls of newspaper bound to the stem with wire.

3. Block out the base with clay if appropriate. If the armature is well padded, the weight of plaster will be reduced.

4. Cover the whole shape with scrim soaked in plaster to form a reinforcing layer before modeling the surface.

5. Add more plaster with fingers or using metal modeling tools. Develop the form, keeping plaster rough to provide a key.

6. When the form has taken shape, smooth down the surface and refine the contours with surforms and scraping tools.

CARVING PLASTER

s an introduction to the carving process, plaster
ffords a cheap and economic material to practice
n. However, plaster does not have the same
sistance as or the permanence of stone, so it
rould not be considered as requiring exactly the
me technique.

To make a block of plaster suitable for carving,
e a strong cardboard box, sealed with tape and
eased to prevent water penetration, and pour a
aster mix into it. Once it has set, the cardboard
in be stripped away and the carving begun.

When carving plaster, it is preferable to keep
e area being worked on *damp*, as this helps
revent fractures occurring by absorbing impact.
owever, when using a rasp, surform, riffler, drill
sandpaper, the plaster should be kept *dry* as
is will not clog the teeth of the tools.

Surforms and plaster rasps are more useful than
nventional rasps when it is necessary to work
e plaster damp, as their design prevents clog-
ng or at least makes it easy to clean them.

The carving can be either left in a state that
lows the carving process or it can be filed or
nded to a smooth finish. If the plaster is still
mp, wet-and-dry paper can be used to achieve a
nooth finish. If the plaster is dry, sandpaper
ould be used. In both cases, coarse grades
ould be used first, followed by finer grades.

arving tools Tools required for carving a plaster
ock include both wood chisels and stone chisels,
allet, rasps, rifflers and sandpaper. When using
isels for roughing out, they should not be
iven too far into the block or they will act as a
edge and may split the block.

Carving plaster 1. Make a
solid plaster block in a casting
box. Draw up rough
guidelines to the design on the
faces.

2. Rough out the basic form
with a flat chisel. Work in
toward the center of the
block to avoid breaking off
the edges.

3. Shape rounded forms with
a claw chisel. Push the chisel
carefully with a small mallet,
developing the carving slowly.

4. The claw chisel makes small
criss-cross marks on the
surface. It is a stone carving
tool, but wood chisels can be
used.

5. Plaster is not a very
resistant carving material, so
the chisels may be pushed
with the hand rather than hit
with a mallet.

6. To eliminate chisel marks
and produce a clean rounded
surface, finish off the carving
with a plaster rasp.

Right This detail comes from
a large sculpture by Henry
Moore called *Internal and
External Forms*. It shows the
texture of carved plaster in a
work formed for casting in
bronze. Marks left by chisels
and rasps make the surface as
active and exciting as the form
itself.

Left Plaster is frequently used
as a component in mixed
media sculpture as it is
versatile and relatively cheap.
It can be cast or formed if a
geometric shape is required,
or more roughly modeled or
carved. In this large
construction, *Black Virgin* by
Michael Kenny, plaster is
combined with wood and
metal.

Forming a hemisphere 1.
The quarter circle template fits to a metal rod set in the center of a wood base.

2. Build thick coils of clay around the metal rod to about 1 in (2.5cm) below the inner edge of the template.

3. Throw a coat of plaster over the clay core. Cover it completely with plaster.

4. Reinforce the plaster coat using scrim soaked in plaster wrapped around the circular form.

5. Build up a thick coat of plaster over the scrim. Rotate the template to scrape away surplus plaster.

6. Complete the shape and let the plaster dry out. Remove the hemisphere and clean out clay from the inside.

7. Fill the small hole left by the rod with fresh plaster. Soak the surface and smooth it with wet-and-dry paper.

SIMPLE FORMING DEVICES FOR REGULAR SOLIDS

A hemisphere can be constructed by setting a vertical axle into a baseboard and constructing a hemisphere using wire netting, or, for small shapes, clay. The netting or clay core should be made smaller than the desired final size in order to allow for the thickness of the scrim and plaster to be used. The axle should be greased to prevent sticking and should project higher than the radius of the finished hemisphere. Next, a template is attached to the axle in such a way as to allow for its easy removal.

With the template removed, the inner core of wire or clay is covered with scrim dipped in plaster—two coats are usually enough. Large scale items may need the addition of mild steel reinforcing rods which should have been pre formed and sandwiched between the coats of scrim. The template should be cut from a zinc plated mild steel sheet attached to a wooden frame for reinforcement. However, depending on the intricacy of the shape to be formed, even masonite could be used if suitably sealed and reinforced.

The template should occasionally be fitted to the axle, and a check made that the scrim and reinforcement are kept below the surface of the required shape. Plaster should then be poured over the scrim, and the template turned around the axle until it scrapes the plaster surface and, in so doing, forms the finished shape. The template will need to be removed and cleaned at regular intervals to avoid any build-up of plaster which may score or mark the surface of the form. Once the form is complete it can be removed from the axle and the inner clay core taken out.

Linear plaster shapes of any reasonable length can be formed by attaching a wooden batten, which is the length of the required shape, to a baseboard. Make sure again that the baseboard is greased to prevent the shape which is being formed from sticking. Make a template so that it slides against the batten. The shape required should be blocked out with clay or netting if necessary. Scrim reinforcement and plaster can be added in the same way as when turning the hemisphere until the shape is achieved by scraping the template along the length of the form.

The thickness of plaster and reinforcement necessary are very much a matter of experience. If the object is to be long and reinforcement added along the length, then it should be rigid enough not to flex too much. This will probably affect the thickness of the plaster used, as the reinforcement should not be placed too near the

al surface of the plaster. Templates should be
signed so as to eliminate undercuts which
uld prevent their removal from the completed
rk, or so that they can be run off the end of the
ape being formed.

FORMING

aster shapes to be used either as forms for
rving or as parts of a larger work can often be
ated by simply pouring plaster into a prepared
rmer, such as a plastic bag or cardboard box,
d leaving it to set.

A useful and versatile device for forming plas-
r is a casting box which, together with a
seboard, enables rectangular solids to be pro-
ced quickly and easily. The rectangularity of
apes cast in this way can be altered by filling
rts of the box with clay or other suitable
aterials to create negative shapes between the
sting box and the plaster. Wood should be
rewed down, either to the base or to the walls of
e casting box, to prevent it from floating when
aster is added. It would also need the applica-
n of separator, as would the casting box.

A baseboard may be either sealed wood or ¼in
mm)glass laid on a pad of polystyrene. When
ing a casting box regularly, it may be desirable
construct the sides out of wood faced with
rmica to make cleaning and release easier.

The sides of the box should be smooth and the
ds cut at precisely 90° to the edges. At one end,
L-shaped bracket should be attached so that it
ojects downward against the end, at the same
stance away from the end of the box as the
ickness of the wood. The box is assembled so
at each L-shape links one board to the other,
rming a square that can be adjusted to a
ctangular shape of any proportion.

Simple cylindrical forms can be cast using a
be made from tin-plate, lightly oiled, tied and
aled around the bottom against the baseboard
ing clay. If more accurate or complex cylindri-
l forms are required, then a turning box may be
ore useful.

Spheres and spherical shapes can be cast using
turning box or, for rough shaping, a balloon,
astic bag or two halves of a ball, which has been
t in half, can be used. A turning box can also be
ed for forming regular plaster cylindrical shapes
at do not include undercuts. Its basic construc-
on is a box without a top or bottom. A metal
aft is fitted across the top of the box, which has
ne end cranked to form a handle. To one side of
is shaft, a wooden plate onto which a template
n be added is attached. The design should
able the top plate assembly to be removed
sily. Now cut a template of the desired profile
om zinc-plated mild steel or some other suitable

Forming a linear shape 1.
The former consists of a metal
template supported upright
against a batten fixed to a flat
board. Make a clay core for
the shape.

2. Mix a bowl of plaster and
throw it onto the clay to form
a covering coat. Eliminate any
air bubbles.

3. Build up the plaster layer
and apply scrim soaked in
plaster as reinforcement along
the whole shape.

4. Completely cover the
scrim with fresh plaster,
working up toward the inner
curves of the template.

5. When the plaster layers are
sufficiently thick, brace the
template against the batten
and draw it along the form.

6. Add more plaster and
scrape it down again with the
template. Repeat until the
linear form is smooth and
perfectly shaped.

Casting box This can be
used to form solid plaster
blocks which can be carved. It
is constructed of four pieces
of wood, each having an angle
iron set at one end (**2**). The
irons hold the sections
together but, as each is
movable, rectangles of
different proportions can be
cast by altering the lengths.
When the box is assembled
(**1**) the irons are secured with
wedges (**3**). The box is set on
a wooden base, coated with a
release agent and sealed
around the base (**4**). Plaster is
poured in and left to set hard.

thin sheet material. The template is half the diameter of the shape being turned, less the radius of the shaft.

When working on a small scale, make the box so that it fits over a bowl, as this will help with collecting and recycling the liquid plaster. When the template has been put in place, scrim soaked in plaster or string is bound around the shaft to bulk out the volume. The shaft should be turned occasionally to make sure the scrim is not catching on the template. New plaster is built up by pouring over this core while turning the handle. As the shape builds up, it begins to scrape against the template and the required shape is formed. The template will need to be removed frequently so that the plaster can be cleared off it. When the turning operation has been completed, the template can be removed and any final smoothing down carried out using wet-and-dry paper. Continue to turn the handle during this process. The shaft should then be removed from the shape and the operation is complete, apart from filling the hole which has been left by removing the shaft.

Turning box The principle here is similar to that of forming a shape, but the plaster is built up on a spindle and rotated against the template, which remains fixed.

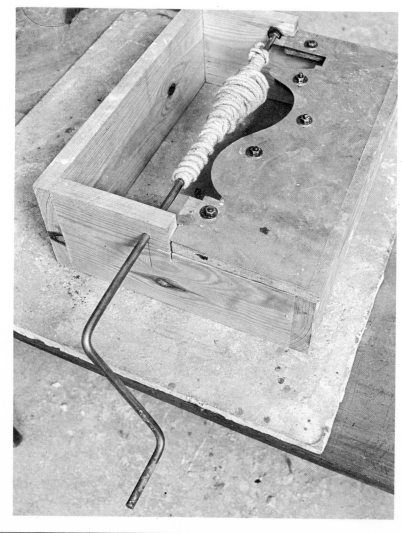

MAKING A HOLLOW REGULAR SOLID USING PLASTER

As well as being molded, modeled or carved plaster can be used as a sheet material and can be built into regular solids such as cubes or pyramids.

Cubes To build a cube, make a former using a baseboard of hardboard or plywood and softwood battening, chamfered to an angle of 45°. The battens should be fixed to the baseboard using screws, so that they can be released and relocated as necessary. The depth of the battening should be the depth required for the final plaster panel. After applying a releasing agent to the former, a quantity of plaster is poured in and allowed to stiffen. More plaster is then mixed, and scrim is dipped into this and applied to the back of the plaster in the former. Take care not to allow the scrim to come into contact with the edge of the former or be pushed through to the surface of the panel. Any additional reinforcement though necessary is now added, and more plaster and scrim applied over this. Finally, the thickness is made up by pouring plaster over the reinforcement and the whole is leveled by scraping excess plaster off with a piece of wood pulled across the top of the battens. Once set, the shape can be removed from the former and the other five panels cast.

As each panel is cast, it should be laid flat on top of the others until ready for assembly. To assemble the cube, the panels are first soaked with water and the edges scratched to form a key. Five panels—four sides and a base—are fixed together by applying plaster as a cement between the chamfered edges and tying the side panels together using rope and wedges or corner clamps. If rope is used, the corners must be protected with packing to avoid damage. The sides are assembled over the fifth bottom panel, and the corners are reinforced internally using plaster and scrim down and along each seam. Finally, the sixth panel is fixed in place using the method described although, of course, these seams cannot be strengthened from the inside. The edges can now be cleaned and the shape is complete.

Quite large, surprisingly strong and rigid box shapes can be formed in this way, without the need for metal reinforcement. Although this type of shape could be made simply using wood, plaster may be more appropriate, and the surface can be subjected to a different and interesting range of treatments, such as fresco paintwork, staining or inlaying of objects and marks. In this way, a wide variety of effects can be achieved. Plaster is a surprisingly versatile medium.

Building a hollow solid 1. Make a rectangular former for plaster slabs by attaching a framework of chamfered battens to a base.

2. Assemble the former and apply a release agent to all the inner faces. Petroleum jelly is suitable for this.

Mix up plaster and pour ough into the former to ake a layer about ¼in mm) thick.

4. Spread the plaster evenly by tilting the mold and tapping it gently on the worktop, forcing out air bubbles.

5. Reinforce the first layer by laying on scrim soaked in plaster. Keep it away from the edges of the shape.

6. Pour in more plaster until the former is completely full. Make sure that the scrim is completely covered.

7. Level off the surface of the plaster by pulling a wood batten evenly across the top. Allow the plaster slab to dry out.

Make as many pieces as are quired for the final form. ak them with water and atch the edges to provide a y.

9. Pour plaster along the edges of each shape to act as adhesive for the joints.

10. Assemble the pieces into shape. Use a thick wood section to guide them into place or if possible use corner blocks.

11. Tie the hollow form with string to keep the pieces in place until the plaster has set.

12. Reinforce inside seams with thick plaster and scrim soaked in plaster.

13. Stand the form upright on a greased base and seal the bottom with clay. Pour in plaster to form a base.

14. When the whole piece has set, fill the outer joints with fresh plaster. When dry, rub them down to a smooth finish.

151

FINISHING

A plaster sculpture may need to have its surfac sealed to prevent dust and dirt building up in th pores. When plaster is still damp, it appears mor dense than when it has dried out, at which stage takes on a more 'dusty' appearance.

Waxing If a dense appearance is desired, then th old technique of waxing will help the surfac retain some of this quality.

The plaster should be warmed prior to trea ment so as to allow the wax to impregnate th pores. The wax, which should be stearin wax possible, should be melted in a double boiler which liquid turpentine is added in the pr portions 1oz (25g) wax to 8oz (200g) turpentin Care must be taken that the wax is not too ho otherwise the turpentine may combust. Also, th turpentine should not come into direct conta with the heat source.

The solution is then applied to the plaster wi a large, soft bristle paintbrush, starting at the to Several coats will be needed, depending on th finish required. The work should then be allowe to cool and, if a polish is wanted, the whole wor should be rubbed with a pad of cotton wool an talcum powder. This process produces a surfac resembling ivory.

Shellac Another method of sealing plaster is coat it with shellac. Make sure the surface is fre of dust and grease, and paint the shellac onto th work with a large, soft paintbrush. After on coat, the surface will be sealed, and subsequen coats are used to build up the degree of polish although too many will fill in detail and darke the plaster. Indeed, this method has even bee used to give work an 'antique' quality. When th polish has been applied and allowed to harden, little dry powder, such as yellow ocher, ra umber or light red, can be mixed with denature alcohol in a saucer and painted into the hollow and creases on the work to darken and 'age' Any color that runs can be wiped clean usir cotton wool and denatured alcohol.

Left *Bust of a Woman* by Pablo Picasso is one of the plaster heads which the artist made in 1932. The main feature of the head is the unusual treatment given to the nose, while the eyes, eyebrows and hair appear rather roughly incised and modeled. The shoulders seem almost untouched. Plaster is only one of the many sculptural media in which Picasso worked.

Right The *Column of the Kis* shows the artist's work in plaster. The piece relates to Brancusi's famous work *Gate of the Kiss* (1937) in which th circle motif reappears. In some ways, the *Column* is itself an abstraction from the artist's early work, *The Kiss*, 1910. This can be seen in the division of the column into two and the proximity of the two halves of the circle like two heads kissing.

Another method used to color a work is to paint the whole work with a color and spirit mix, and then remove the unwanted color, again using pad of cotton wool and denatured alcohol. Care should be taken not to dissolve the shellac sealing coat by rubbing too hard.

Linseed oil Another medium used for sealing the surface of plaster is linseed oil, but this tends to darken with age and may, therefore, tend to defeat the purpose of sealing. However, it does give a mellow quality to the plaster and could be used to advantage. Where possible, immerse the warmed plaster sculpture in linseed oil for several hours, or, failing this, paint on the oil until the surface is saturated. The sculpture should then be allowed to drain and, when dry, rubbed carefully with a soft rag to produce a polish.

Finishing with wax 1. Heat a mixture of wax and turpentine in a pan. Meanwhile warm the plaster block in an oven.

2. Brush the liquid wax over the plaster surface, working first in one direction, then across to form a thin layer.

Adding surface color 1. Draw into the surface with a sharp metal tool. Lay on plaster colored with powder paint.

2. Scrape away the colored plaster with the flat edge of a knife, leaving color only in the engraved lines.

Below The casting box for this work, *Settlement* by Barry Midgley, forms the frame for the finished work. The shapes were created using sand, placed on top of the layer of glass in the bottom of the box. The stones were placed in the sand and the plaster poured on. After the plaster had set, the sand was poured out.

COLORING PLASTER

Powder color added to the water prior to mixing in the plaster can be used to produce a colored plaster, although too much powder may affect the setting or the strength of the plaster. The earth colors are safest.

This method should be used for making a plaster mold, from which a plaster cast is to be made. The colored plaster is the first coat of the mold, the subsequent coats being a normal mix. When chipping away the mold to reveal the cast, the color shows when the mold is nearing the cast and very great care should be taken to prevent damage to the surface of the cast. If color is used in a finished plaster work then no work should be carried out on it after casting, if surface changes of color are to be avoided.

If color is to be applied to the sculpture on completion of the forming or casting process, then the surface will need sealing if gloss or enamel paints are to be used. Shellac is the quickest means of sealing the surface, as paint can be applied within approximately 30 minutes, when the shellac has dried. Emulsion or acrylic paints can be applied directly onto the plaster without the need for a sealing coat.

JOINING, REPAIRING AND FIXING

Because plaster cannot absorb shock through sudden pressure, it can easily be broken. Therefore, careful handling is always necessary. When a work is broken or cracked, repairs can be difficult for any sculptor.

Simple blemishes on a work such as cracks, or pinholing, caused by air bubbles being trapped against the surface, can be removed by filling with a weak mixture of plaster, after first thoroughly wetting the plaster which is to be repaired. If the work to be repaired is old and dry, the whole object should be immersed in water until air bubbles stop rising to the surface. If this is not possible, water should be poured over the work until it stops absorbing water in the repair area. Dirt and grease should be removed and a key for the new plaster formed by scraping the surface of the parts to be repaired. After application of the new plaster, the repair can be gone over with a damp brush to blend it with the surrounding area. The surface should then be left to dry.

Should the repair require two parts that have dried to be joined, the fractured faces of each can

Left This striking portrait head of Sir James Frazer is an example of the work of the French sculptor, Antoine Bourdelle. Bourdelle worked for a time with Rodin who was a great influence on Bourdelle's work. This head conveys an impression of great concentration. Traces of the tools the artist used can still be detected on the surface.

Joining plaster forms 1. Trim the sections to the same size by cutting through them with a general purpose saw.

2. Provide a tooth on the seam lines by scratching across them with a knife or metal tool.

3. Wedge one section with seam edges upwards and horizontal. Pour fresh wet plaster along each seam.

4. Put the second section in place and press the two halves firmly together.

5. Reinforce the inside seams by reaching into the form and laying on more plaster.

6. When the joints are firmly set, smooth down the outer seam lines with a surform.

be painted with shellac and, when dry, a second thickly mixed coat of shellac used as a glue to fix the parts together. Alternatively, carpenter's glue, the type that is melted in a double boiler, can be used. The parts should be held firmly together while the shellac hardens and the excess that has been squeezed from the joint removed with a sharp knife or scalpel. To help hide the joint, it can be scraped carefully with the knife to create a surface crack along the joint. This can be filled with a weak plaster mix in the way already described.

PVA (polyvinyl acetate) woodworking adhesive is also useful for repair work and has the advantage of drying to a clear finish. Surfaces that are to be joined should be absolutely free from dust and grease before the adhesive is applied.

A joint that will be under stress is best reinforced with metal rods. These should be fixed with plaster into holes drilled into one piece, so that half the rod protrudes, and, when set, should fit into holes drilled into the second piece. The joint can then be completed by pouring plaster into those holes and onto the face of the break. The pins should be placed into their respective holes, and the joint squeezed firmly until a bond has been made.

Right *Spring* by the French sculptor Aristide Maillol is made from plaster washed with blue. The figure is typical of Maillol's interest in simplicity of form and massiveness of volume. For much of his work, he concentrated on drawing and modeling the same type of female figure.

Below This small sculpture, *Female Vine Leaf*, by Marcel Duchamp was created in 1950. It is made of galvanized plaster. Duchamp's wide ranging talents were exercised in many different media.

einforcing a joint I. Drill
oles along both edges to be
ned and cut small metal
ds of suitable size. Make
re holes are correctly
gned.

2. Fill the holes on one section with fresh wet plaster and insert the rods.

3. Roughen the edge of both sections by scratching the face with a metal tool.

4. Pour wet plaster along the roughened edge. Make quite a thick layer to cover the whole surface of the joint.

5. Set down the plaster slabs on a flat surface and locate the rods in one section to the holes in the other. These should be a little larger to help with fit.

6. Press the two halves firmly together. Wait until the wet plaster has dried and then rub down the seam with a surform.

ending a break I. With a
ft brush, coat the faces of
ch broken piece with a thin
yer of shellac to seal them.

2. Apply a thicker coat of shellac to both surfaces to act as adhesive in the repair.

3. Press the shellacked faces firmly together and leave them for about 1 hour or until the joint feels quite firm.

4. Cut a shallow V-shaped groove along the surface of the plaster, centered on the seam line.

5. Fill the groove with plaster applied with a flat spatula. When this has dried, rub down and finish the surface.

Left This plaster model for a monument by John Flaxman shows one of the main possible uses of plaster, as a medium for making models of work which will be executed on a larger scale.

A hole in a hollow form, such as a portr[ait?] head, can be mended simply by filling the fo[rm] with damp newspaper and pouring plaster i[n] the hole against the paper. Another method is [to] fix a piece of string to the center of a piece of ca[rd] by piercing it, and tying it to a nail. The car[d is] then pushed through the hole in the form a[nd] held firmly against the inside of the hole [by] pulling the string tight. Plaster can then be used [to] complete the repair, and the string removed af[ter] the plaster has set.

Bolts can be used to join plaster sectio[ns] together, either by drilling the sections to [be] joined and bolting in the usual way, or by sett[ing] the bolt head into the plaster when casting, so [the] thread is exposed once the former or mold [is] removed. If this method is used, the bolt sho[uld] be primed to prevent rusting, which may stain [the] surface of the plaster, and the exposed thre[ad] should be greased to prevent plaster adhering [to it].

Left German-born sculptor Wilhelm Lehmbruck created most of his work from artificial stone and bronze. But he was also capable of creating expressive work using plaster. Lehmbruck's work often produces an air of inner contemplation, as does this small work in colored plaster completed in 1911.

Filling a hole 1. Cut a piece of card large enough to cover the hole and attach a piece of string through the center.

2. Push the card through th[e] hole and pull it back against the inner surface. Start to pour plaster into the hole.

3. Continue pouring slowly until the hole is filled. When the plaster has set, cut off the string at the surface.

4. When the plaster has dri[ed] work over the repair with a surform to finish it flush wit[h] the original surface.

MARINO MARINI (geb. Pistoja 1901) Arcangelo 1943.
LEIHGABE

SAFETY

Dust Plaster dust, like all dust should be kept to a minimum.
Skin Contact with the skin should be avoided by rubbing petroleum jelly or a barrier cream well into the hands. Plaster dries out natural oils from the skin and excessive contact can produce serious skin complaints. When working with plaster, hands should be washed after each mix before the plaster hardens, a problem that can be quite painful for plaster mixers with hairy arms.
Lifting You should take the usual precautions which should be observed when lifting heavy weights.

General Plaster is a relatively safe, stable and cheap material to use and well suited to the needs of an inexperienced sculptor.

Far left The quick-setting properties of plaster can be used to create interesting effects of roughness in texture, as evidenced here in *Archangel*, sculpted here by the Italian painter and sculptor Marino Marini in 1943. Marini was greatly influenced by the techniques of Rodin.

Left The Rumanian-born artist Constantin Brancusi worked in many different media. He often worked on the same subject in different media. For example, *The Cock* was originally carved from a single piece of wood. Plaster was just one of the many media Brancusi used.

CONCRETE

HISTORY

Concrete is a relatively new sculptural medium, although it has been used in architecture for some time. Its use has been limited partly because it has been considered a poor substitute for stone, lacking stone's inherent character and historic importance in the development of sculpture.

However, its popularity has grown with t[he] development of architectural techniques whi[ch] employ concrete for forming a building's exter[nal] skin. These developments have led to the reali[za]tion that the processes of shaping and formi[ng] concrete give the medium a unique quality t[hat] can be exploited by the sculptor.

Since the 1950s, sculptors have developed [a] technique by which they can hollow cast cime[nt] fondu, a gray-black type of concrete, and this [has] done much to popularize concrete as an econom[ic] and permanent material for outdoor locatio[ns]. Other important features of concrete are that i[t is] relatively cheap to make, quick to use, a[nd] extremely fine surface details can be produced.

Concrete is a mixture of cement, aggregate—a
[sub]stance that adds body to the cement—and
[wa]ter. There are two types of cement. Portland
[ce]ment is composed of calcium aluminum silicate
[an]d is similar in appearance to Portland stone,
[an]d high alumina cement or ciment fondu. This is
[co]mposed of alumina and is gray-black in color.
[C]ement is made by grinding the raw material to
[a f]ine powder and heating it in a furnace to form a
[cli]nker. This is finely ground to create a powder
[th]at, when mixed with water, forms a paste that
[wil]l remain workable for a reasonable time before
[se]tting to form a dense mass. The act of mixing
[wi]th water triggers a chemical reaction that will
[oc]cur even if the mixture was placed under water.

To increase the strength and durability of the
cement mixture, aggregates are added to form the
paste. There are two main groups of aggregates—
fine and coarse. Fine aggregates include stone
dust and silver sand. Coarse aggregates are normally granite or marble chippings. The basic
criteria for an aggregate are that it should not be
liable to structural weakness, nor should it react
chemically with cement. Furthermore, it should
be clean, pure, inert and strong. Aggregates can
give a concrete mix a wide variety of qualities,
depending on the· combination of aggregates
used. These vary from a fine cast stone appearance to an open, exposed aggregate surface, like
that used on many modern buildings.

Sculpturally, concrete is used in one of three
main ways. It can be cast solid from a mold, in
which case a combination of fine and coarse
aggregates may be used and the mixture vibrated
to ensure good surface reproduction and the
elimination of air pockets. Concrete may be
hollow cast from a mold. For this, only fine
aggregate is added to the cement, and strength is
provided by the use of pieces of fiberglass.
Concrete can also be worked by direct modeling.
This process is not very popular, but it does
provide a means of working on a large scale
relatively cheaply. This use is perhaps best illus-
trated in making yacht hulls. If a concrete mixture
is to be applied directly onto a supporting armature, lime can be added (approximately three
parts cement to one part lime) to give the mixture
greater plasticity.

Below This is one of the fore-runners of Henry Moore's famous reclining figures. It was made in 1927 of cast concrete and is 25in (62cm) high. The position and style of the figure was influenced by Moore's visits as a student to the British Museum in London, where he was particularly drawn to non-European art, to the African and ancient Egyptian exhibits as well as to the pre-Columbian art of Mexico. The coarse effect of the concrete emphasizes the massive shaped arms and legs which give such strength to this sculpture. The interest in strong massive line can be seen in the works of other English and European sculptors of this period, including the French sculptor Gaudier-Brzeska and the Russian-American artist Archipenko.

Above This modern concrete sculpture called *Artigas* by J. Gardy shows how well the medium can blend with a natural setting. The reflections in the lake add to the work's appeal.

Tools for concrete

Many of the tools used with concrete are identical to those used in and around the home. These include a bucket (**1**) for mixing or holding the concrete, a spade (**5**) for mixing, a selection of trowels (**4**) and scrapers (**11**) for applying the concrete to the work. If casting solid, tap the box with a wooden mallet (**2**) to help eliminate air bubbles. A paintbrush (**8**) is a convenient implement for applying the thin goo coat.

Sacking or hessian (**3**) is handy for keeping the concrete damp while it cures. The concrete can be smoothed with a float (**10**). For finishing, use a file (**9**), stone chisels (**7**) or carborundum discs (**12**) attached to an electric drill (**14**). For drilling, a masonry bit (**13**) should be used with the drill. Working with concrete can be messy. It is best to keep your tools and work area clean. A scrubbing brush (**6**) is indispensable.

EQUIPMENT AND TOOLS

A mixing box is a useful item to have wh working with concrete, as is a measuring box i which the dry ingredients can be poured so t volume can be measured accurately. This ensu that consistent proportions can be achiev should more than one mix be needed and he avoid changes in color and density in the w being undertaken. Having mixed the constitue of the concrete dry, water is added to make mix plastic. This should be added a little at a tin until the required consistency is reached. Sa and aggregate, when purchased from a builde yard, will probably contain a high percentage water, and allowance must be made for this wh calculating ratios of sand to cement.

Apart from mixing and measuring boxes, use tools include a spade and an old brush cleaning tools and work area, a paintbrush apply the 'goo' coat when hollow casting, sacks keep work damp during curing, a bucket a assorted trowels and scrapers to apply or work mix. A stick of wood is useful as a 'rod' puddling concrete that is to be solid cast. Wh vibrating concrete for solid casting, a wood mallet is useful for tapping the side of the b containing the concrete.

Generally, because concrete is either mode onto an armature or cast from a mold or form it is rarely necessary to cut into a concrete ma but, should this be necessary, special carbide di specifically designed for the purpose can be fitt to an angle grinder. However, when using su equipment, care must be taken to follow manufacturer's instructions, safety goggles sho be worn, and adequate safety precautions take

Some finishing work can be carried out concrete with other tools. These include sto chisels, files and carborundum papers or whee although it should be borne in mind that, on a c surface, further working tends to show up a different color or texture.

Concrete can be drilled using a masonry d bit and a hammer drill. However, an alternat method suitable for more delicate works or la diameter holes is to include a wooden dowel the mold or armature, so that it can be drilled using a hand drill, leaving a clean hole of correct diameter.

Slabs of concrete may be joined using conve tional methods of fixing, such as bolts. They also be designed to slot together or to be join with doweling. Such considerations may be more importance on large works where, reasons of weight or to protect vulnerable proj tions, the work needs to be assembled on si These possibilities should always be borne in mi

TECHNIQUES

ne strength of concrete depends on several ctors. The first is the water content of the ixture, basically, the more water in the concrete e weaker it is. The second factor is the type of gregate used, as strength is related to the rength of the individual components. A third iportant element is the curing of the mixture. uring is the process in which the mixture dries. is very important that the drying time is ntrolled, so that the concrete does not harden o quickly. If it hardens too fast, it will not be iiformly strong. To ensure a good curing, keep e concrete damp. The best way to keep ciment ndu moist is to wrap it in damp rags or sacks for least eight hours, and preferably 24 hours. In e case of Portland cement, the concrete should e kept damp for about 10 days after being moved from its mold.

The strength of concrete is also related to the e of steel reinforcement. If concrete is properly ixed and cured, it has good compressive rength but relatively poor tensile strength, in her words it would crack easily. To provide eel reinforcement, incorporate mild steel rods mesh into areas that will be subjected to tensile ress. If steel reinforcement is used, it should be mpletely encased in concrete or sealed in order avoid rust stains on the surface of the work.

Strips of fiberglass, known as glass fiber mat, e often used either in direct modeling or for inforcing hollow cast shapes. This can be em oyed either as supplementary to or as an ternative to reinforcement with mild steel bars. lass fiber mat can be shredded and mixed with ment to form a binder or impregnated with ment and tamped—or forced—into place gainst the surface coat of the hollow cast section.

Concrete as a sculptural medium has many lvantages, particularly if it is to be used out-of- oors. It can withstand various climatic con tions and is resistant to scratches and knocks, id, if properly reinforced, can be molded or odeled into almost any shape. A large number textured finishes are also possible. It is rela vely cheap to work with and few specialist tools re needed.

The main disadvantage of concrete is that it is fficult to add additional material to concrete at has already cured. If concrete is added after a ork has been finished, some cracks may appear etween the old and new areas of concrete. ecause of this, it is best to plan the work well, aking sure that the work is supported by a well esigned armature, so that the sculpture can be mpleted before the concrete cures. So sculpture concrete requires good planning and timing.

PREPARATION

When mixing cement and aggregate, the ratio of each will vary depending on the type of work being undertaken. The main considerations are whether the concrete is to be poured solid, laminated in a mold or applied directly onto an armature.

To make a hollow fondu casting, first mix neat cement with water to form a creamy paste, usually referred to as 'goo'. Apply a layer of this with a brush to the wall of the wet mold, and then lay a mix in the proportion of one part cement to two parts sand over this, followed by a similar mix reinforced with glass fiber mat.

If the concrete is to be poured into a mold, then a coarse aggregate can be used in the mix. A good general mixture would be one part cement, two parts sand and four parts coarse aggregate, such as granite chippings. The size of coarse aggregate which can be used will depend on the volume of the sculpture, as the greater the volume, the larger the aggregate size that can be incorporated in the mix.

Below This piece by Martin Ives shows how concrete can be combined with other media. The ring of concrete, which is almost 6 feet (2 meters) tall, has pieces of straw in it. The center of the ring is filled with hazel twigs.

Modeling I. Mix up concrete to the consistency of a stiff paste and add shredded glass fiber matt for the first coat.

2. Model this onto the armature with your fingers. Use barrier cream to protect skin when handling concrete.

3. Allow the first layer to stiffen slightly and then model over the surface with a smooth paste of concrete only.

MODELING CONCRETE

Working concrete directly onto an armature requires a good understanding of the final shape wanted, as the armature must be designed to withstand the weight of concrete applied. To help keep the amount of concrete used to a minimum, it is best to construct the armature from welded mild steel bar or tube with expanded metal, which can be used to form the 'skin' of the shape being created. If the armature is well designed, the amount of concrete needed will be greatly reduced.

Having constructed the armature, it should be covered with a stiff concrete mixture reinforced with glass fiber matting to help bind the concrete into a homogeneous mass. Work should be continuous until the entire armature has been covered. If work has to stop for a few hours, the edges should be roughened and water applied before continuing. If more concrete is to be joined to some that has set, the surface which is to be worked on should be roughened to form a key and a proprietary sealant applied before the fresh concrete is added. The final surface should be applied while the first is still wet, in order to ensure that the two surfaces bond. If this is not possible, the same procedures for starting work again must be carried out.

Left *Composition* by Henry Moore was made of carved concrete in 1933. It is 23in (57.5cm) high. Moore used this unusual way of working with concrete to explore and integrate Surrealist influences into his work. The use of hollows and contrasting curved forms are characteristic of his work.

SOLID CASTING

[W]hen casting concrete from a plaster mold, the [m]old should be soaking wet or sealed to prevent [w]ater being absorbed from the concrete mix, as [th]is would adversely affect the final strength of [th]e concrete. If the mold is wet, a bloom will be [pi]cked up on the surface of the concrete. In both [ca]ses, the mold should be kept damp while the [co]ncrete cures. The concrete mix should be as [st]iff as possible, while still being workable. The [re]ason for keeping the concrete stiff when solid [ca]sting is that this prevents the larger aggregate [p]articles from settling to the bottom of the mold, [w]hich would create a mass that varied in density. [T]he concrete should be 'puddled'. This process [en]sures a good surface reproduction and elimi-[na]tes air bubbles. Puddling involves pushing a rod [u]p and down in the mix to compact it. Concrete [ca]n be added in several stages when this method [is] used. Care needs to be taken not to agitate the [ro]d too rapidly or the mold will get damaged and [ai]r bubbles will form. As the mold is filled, it [sh]ould be vibrated by being gently tapped by a [w]ooden mallet; this also ensures an even density [of] mix.

Apart from plaster molds, wooden formers or [sh]uttering can also be used in concrete work in [m]uch the same way as in plaster work. These [ne]ed to be sealed with grease or oil, and the [w]hole work should be covered with damp sacks [w]hile the cure is achieved.

[B]elow Wendy Taylor's Brick [Kn]ot (1978) uses brick and [co]ncrete to achieve an effect [of] lightness which belies the [m]edium she is working in. The [ab]stract geometric forms are [ty]pical of her established [st]yle.

Solid casting 1. Construct a mold or former for the cast. Coat all inner surfaces with a release agent.

2. Drop a layer of stiff wet concrete into the mold. Use a rod or batten to puddle it, but do not create air bubbles.

3. Bang the mold repeatedly on the bench top to settle the concrete and spread it evenly.

4. Bend an iron rod to fit the mold and place it into the concrete layer to provide reinforcement.

5. Drop in more concrete over the reinforcing rod and fill the mold right to the top.

6. Make sure the concrete is evenly distributed in the mold by tapping round the outside with a mallet.

7. Level off the top of the wet concrete by drawing a wood batten across the mold.

8. Cover the mold with damp sacking and leave it to cure.

Below Meeting Place by Spanish sculptor Eduardo Chillida was finished in 1973. This sculpture typifies the austerity of form that Chillida brings to his work. The wide sweep of the solid block forms are served well by the medium of concrete in.this striking piece which measures 8 feet (2.5 meters) by 14 feet (4.4 meters). This differs from his earlier work which was characterized by jagged or twisted ribbons of metal.

HOLLOW CASTING CIMENT FONDU

Generally, a plaster waste mold is used when making a hollow casting. This should be strong enough to absorb the compacting process and the soaking. If the plaster mold is dry, it should be sealed with two layers of shellac and a thin coating of oil. Any metal reinforcement that may be necessary to strengthen the concrete should be bent and cut to shape. Prepare a 1½ oz (42g) glass fiber mat by cutting it into manageable sizes and splitting it into two thinner layers in order to facilitate handling when laying up the mold.

A coat of neat cement or 'goo' is applied with a brush to the surface of the mold. The thickness of this coat will be about ⅛in (3mm). A second coat composed of one part cement to one part aggregate (silver sand), mixed to a slightly stiffer consistency, is applied immediately over the 'goo' to form a thickness of approximately ¼in (6mm). It should be pressed well into the mold in an even layer, using a spatula or fingers, and care should be taken to ensure all projections are fully covered, while, at the same time, ensuring it does not displace the 'goo'. If a piece mold is being

worked on, only one part at a time should b completed, the caps first. Into this second laye glass fiber is stippled using an old paintbrush ensure complete impregnation of the fibers. second layer of the sand and cement mix applied, and any steel reinforcement placed this layer. The steel should be completely covere with cement or it will corrode.

A second layer of glass fiber is added, and further layer of sand and cement mix used build up the final thickness. It can be stiffer tha the previous layers and used to ensure that ar possible weak spots are adequately strengthene The seams should be cleaned and the edges of th concrete slightly angled back to allow close co tact between the mold sections.

When all the mold pieces have been laid u they can be left to form an initial set. This take approximately three hours. However, the par should be joined as soon as practicable after th time. If they are left unjoined until they harden, sealant should be used on the seams before th parts are joined.

The caps of the mold are joined by applying layer of 'goo' around the seams and squeezir against the main mold section. Where possib

Below *Barriera* by Mauro Staccioli made in 1971 measures 2 feet 8in (80cm) on all sides. It is made of cement and iron. He uses his solid square and triangular forms with protruding spikes to make an impact on the environment and act as a contrast to the surroundings.

Hollow casting 1. Mix up a creamy paste of ciment fondu and water, and brush it into the mold to about ⅛in (3mm) thick.

2. Cut glass fiber matt into small pieces and separate each piece into two thin layers by pulling it apart.

3. Mix up a quantity of concrete, using equal parts o cement and silver sand. Use stiff mix.

4. Press the stiff cement into the mold, making a layer of about ¼in (6mm) thickness. Add extra weight in the corners.

5. Pat in a reinforcing layer of glass fiber matt soaked in the concrete. Cover the mold with damp sacks and leave it to cure.

6. Chip away the plaster mo and brush off the cast surfac The plaster leaves a soft bloom on the surface.

...e joint should be reinforced from the inside by ...minating a layer of glass fiber over the seams. ...i completion, the mold should be covered with ...mp sacks and allowed to cure.

FINISHING

...hen a concrete sculpture is released from its ...old, in particular a plaster mold, it has a bloom ...ich it picks up by dissolving minerals from the ...ster. This is often considered to be an attract-...e feature which is retained. If the work demands ...polish, then it can be treated with a shoe polish. ...the case of ciment fondu, a bronze patina can ...produced by brushing the surface of the ...lpture with ordinary black shoe polish, using a ...ede brush which has brass bristles. Finishes that ...itate other materials should be used with cau-...n as they may well work against the structural ...ality of the material, but this kind of decision ...ust be made using experience.

...Color can be incorporated either as an addition ...the original mix or rubbed into or painted on ...e sealed surface of the concrete. Materials for ...aling and coloring concrete are produced by ...ecialized firms and can be purchased at buil-...r's and plumber's merchants.

SAFETY

Dust Keep concrete dust to a minimum by ventilating the work area.
Skin irritation Concrete draws out the natural oils from the skin and can cause dermatitis. In order to avoid this, protect hands by wearing surgical gloves or by rubbing a barrier cream into your hands. When working with concrete, hands should be washed after each mix and before the concrete hardens, so that it does not harden on the skin.
Heavy weights If you observe the usual precautions for heavy weights, concrete will be a safe and relatively cheap material which is well-suited to the needs of the novice sculptor.

Barrier cream

Cleansing cream

Protective gloves

...rface finishes Cast ...ncrete picks up surface ...alities from the material ...ich forms the mold. The ...ee examples (from **left** to ...**ght**) show blocks cast against glass, wood and creased polythene. The block on the right has been treated with boot polish to give it a heavy black sheen.

PLASTICS

Right Naum Gabo created his work *Column* in 1923. It is about 4 feet (1.04 meters) high. It is made from a variety of media – perspex, glass, metal and wood. One of the founders of Constructivism in Russia, Gabo was one of the major innovators in sculpture in the twentieth century. During the 1920s, Gabo used transparent materials such as plastic extensively. This example shows how the materials have been combined to produce an apparently simple sculpture with clean lines.

Below Claes Oldenburg's *Giant Ice Bag* is an example of the artist's use of plastics to create images which are startling because of their scale and soft texture. Oldenburg's approach turns quite everyday objects into soft collapsing structures which can both amuse and fascinate.

HISTORY

Plastic is generally considered to be a mode[rn] material, although, surprisingly, the first pub[lic] announcement of its invention came in London [at] the International Exhibition of 1862. The m[a]terial concerned was the cellulose nitrate-bas[ed] substance 'Parkesine', developed by Alexan[der] Parkes and D Spill, two English metallurgis[ts]. Parkesine was primarily a substitute for existi[ng] materials, such as ivory, hard woods and t[or]toiseshell, which were already in short supply. [It] was never really exploited, and it was left to t[wo] Americans, John Hyatt and his brother, Isaiah, [to] patent a similar plastic, 'Celluloid' in 1869 and [to] begin commercial manufacture.

The next 70 years produced a chemical rev[o]lution. The phenol-formaldehyde-based 'Bak[e]lite', developed by Leo Hendrik Baekela[nd] (1863–1944), came in 1907; 'Polythene' was cr[e]ated in Britain in 1933; 'Plexiglas' acrylic she[et] was patented in America during the same ye[ar] while 'Perspex' appeared in Britain in 1936. T[he] same 70 years also saw important changes in t[he] arts. Plastic played a part in some of these. [In] Moscow in 1920 the Soviet brothers Anto[ine] Pevsner (1886–1962) and Naum Gabo (189[6–] 1977) published their *Realistic Manifesto* in whi[ch] they attacked the current principles of art a[nd] declared a new direction, which became known [as] Constructivism. They rejected solid, hea[vy] masses and volumes in sculpture, introduci[ng] light, airy forms constructed with transpare[nt] sheets, initially celluloid, which were intended [to] demonstrate static forces and kinetic rhyth[ms]

thin particular areas. Gabo in particular pur-
ed the use of plastic, developing complex non-
urative inter-penetrating acrylic constructions
ring the 1930s and 1940s while in England.
One of the founders of the Bauhaus, the
ungarian László Moholy-Nagy (1895–1946),
th the famous *Light and Space Modulator* series
ed acrylic sheet in combination with other
aterials and projected light. The light was
rtially absorbed, refracted and reflected to
nerate new fields of visual experience around
d within the basic structures.

The use of natural and artificial light provides
e clue to the main directions taken by plastic
ulpture in the last 20 years. Sculptors have
plored many of the avenues opened by the
rly pioneers in kinetics and light sculpture.
ectronics have given the sculptor the means to
ntrol the levels and hues of light in their
ructures. Industrial processes have added the
e of heat and pressure to generate new and
citing forms in the sculptor's vocabulary. Plastic
s recently found its way outside the confines of
e studio and the object. It is widely used by
tists working on temporary environmental or
stalllation ideas, becoming an integral part of
any performance events, such as the silver
flatables made by American Andy Warhol
orn 1930) which floated freely in the gallery
ace. The Bulgarian Jachareff Christo (born
35) has wrapped objects, buildings and even
hole sections of coastline in synthetic sheet. The
lymer chemist, from Parkes' early beginnings,
s now provided a range of colors and types of
astic to satisfy many of the sculptor's needs. This
edium still has great potential for the sculptor.

Right Claes Oldenburg's
Giant Soft Fan (1966–67) is
about 10 feet (over 3 meters)
tall and is made of vinyl filled
with foam rubber, wood,
metal and plastic tubing. The
gigantic size of the fan gives it
a surreal effect while the
softness and looseness of the
material supplies a humorous
comment on the 'value' of the
fan in society. In the same
period Oldenburg created
other gigantic versions of
household objects and
foodstuffs.

Tools for plastics

Different tools are required depending on whether rigid plastics or flexible plastics are being used. For expanded polystyrene, a selection of wire tools (**2**) are useful. It is important to heat the heads of the tools in a gas flame. The tools have wooden handles, which should, of course, not be placed too close to the flame. The various shapes of the tools determine the amount of polystyrene and the shape which can be created. For filing down the polystyrene, use surforms (**1**). These come in a variety of shapes and sizes. Before

cutting rigid plastics, make sure that all tools are very sharp. This will help ensure a neat, clean cut. A general purpose saw (**4**) is useful, as are craftknife (**9**) and metal file (**8**). In order to achieve a surface texture, use either an electric engraving tool (**3**) or a scribe (**6**). A drill (**7**) is necessary for making holes before pieces of plastic are joined, while a G clamp (**10**) is handy for keeping work steady. Safety is an important consideration when working with plastics. A face mask (**5**) should always be worn if dust is likely to occur. A small amount of cutting oil or

coolant will be useful to stop the tools overheating during use. Working with plastics tends to generate heat. You should be careful that it does not become excessive.

TYPES AND TECHNIQUES

There are two general families of plastics—rigid plastics, which include acrylics and polystyrene, and flexible plastics, such as the PVC (polyvinyl chloride) and polythene families. Plastics are extremely versatile materials and different techniques can be applied to them. They are mainly used in construction, but carving and turning are also possible. However, they are expensive, so it is important to plan the piece carefully. First make detailed drawings and designs, and decide the scale of the work. Also, think about the most appropriate fixing method for the work and whether plastic is the most suitable medium for it.

The best results are achieved with plastics which are worked in a clean and dust-free area. Make sure that bench tops and other working surfaces are free from nail heads, dried glue or other foreign matter likely to scratch the surface of the plastic. Work tops can be covered with soft cotton cloth or felt. Unfortunately, once marked, plastic will never fully regain its original quality. It is advisable, therefore, to leave any backing paper or protective coating in place until the last possible moment.

Plastics generate an electrostatic charge, particularly when being handled or machined. This attracts dust to the surface very quickly. When a piece is finished, it should be washed with warm water and a mild detergent. Then the surface should be dried with a soft cotton cloth or chamois leather, and finally an antistatic agent applied. These can be obtained at most record stores and come as liquids and, for large areas, as aerosols. Smaller areas can be treated with an antistatic pistol.

RIGID PLASTICS

Acrylics Acrylics are available in four different forms: as sheets, blocks, rods or tubes. They all come in transparent form, although sheet acrylics are also sold in opal and opaque, and rods of acrylic are sometimes sold in different colors. They come in a range of thicknesses and diameters. Sheet acrylics are sold in ⅛–¼in (3–6mm) thicknesses; blocks come in 1–5in (25–125mm) thicknesses and rods and tubes in diameters of ¹⁄₁₆–1in (1.5–25mm).

Acrylics, such as perspex or oroglas, are light, strong, homogeneous materials with no grain irregularities. They will pipe light internally even when the plastic has been bent or shaped, transmitting the light from the cut edge or rod end.

Acrylics are relatively easy to work. They can be sawn, drilled, routed, turned and milled in much the same way as non-ferrous metals. Standard hand and machine tools are suitable. All tools should be very sharp, and, if possible, tungsten carbide tipped. A blunt drill or saw quickly causes overheating and binds. Use a little cutting oil or coolant to help prevent this.

When drilling, always clamp work firmly to a wooden backing sheet to stop vibration which might cause the edges to chip. High speed twist drills are used, their cutting heads being ground to a zero or negative rake. Circular saws with thin, hollow ground blades of 8 to 14 teeth per inch (2.5cm) are best for cutting straight lines. Jigsaws and band saws are preferred for curves and more complex shapes. In general, high machine speeds and slow feeding are the rule for working with acrylics.

Acrylics can be joined with self-tapping screws, bolts or adhesives. Care should be taken to match the drill size to the screw or bolt size. Under or oversize holes can lead to stress and possible cracking. Soft leather or rubber washers will help ease the stress around the holes.

Solvents such as chloroform and ethylene dichloride can be used for simple joints. However, the best general adhesive is a two part cement which can be used for up to 20 minutes after mixing, and produces a strong and durable bond, which is resistant to water and weather. The adhesive can be applied by brush, glass rod or syringe. It may, however, attack acrylic surfaces, and care should be taken to avoid unwanted spillages which may be dangerous.

Acrylics are thermoplastics and so, if heated to 308°F (150°C), soften and become rubbery. They can be stretched and formed into three-dimensional shapes. On cooling, they become rigid again and retain their new shape. For large sheets, hot-air or infra-red ovens are used. On a smaller scale, domestic ovens can produce a successful result. Localized or edge bending is possible with hot-air blowers in combination with simple wooden formers. These blowers may have special attachments for heating rods and tubes. The use of vacuum and air pressure with heat is also suited to acrylics. Blow forming can produce particularly spectacular results.

Polystyrene The two main types of polystyrene are toughened and expanded. Both of these are available in sheet form, but expanded comes in blocks or granules as well. Toughened polystyrene comes in a number of colors, including black and white and in various thicknesses. Expanded polystyrene comes in a range of sizes. Toughened polystyrene sheet can be readily used for small box or plane forms. It is cut easily with a guillotine, scissors or a modeling knife and

Types of acrylic
Available in four different forms, acrylics also come in a wide range of translucencies and colors. The forms include cylinders (**1**), rods (**9**) and sheets (**6**,**7**). All of these forms can be purchased in a range of thicknesses or diameters: sheets range from 1/8–1/4in (3–6mm), blocks from 1–5in (25–127mm) and rods come in diameters of 1/16–9/10in (1.5–23mm). Colors available include turquoise (**2**), brown (**3**), orange (**4**), opaque white (**5**) and black (**8**). All these forms of acrylic can be sawn, drilled, turned and milled in a very similar method to that used for non-ferrous metals. The color is obtained by the addition of pigments or dyes which do not affect the workability of the material.

Blocks for holding the pattern for the sculpture

Wooden frame for clamping plastic over the top of the bed

Wooden bed in tray

Pipe leading to vacuum cleaner

Central hole for vacuum pump

Vacuum former One way of shaping plastics which is ideal for the beginner or inexperienced sculptor is using a vacuum former. It is particularly good for low relief work.
Only a small amount of vacuum and heat are needed to shape the plastic. The vacuum can be created using a pipe attached to a domestic vacuum cleaner.

Right This work is *Tower* by the British sculptor Anthony Benjamin. About 2 feet (60 cm) high, it is made from bronze and plexiglass. The work makes interesting use of different planes and areas of reflection. The work was created in 1966. During the 1960s, there was considerable interest in the potential of plastics as a sculptural medium, and this has continued until today.

can be scored and folded in a similar way to ca Standard polystyrene adhesives of the type u for model aircraft kits bond the sheet.

This is perhaps the most useful material for with a home-made vacuum former. Its soften point is 176°F (80°C), and only a small reduct in air pressure is needed to stretch the sheet. I the beginner, vacuum forming is best used a means to develop low relief work. Professio results can be obtained with this process.

With the vacuum former, patterns can be ma cheaply and easily using combinations of woo clay, modeling clay, card and metals. The m point to be aware of is that the draft of the patt is limited by the depth of the vacuum box, the should be no undercuts on the pattern. Sm holes should be drilled through the pattern wh ever air might be trapped between forms. Th will allow the air to vent freely, drawing plastic into the hollow. The deeper the draw thinner the sheet becomes. But excessive dr will rupture the sheet and the forming will ruined.

Expanded polystyrene has altogether differ uses and characteristics. It has a cellular struct and a low weight to volume ratio, making it id for large-scale work. Surface finishes, thou versatile, are generally visually unpleasant. Po styrene is, therefore, recommended mainly a

Cutting acrylic sheet 1. Draw around a paper template, marking the required shape on the backing paper of the acrylic.

2. Cut out the shape on a band saw, working fractionally wide of the mark. Use a metal cutting blade as acrylic is very tough.

Bending acrylic sheet
Clamp the acrylic under a t strip of metal on a wooden Hold the protruding end between asbestos and woo so only a narrow line is exposed along the width. Direct the hot air blower o this area (**1**). The metal stri helps to spread the heat. A the plastic heats, work it gently up and down and wh it is ready to bend put aside the blower and form the be evenly with both hands (**2**). varying the angle and direction of each bend you can form a complex shape As the edges may flare whe heated it may be advisable cut the original sheet over t required size and trim it wh bending is completed.

3. Grind down the edges to finish accurately on the mark, using a bench grinder. Saw cuts cannot give the necessary precision.

4. To make marks on the surface of acrylic sheet, peel away backing paper and draw with an electric engraving tool.

se material to which more interesting surfaces
ilt up. For example, plaster, resins and ad-
sive sand and sawdust mixes can be applied.
tting and carving can be done with single-
ged razor blades, hand saws, knife-bladed
ndsaws, rasps and surforms.

Heated carving tools for working with ex-
nded polystyrene can be made cheaply from
ck metal wire bent to the required shape and
unted in a wooden dowel handle. These are
en heated over a gas flame before cutting.
gular cleaning of the tool will prevent melted
stic deposits building up. Abrasive paper is
al. These tools are useful for cutting away
ernal volumes. Hot-wire cutters are another
ernative and are available in small battery
erated and larger tabletop models.

Joining polystyrene with adhesives can present
me problems. Solvent-based types can corrode
e material. If in doubt, try a test sample.
nerally, latex and PVA-based adhesives are
e safest and produce strong bonds.

Corrosion can be used to give textural effects to
rfaces. Liquids, such as cellulose thinners,
rbon tetrachloride and nail polish remover,
en sprayed will etch the surface of polystyrene.
ey can be difficult to control, but paper tem-
ates or stencils will protect those areas not to be
ated. Never use mouth sprays for these liquids.

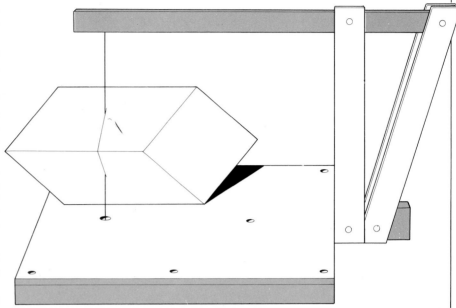

Table top hot-wire cutter
Although a hand-held wire
cutter will suffice for most
jobs, for large-scale work a
table top cutter may be more
appropriate. With a hot-wire
cutter, you can cut more
intricate shapes than with the
hand-held model. Electric
cutters work on the principle
that an electric current passes
through the wire, softening
and cutting the material. The
wire should be made of nickel
chrome.

rning acrylic rod Turn
sawn end of acrylic rod on
the to give it a clean edge.
the lathe to a negative
e, so it cannot dig into or
the acrylic.

Polishing acrylic sheet The
polishing wheel is made of
layers of canvas which hold
together in a tight mass when
in motion. Canvas abrades as
well as polishes the acrylic,
removing any scratch marks.
Set the wheel in motion and
apply polish from a block (1).
Peel away all backing sheet
from the acrylic and hold the
edge lightly against the wheel,
moving it gently up and down
(2). Stand slightly to one side
of the polisher and avoid
trapping corners of the acrylic
between the canvas layers of
the wheel.

**Joining acrylic sheets at a
right-angle 1.** Clamp the
sheet and cut two pieces,
using a sharp general purpose
saw.

2. Peel off part of the backing
and scribe a line very close to
the cut edge. Miter the edges
up to this mark with a file.

3. Butt the two mitered
pieces together, angled edges
down, on a flat surface. Put
clear adhesive tape along the
join and rub it down.

4. Turn the sheets over and
apply adhesive along the V-
shaped groove formed by the
two miters. Use a small
syringe or dropper.

5. Support the acrylic sheets
in a wooden jig to hold them
at a 90° angle while the joint
sets firm.

6. Avoid removing all backing
paper for as long as possible,
so most of the acrylic is
protected while you work.
The final result will be clean,
firmly jointed sections.

Vacuum forming 1. Make up a relief pattern for the work using wood and clay. The underside must be absolutely flat.

2. Drill small vent holes in the baseboard to ensure tight forming. The pattern must have no undercuts or right-angles.

3. Place the pattern into the bed of the vacuum former. It should rest below the top edge with ⅛in (3mm) free surround.

4. Lay a sheet of toughened polystyrene over the bed. Clamp it down firmly under a wooden frame with G-clamps.

5. Turn on the vacuum and heat the plastic with a hot air blower until the suction draws it down over the pattern.

6. Vacuum formed plastic can be colored in several ways. Here it is worked on with oil pastels and turpentine.

Cutting and joining expanded polystyrene 1. Mark the block with a felt tip pen. Cut along the mark with a hot-wire cutter.

2. Cut all the sections needed for the sculpture. In this example they are interlocking shapes and there is no wastage.

3. To shape a curve, cut off surplus material with a saw or hot wire and use a surform to round off the edges and corners.

4. On each section apply a latex based adhesive to the faces which are to be joined.

5. Locate the shapes and press the glued surfaces together. Insert a thin wooden peg to secure them while they are drying.

6. A wood glue mixed with acrylic pigment and sawdust is used here as finish. Two coasts are needed and it is sanded when dry.

FLEXIBLE PLASTICS

Polythenes and PVCs are both flexible plasti[c]. They can be bought as flexible sheets, althou[gh] polythenes come as tubes and bags as well. B[oth] are available in clear colors, while PVCs come [in] opaque colors also. PVCs and polythenes a[lso] come in a variety of sheet sizes and gauges.

Flexible plastics are mainly used by the sculp[tor] as 'containers'—to contain air with inflatabl[e] kapok or cotton waste for soft sculpture. D[ry] liquids, polystyrene granules, sand, soil and va[ri]ous aggregates have all been used to create fl[uid] and organic forms.

When marking out designs, use paper te[mplate] plates as a guide. Ballpoint pens or tailor's ch[alk] mark clearly. Cut with scissors or modeling kni[fe]. Take care the blade does not slip.

There are a number of ways of joining flexi[ble] plastics. Special adhesives are made for PV[C]. Non-solvent types are particularly recommend[ed] for inflatables. No permanent adhesive is av[ail]able for polythene.

PVC can also be sewn together on a standa[rd] sewing machine. Use strong thread and 10 to [12] stitches per inch (2.5cm), six to eight stitches p[er] inch (2.5cm) for polythene. A useful tip is [to] place tracing paper underneath the sheets be[fore]

Blow forming The blow forming table has a clamping ring in the middle surrounded by toggle clamps. A hole at the center of the ring admits the compressed air supply and is covered by a loose felt pad to prevent a direct blast of air onto the plastic. Acrylic sheet is cut in a circle slightly larger than the clamping ring. With the backing paper removed, it is heated in an oven and, when rubbery, it is taken from the oven and clamped down on the table under the clamping ring. This must be done very quickly before it cools. Asbestos gloves are used a[s] protection from the hot sh[eet.] Compressed air is released slowly into the ring and the sheet inflates into a dome shape, the height controlle[d] by the amount of air let in.

wn. This aids the movement of the sheets under e machine foot. If sewn seams are backed with ar adhesive tape, they produce seals which are rly airtight and satisfactory for most purposes.

Welding is the most permanent method of ining flexible plastics. A number of electrically ated hand irons are made for polythene weld- g; and there are also larger table models. Heat lding is very much a matter of trial and error, lding times vary according to the gauge of astic being handled.

Hot-air blowers with specially designed nozzles d a small type of pressure roller can be used to ld PVC. This method requires considerable actice, but gives excellent results when it has en mastered.

High-frequency welding techniques can also be ed with PVC. This is the most sophisticated ethod, but demands high capital outlay for the uipment. The welding electrodes are made of pper or brass, and can be bent into any flat ofile pattern, limited only by the size of the achine's welding bed. This is, therefore, not so itable for the beginner or inexperienced ulptor.

Plastics are a relatively recent sculptural medium. wever, they have great potential, as scientists vent new substances. One of the most interesting pects of work with plastics is the way some plastics, pecially the rigid variety, can interact with light.

SAFETY

Manufacturers of the different types of plastic supply detailed literature dealing with specific hazards of their products. Read these carefully before starting work. Safety notes with solvents and adhesives must also be observed. There are five general areas of safety:

Fire All the plastics described here are inflammable. The temperature at which they ignite and the ferocity with which they burn vary, but all release toxic fumes as they decompose. Never leave material on or near paraffin stoves, central heating boilers, gas rings or open fires of any kind. Try and store plastic away from living areas. Outside in a garden shed is ideal. Always keep a fire extinguisher or at least a sand bucket in the studio.

Toxic fumes In addition to fire, many plastics release toxic fumes when overheated during machining. Use a coolant to help avoid this. Harmful styrene fumes are released in small quantities when cutting polystyrene with heated tools. It is essential to

ventilate your work area adequately. Extractor fans can be fitted to your studio windows at reasonable cost. Solvents and adhesives can also produce potentially dangerous fumes. Chloroform is an obvious case. Fumes can cause nausea, irritability, drowsiness and, in extreme cases, coma. Fume masks help reduce these risks.

Dust Acrylic machining is the main dust producer. Liquid coolant helps absorb dust in certain processes, but, with grinding, filing or hand-sawing, this is not practical.

Dangerous solvent

Safety mask

ining PVC 1. Seam two eces on a sewing machine ng strong thread and edle. Run tissue through der the PVC.

2. To make a seam suitable for use in inflatable sculptures, flatten down the seam with a wallpaper seam roller.

3. Lay adhesive tape down the seam covering both edges of the PVC. If curves are required in the seam make darts before taping.

4. Turn over the PVC and smooth it out along the seam line. This is strong and airtight.

n and fell seam 1. This is PVC sculptures which will ld water. Apply adhesive ng the edges of each piece.

2. Align the pieces together and rub down the seam with the roller to seal it quite flat.

3. Apply glue to one side of the seam and turn it down to form a double thickness. Flatten it down again with the roller.

4. Unfold the PVC and smooth out the seam. The strength of the adhesive and doubling of the seam make it watertight.

Hot air blower The hot air blower is used to form plastics using a mixture of heat and air. The tool is electric powered and comes with a variety of possible attachments. It is extremely useful when working with plastics.

CONSTRUCTED METAL

Above This Chalcidian helmet was made in Greece between 559 BC and 500 BC. It is 2 feet 5in (72cm) high and is made of bronze with a silver and ivory inlay.

Above right This ornate jar made in Egypt dates from the eighteenth century BC. Silver and gold used in its manufacture both show the decorative animal forms, either worked into or onto an object. This represents an early attempt to build up a construction of separate forms to make one whole.

HISTORY

Metal as a medium in which to construct rath than cast sculpture only developed in the twe tieth century. It is, in many ways, a product industrialization and the processes developed industry. The first important all-metal co structed sculptures were made by the Spani artist Pablo Picasso (1881–1973) just after 190 These were influenced by metal masks made his compatriot, Pablo Gargallo (1881–1934 Picasso's *Guitar* of 1912, which was made fro sheet metal and wire, constituted a major bre with the tradition of cast sculpture. Picasso inventiveness imbued the medium with a fres ness and vitality which is still evident today some 70 years later. The mood of change arou the turn of the century and heavy industrializatic all brought about the kind of atmosphere in whic traditional sculptural values no longer seeme adequate. Sculpture, especially through this ne medium of constructed metal, began to reflect th vigor of the industrial age.

In Russia, where revolution was transformir the thoughts of the people and the make-up of th country, the Contructivist sculptors were trying create a movement in line with the cult of th engineer. Vladimir Tatlin (1885–1953) had me Picasso and seen his small relief sculptures. Mixe with Tatlin's own ideas, this new use of materi led to the Constructivists producing the fir abstract sculpture, free of any representation. 1919 Kasimir Medunetsky constructed his *A stract Sculpture, Construction No 557* from ti brass and iron. This piece shows complete a straction, but also reveals a certain awkwardnes

Far left *Construction: Metal Violin* is an example of Picasso's early work in metal. It was created in 1915. The metal was painted in several colors. Some of the surfaces of the work were painted in plain colors, while others were given a pattern. In its many different surfaces and textures, this work shows the influence of Cubist ideas about form and space.

Left This is one of the early abstract heads of Naum Gabo, the Russian Constructivist which was made following Cubist ideas. The iron planes used in this sculpture are surprisingly evocative and give a certain strength and presence to the whole sculpture. The edges of the plane delineate the form and there is no barrier between internal and external space. Gabo—who is standing by the work—saw Constructivisim as a 'general view of the world, an ideology that is grounded in life'.

if it was an engineer's model rather than a ɪlpture.

ɪn 1930 Picasso made *Construction in Wire*, a ally open space frame, which, although figura- e in content, was a radical change from the itude that sculpture was only about mass and ɪd form. This elevation of materials, which ɪviously would only have been considered for ɪquettes or models, to the stature of sculpture ɪved the way for the adventurous use of metal in ɪnstructional sculpture. Picasso began to sup- ɪment his materials by selecting metal scrap ɪich could aptly convey his ideas. About this ɪe, Picasso was joined in Paris by fellow ɪaniard, Julio Gonzalez (1876–1942). Gonzalez ɪne from a background of silversmithing, and ɪroduced Picasso to forging and welding tech- ques. Hammered surfaces and spikes gave Gon- ɪez's sculpture an aggressive feel, which can be ɪn in the *Cactus* figure pieces (1939–1940). He ɪalt with shapes based on masks and armor ɪd, although aggressive, they are very lyrical.

Toward the middle of this century, many sculp- ɪs felt that it was important to convey in their ɪrk their attitude to man's position in society, ɪl feelings of alienation and anxiety. This was a ɪad phenomenon involving many media, but ɪtal sculpture became one of the most appropri- ɪ. Such was the case with Theodore Roszak ɪorn 1907) who created bird-like forms in ɪlded steel. His *Night Flight*, created between ɪ8 and 1962, conveys a feeling of impending ɪl.

ɪhe general mood manifested itself in an inter- ɪ in mythology. In Britain, the Scottish-Italian ɪlptor Eduardo Paolozzi (born 1924) welded ɪeformed aluminum and bronze industrial

shapes into god-like pseudo machines as in the 1962 work *Hermaphroditic Idol No 1*. The French sculptor Cesar Baldaccini (born 1921) used metal found objects to construct welded winged figures with elaborate surfaces. In some instances, the found objects provided a direct reference back to the industrial society that the sculptor was parodying, as was also the case with the large motor-like sculptures by the American Jason Seley (born 1919) which were made entirely from chrome-plated automobile bumpers.

More significant in the development of sculp- ture generally was the American artist David Smith (1906–1965). His early forged steel sculp- tures, such as the 1951 *Hudson River Landscape*, were open and calligraphic in form. His wit and inventiveness were prodigious, as even left-over cut-outs were transformed into sculpture. By the early 1960s, his work had become more abstract, simple, and contemplative, as can be seen in the box structures welded together into the columns or arch formations of the *Cubi* series. The process of welding is central to the make-up, visual balance and sense of form in these last pieces by Smith. Another central figure in constructed metal sculpture is the Englishman Anthony Caro (born 1924) whose use of industrial metal beams and simple treatment of steel has done much to further abstract sculpture. In Caro's *Early One Morning*, for example, the simple steel units actually describe their own environment into which the spectator can physically enter.

The development of constructed metal sculp- ture has been one of liberation, ·thanks to its flexibility and durability. This, coupled with its direct links to the rise of industrial society, has made it a part of sculptural advancement.

MATERIALS

Not all of the wide variety of metals available [to] the sculptor are practical for general use, for [a] number of reasons. To the student, with limit[ed] workshop facilities and little money, cost a[nd] ease of working are especially relevant. T[he] expensive metals—gold, silver and tin—are n[ot] really suitable for sculpture, except on a sm[all] scale, and will more often be used by a silversm[ith] or jeweler. The metal generally called tinplate [is,] in fact, thin, mild steel coated with a thin layer [of] tin for protection against rust. Aluminu[m,] bronze, and brass are available in various for[ms] and can be fixed mechanically. However, th[ey] present some problems in welding, as they ne[ed] specialized equipment.

Copper is very malleable, and therefore is id[eal] for beating into shape or riveting, and it is eas[ily] soldered. However, bronze, brass and copper a[re] too expensive to experiment with on a large sca[le,] and none of these materials can compare with t[he] versatility of mild steel for construction purpos[es.] Mild steel can be soldered, brazed and weld[ed] quite simply, if it is thin enough. This is only o[ne] of the alloys of iron. Another alloy, stainl[ess] steel, has been used by many sculptors. Howev[er]

Tools for metal sculpture

A certain number of specialized tools are required when working in metal. Pictured here are a large claw hammer (**1**), a small ball hammer (**2**), a punch (**3**), a pop riveter (**4**), an electric drill (**5**) and tinsnips (**6**). A choice of chisels and wrenches are often used, and an engineer's vice is an essential piece of equipment. Most of the work involved in metal

construction falls into two categories—cutting and bending or shaping. For cutting, power or hand tools or heat is used. Heat cutting requires oxyacetylene equipment. Harder metals also have to be heated before bending and shaping. Thinner metals do not require such treatment and can be shaped with hammers like those pictured (**above**). When working with metals safety precautions should be strictly observed,

especially when metal is being cut. Protective clothing, including gloves and a dust mask, is essential. Steel-capped shoes should be worn for protection in case any metal is dropped. Oxyacetylene equipment is highly specialized and should only be used under strict supervision. Pipe benders should also be used with great care and supervision.

Types of metal

Although not all of the forms of metal available to the sculptor are suitable for the amateur who must pay attention to cost and ease of working, it is important to be aware of the qualities and the availability of metals before choosing a medium. Aluminum can be obtained as a cylindrical bar (**3,1**) or a hexagonal bar (**2,6**). Copper (**4**) and brass (**5**), here in sheet form, are two of the most popular metals. Steel

generally comes in the sam[e] form as aluminum—cylindr[ical] (**7**) or hexagonal bars (**8**)— it is also available in sheets.

Tin offcuts As well as flat metal sheets hammered ou[t] from the walls of the cans, [thin] strips of metal are obtained by trimming off seams and rims. You may also find a u[se] for the round sections of th[e] top and bottom of the can. This is a cheap and easy wa[y] to find a source of metal (**right**).

is metal is rather impractical for the beginner.
There are four basic sources of metal. It can be
ught new in all forms from commercial stock-
lders, builder's merchants, and much interest-
g metal can be found in industrial scrap or
scued from household waste. Both the Swiss
ulptor Jean Tinguely (born 1925) and the
enchman César (born 1921) extensively used
d industrial components from scrap yards, and
e American John Chamberlain (born 1927)
ed crushed cars which came straight from the
eaker's yard.

An almost overwhelming variety of material
n be found in this way and this method is, of
urse, much cheaper than obtaining new ma-
rial. Any form of metal of usable size —
ether sheet, plate, bar, tubing, mesh or I-
am—is costed by its weight of metal. In addi-
on, very small scrap will often be sold for a
minal sum to artists. Scrap metal offers a large
mber of interesting shapes which lend them-
lves readily to construction methods. In the
me, the sort of materials available will be on a
ch smaller scale, but nevertheless very useful
ings are often found. Tin cans, for instance, can
opened up with metal cutters or tinsnips to
ovide a good source of thin steel suitable for
ldering or riveting.

Left Julio Gonzalez's *Tunnel Head* (1933–1935) is a construction in sheet steel. With an economy of line, using curved, bent and flat surfaces, he creates total darkness within a continuous surface by the almost complete sealing-off of the void in *Tunnel Head*. He achieves a striking effect through the use of strong bold lines.

Below The French sculptor César is renowned for his work with found objects, particularly cars which he crushes with a hydraulic press. He calls his works *Compressions dirigées* (*Directed Compressions*). He is interested in the surface textures created.

Cutting and flattening a tin can 1. Remove the top and bottom of the can, and cut down one side of the seam with tinsnips.

2. Using gloves to protect your hands, grasp each edge of the metal and pull out the can to flatten it.

3. Place the metal down on the work bench and hammer it out along the edges to ease the buckling.

Cutting metal on a guillotine 1. Place the metal flat on the bed of the machine, positioned under the blade. Press down the foot pedal.

2. The foot pedal activates a toothed grip which holds the metal in place and then draws down the blade.

Safety The importance of safety cannot be overstated when dealing with metal cutting machinery. It is vital for you to pay attention to all safety procedures. Always have the machine's safety guard in position, as the manufacturer suggests. Also it is important to wear gloves, so that your hands and fingers are not cut by the sharp edges of the metal or the blade.

Bending metal 1. Place a wood block at the edge of your work bench, and position the metal sheet to overlap the wood.

2. Align a second block with the first to hold the metal in place, and clamp them firmly to the worktop.

3. Hammer along the overlap of metal to flatten it down against the lower block, making a clean sharp bend.

MARKING OUT

Before undertaking any sculpture in metal it important that all the processes—such as shapin fixing, and drilling—should be well planned a marked out, especially if the sculpture is going be an awkward shape, which may make drilling cutting difficult. Ordinary blackboard chalk w prove a useful item of equipment for marking on steel prior to cutting. The chalk line w remain easily visible when using oxyacetyle cutting gear. Where precision is required, engineer's scribe should be used. To make t more visible, a marker usually called 'enginee blue' is painted onto the metal and the li scribed through it.

Where a completed sculpture is very heavy a therefore needs to be split into sections for ease transport and reassembly, cutting lines should envisaged during construction. Where two pie have to be bolted and holes drilled, accuracy essential, and it is useful to mark the center of t hole with a punch. If a large hole is required, i best to drill a pilot hole of a smaller size first.

CUTTING

Cutting is an important operation which al needs careful planning and thought. It is impo tant to consider the physical properties of t material which determine how it can be cut. addition, the type of cut may influence the imp of the sculpture and the effect it achieves.

There are three main means of cutting—usi hand tools, power tools, and heat. The hand to are the cold chisel, hacksaw, tinsnips and manu ly operated guillotine. The most commonly us power tools are the power guillotine, bands and mechanical hacksaw. Heat cutting requi oxyacetylene gear. This should not be attempt by a beginner, as it requires both special equipment and strict supervision.

Hand tools can only be used effectively on t metals and short runs. The hacksaw is useful cutting tubes, bars, and rods, as long as th diameters are not greater than the depth of t saw. However, it is not so practical for she metal as the saw's frame prevents it from going deep enough. A sheet saw may be used to sheet metal by hand. The manual guillotine c only be used with thin sheet metal, unless it geared. It will only make straight cuts, althou external curves can be achieved by snipping small bits at a time. Both guillotine and tinsn will affect the shape of sheet metal. If this is r desirable, the sheet must either be flattened af cutting or a different method employed.

The mechanical hacksaw and bandsaw are or

seful for taking the hard work out of cutting. The power guillotine, on the other hand, is a very seful piece of equipment, as it can chop through ick section steel.

However, the most versatile method for cutting etal is oxyacetylene equipment. This uses a rced flame of oxygen and acetylene, which eats the metal to melting point. Then an extra ast of oxygen oxidizes the metal, forming a ole. The advantage of this method to the sculpr is obvious, because, using different cutting ps, it can cut anything from the thinnest sheet to ery thick plate. With practice, a smooth and ven cut can be achieved. Unlike the other ethods of cutting, it can cut from the center of a eet of metal without the cut having to be started the outer edge. However, the equipment is ecialized and should only be used under strict pervision. It is also vital to follow all safety gulations or advice when using this equipment.

BENDING AND SHAPING

here are various ways of bending and shaping etal, ranging from the simple process of hamering to the precise process of box bending, all which produce different results. Non-ferrous etals should be annealed before shaping. With pper, copper alloys and silver, this means eating the metal to a dull red and quenching it in ater. Aluminum is annealed to a much lower mperature. It can then be hammered out, using ft mallets and concave wooden formers or ndbags. Very thin mild steel sheet can be aped without heat, using steel hammers which ill produce a more rugged surface than that of a ooden mallet.

Thicker steel sheet and plate needs to be rged. This means heating the metal to red heat nd hammering while it is still hot. This involves sing a forge, which is an open coke fire raised to high temperature by a forced jet of air. The etal is held in tongs and beaten out on a stout nvil. Julio Gonzalez used this technique to roduce vigorous sculptures. However, this is not practical technique for the beginner.

A rolling mill can be used to produce smooth irves in one direction only on thin sheet metal. ne of the rollers has a series of grooves running round it which enables rods and bars to be irved evenly.

The effect of expansion due to heat may be sed to bend thicker plate in one direction. A ntrolled line of heat applied on one side of a ate by an oxyacetylene flashlight will cause the etal to expand, thus curving the plate the other ay.

Angled folds in thin sheet metal can be made a box bender. If more than one fold is wanted,

these must be carefully planned to allow easy removal from the machine.

In his sculpture *Open Bound*, the British sculptor Phillip King (born 1934) used a box bender to produce square boxes of steel to reinforce the honeycomb structure of the piece visually. The box forms are used in combination with expanded steel mesh.

Another useful piece of equipment is the pipe bender for bending tubes and bars. The most common type has a long lever which is pivoted about a grooved wheel. The tube or bar is held in the concave part of the wheel and is bent around it by a corresponding grooved block set in the lever. To prevent the tube collapsing during the process, a spring can be inserted into the tube, but this is not necessary if it is bent in gradual stages. A hydraulic bender will do the same job with less effort and is a smaller piece of equipment. Much of this equipment is specialized and expensive. Great care should be taken when using it and expert supervision is essential.

Metal bending machine
This produces a clean, angled bend along the edge of thin metal sheet. The metal is pushed into the jaws of the machine with the edge overlapping the machine bed (**1**). The top section of the machine is clamped down on the metal and the bottom section drawn up over it (**2**). The two parts lock tightly together and trap the metal to form the bend (**3**).

Joining metal 1. Interlock the trimmed and bent edges of two flat sheets of metal. The edges must be absolutely straight.

2. Hold the pieces in place and hammer down the seam. Work from each end toward the center. Make the seam line quite flat.

3. Mark out holes for rivets at each end of the seam. Place a punch on the metal, hold it vertical, and tap it with a hammer.

4. Place the metal sheets on a wood block and drill through the punched marks to make rivet holes.

5. Fit an aluminum rivet into a pop riveter and secure the seams.

6. Continue to work in the same way, joining the sheets to make the shape required.

7. To join two ends of a flat sheet to form a cylinder, find a support which will fit inside the curve, on which the seam can be drilled and hammered.

Right *Metal Column* is a constructed metal piece by the British sculptor Andrew Fyvie. It stands several feet high and is entirely constructed from jumbo size tin cans by the processes described in the step-by-step sequences. The form derives from the artist's interest in the simple, powerful solidity of tree trunks. The spirals of the tin sheets suggest organic growth. The sculpture is hollow and, in fact, relatively fragile, but at the same time evokes the strength of a heavy, old tree.

In metal sculpture, the fixing or joining processes are more important even than cutting processes in determining the approach to the work. Therefore, it is important to consider, for example, whether the joins should be concealed or should form an integral part of the sculpture. For example, when arc or oxyacetylene welding is used, the weld line can be left as an obvious join between two areas, or it can be ground down to produce one continuous surface. Oxyacetylene welding utilizes a forced flame of oxygen and acetylene which brings the metal up to red heat. For joining, a filler rod of the same material is placed in front of the flame to help fuse the metal. Although a weld can be achieved without the filler rod, it helps to fill any slight gap between the pieces of metal and prevents any tendency for the metals to run away from each other when the right heat is reached.

An arc weld is made by producing a powerful localized electric current through the pieces to be welded. A negative cable is clamped to the work and a circuit is made by the positive electrode (the filler rod) being introduced to the point of the weld. As in oxyacetylene welding, the filler rod is made of the same metal as those being joined. This means that only identical metals may be joined by these methods.

Different metals can, however, be joined by brazing. This is similar to welding, but uses a lower heat and a copper-zinc brazing rod. The metals must be cleaned and fluxed to obtain a good join. Fluxing is a method of ridding metal of

Blueing metal The surface of the metal is heated continuously with a blowlamp until it changes color. If using tin cans to provide the metal this process will also clean off any dirt or scraps of labels.

purities using chemicals which coagulate any pure substances. With practice, both welding and brazing can be used to fix metals of different thicknesses and sizes. This can greatly add to the quality of a sculpture.

For reasons of convenience, it may be necessary to make a piece of sculpture that is easily dismantled. In this case, bolting would be preferable to welding as a means of joining. Used thoughtfully, bolts may also add to the effect of the finished work.

Bolting and riveting are also suitable for joining thin materials, as they eliminate the distortions caused by joining methods which use heat. The only extra piece of equipment needed is a drill to make the holes for the rivets or bolts. For very thin metals or wire construction, soldering may be necessary. This relatively simple method requires only a heating element and solder. The join does not have great strength but is adequate for small work.

Left *Orion* is an example of the metal sculpture of the French artist Hajdu. Completed in 1968, the work was constructed from polished aluminum. Much of Hajdu's sculpture features pierced forms with jagged edges. As well as using aluminum, he also works frequently in marble, copper and lead.

FINISHING

The surface of metal sculpture may be painted or treated in various ways to change its appearance and make it suitable for an outdoor site. Paint will prevent steel from rusting, but it is also generally used to unify an image by covering a sculpture with a single color.

Parts may be emphasized by introducing more dominant colors, or made to recede by painting in a way which contradicts the original contours. One possible disadvantage of painting steel sculpture is that the raw quality of the steel may be lost. In some cases, it is preferable to paint the bare metal with clear varnish. To overcome the problem of the outside durability of metal sculpture, some sculptors have used stainless steel, which has a distinct individual character. For instance, David Smith has used stainless steel which he polished or burnished with a grinder, giving the pieces a dazzling, reflective surface.

It is possible to achieve an overall dense surface on mild steel by allowing a coating of rust to develop. This process can be accelerated by wetting the metal with a weak acid. Any surplus flaking rust built up must be brushed off and then varnish may be applied. This will tone down the rust color and keep it stable for some time. To prevent any rusting at all there are several proprietary brands of rust inhibitor and converter. Once applied, these can be covered with paint or varnish.

Weather proofing only has to be taken into account when sculptures are going to be placed outside. For smaller indoor pieces, more liberties may be taken.

SAFETY

Hazards abound in any area where sculpture is being made, and this is especially so with metal sculpture. Therefore all possible precautions should be taken to lessen the risks.

Clothing Generally, stout clothes are advisable, but, where specialist operations are carried out, protective clothing is essential. Goggles should be worn to guard against sparks or chips of metal entering the eyes; earmuffs will deaden excessive noise; and hard hats will protect the head from falling objects. Leather aprons, caps, gauntlets and thick trousers will prevent the danger of burns when cutting, welding or grinding, as sprays of molten metal are created when cutting with oxyacetylene flashlights.

Footwear It is important to wear appropriate footwear. When handling heavy objects that are likely to fall, it is vitally important that the toes are protected with heavy shoes, preferably with metal toecaps.

Eyes and skin Apart from these obvious dangers, extreme care is needed when arc welding, as the light produced by the arc will seriously damage the retina of the eye. Overexposure can cause skin cancer, so the proper face guard must always be in place before applying the electrode, and work must be screened from other people.

Ventilation There should be good ventilation at all times, as a build up of the fumes produced by the arc are toxic.

Electricity Arc welding will not result in electric shocks as long as neither the work nor your hands are wet.

Gas When welding with gas, common sense should ensure that nothing goes wrong. The cylinders must be placed away from the work and from any source of heat, and the hoses kept tidy and off the ground.

Safety instructions These are only general safety precautions. All pieces of equipment have particular rules for usage with which the user must be familiar and which should be adhered to.

Safety goggles

Safety gloves

Safety spectacles

KINETICS

HISTORY AND BACKGROUND

The representation of movement in sculpture and painting has always been a definite aim of many sculptors, but it has made itself felt in static form. The background to the beginnings of kinetic or moving sculpture also has other roots including the interests of scientist engineers as well as artists. From the early experiments in clockwork mechanisms in the sixteenth century to the complex mechanical toys of the eighteenth century, there has been a desire to create the novelty of independently moving objects.

The situation where movement could become an art form was helped when sculpture was freed from traditional restraints by artists such as Marcel Duchamp (1887–1968). While working on changing people's ideas as to what constituted a work of art, Duchamp created his *Bicycle Wheel* (1913), which was the first mobile 'art' piece. As the name suggests, this was just an upturned bicycle wheel which was mounted upon a wooden stool. Although the reason for producing the piece was not that of making moving sculpture, the wheel would have moved if anyone pushed it.

Since Duchamp, movement has been used in sculpture in widely diverse ways. It has been used to multiply the compositional variations of a piece, to comment on the mechanical nature of society, and to introduce an element of time in a work. Ideas ranging from simple to very complex have been employed by kinetic sculptors. The Russian Constructivist sculptor Naum Gabo (1890–1977) made his *Kinetic Construction, Standing Wave* in 1920. Powered by an electric motor, it is a single oscillating metal rod, which is transformed into a seemingly solid volume when in motion. In contrast to the simplicity of Gabo's construction, *Light Space Modulator* by László Moholy-Nagy (1895–1946), which was conceived in 1922 and made in 1930, consisted of an arrangement of polished metal plates and screws rotating in a synchronized motion, powered by the same motor. Designed to stand alone on a theater stage during the interval of a show, the surfaces of the sculpture reflected 116 different colored light bulbs onto surrounding walls. In addition to the elements of movement and light, Moholy-Nagy envisaged a suite of music to accompany the action, but this was never brought to fruition. This type of complex visual display was taken to an extreme later by the Hungarian-French artist Nicolas Schöffer (born 1912). He built large towers of moving and reflecting surfaces and flashing lights. His work was financed by commercial sponsorship.

In the work of both Moholy-Nagy and Schöf-fer, the motor was a means to an end; its so[le] function being to drive the moving parts of t[he] sculpture. It therefore remained hidden fro[m] view. As a contrast, the Swiss sculptor Je[an] Tinguely (born 1925) based his major work on t[he] motor-machine itself. His earlier pieces we[re] mobile shapes, powered by hidden motors, b[ut] in the work for which he is best known, t[he] emphasis is on the often useless and waywa[rd] nature of mechanical hardware. In the *Metama[tic]* series, produced in the late 1950s, petrol moto[rs] mounted upon freely moving, wheeled tripo[d] drive mechanisms which produce continual a[b]stract drawings on rolls of paper. In the larg[e] sculptures such as *Hannibal No 1*, the mechanis[m] becomes the sculpture, creating aimless motio[n] with rusting wheels and cams which gradual[ly] wear themselves out. Most bizarre of all was t[he] *Study No 2* for an *End of the World* (created [in] 1962), which, after being set up in a desert [in] America, was exploded in a ritual-like 'ha[p]pening'.

As with Gabo's kinetic construction, some [of] the most evocative images have come from t[he] use of natural forces or simple mechanical mov[e]ment. The American sculptor Alexander Cald[er] (1898–1976), best known for his invention of t[he] term 'mobile', first used motors to power h[is] moving sculptures, but soon relied solely on a[ir] currents to set them in motion. The mobiles u[se] simple counter-balanced weights, usually roun[d]ed flat metal shapes suspended from elegant[ly] poised rods with very simple wire joints. Anoth[er] American, George Rickey (born 1907), mak[es] groups of slender needles balanced near the[ir] thicker ends. In some of the smaller versions, t[he] needles lie horizontally at rest, while in the larg[e] ones they are in equilibrium vertically. In t[he] large examples, Rickey developed elegant pivo[t]ing arms radiating from central columns upo[n] which the needles rest in a cluster. In a stron[g] wind the needles fan out to produce endle[ss] variations of composition.

In the 1960s and 1970s sophisticated electron[ic] sensing devices were developed prompting t[he] emergence of increasingly clever 'toys' which g[o] beyond the realms of sculpture, in some case[s] going back to the eighteenth century concept [of] mechanical novelties. Two artists, howeve[r] whose sculptures are interesting because of the[ir] straightforward simplicity, are the Greek sculpt[or] Takis (born 1925) and the French painter an[d] sculptor Pol Bury (born 1922). Takis used ele[c]tromagnetism to motivate slender antenna[e] tipped with discs of metal, which quiver when a[n] overhead electromagnet is turned on and off. T[he] significance of these very minimal pieces lies [in] the magical quality of the movement created b[y] the invisible force of magnetism. Bury's work

Far left *Bicycle Wheel* by the French artist Marcel Duchamp was one of the first kinetic sculptures. It consisted of a wooden mount on which was placed a bicycle wheel. Duchamp was one of the first major sculptors to become interested in kinetic works.
Below The *Light Space Modulator* was a simple construction, which was extremely influential in kinetic sculpture. This picture shows a reconstruction made in 1970. The *Light Space Modulator* used a motor to power several metal plates and screws which rotated in a synchronized motion.
Left A work by Naum Gabo is his kinetic sculpture *Standing Wave*. The work dates from 1920. It shows how effective a simple image can be. The movement of the metal rod, caused by the electric motor, creates an impression of constant movement. One of the main features of kinetic work has been a willingness by the artists to experiment with widely different forms and materials.

very different as the movement of the sculpture is so minimal that in fact it looks virtually motionless. Wooden cubes and balls in a rack twist and shift almost imperceptibly, and matted strands of nylon mounted through boards switch around in minute amounts which seem to imply stretching and growing rather than movement in space. Even though kinetic sculpture has become increasingly sophisticated, simple interpretations have often been the most successful in capturing the essential quality of movement.

Below This ceramic work by the Spanish artist Joan Miro is an example of the use of water in sculpture. The green ceramic gargoyle, made in 1968, epitomizes Miro's zany approach to his art.

TECHNIQUES

Kinetic sculpture can be achieved by two bas[ic] means of propulsion—mechanical power, such a[s] electricity or internal combustion, and natur[al] forces, which include falling water, wind, ga[s], heat, magnetism, and solar energy. The natur[al] sources of power are often used when ecologic[al] factors are considered and a definite decision [is] taken against the use of motors. Among th[e] sculptors who do use motors there is also [a] division between those working with technolog[y] and those commenting on it. For exampl[e] Nicolas Schöffer's towers make conscious use [of] technology, whereas Tinguely's sculptures make [a] comment about machine technology from th[e] outside. His attitude to the machine is slight[ly] anarchic and disrespectful; by making h[is] machines 'un-machine like' he draws attention [to] the relative importance of machines and the[ir] place in life today.

Circumstances ultimately determine whic[h] power source can actually be used. Where [no]

Below This kinetic sculpture entitled *Fountain* is by Pol Bury, one of France's leading kinetic sculptors. The work measures about 12 feet (4 meters) across and is made of stainless steel. It is in a lake near a French art gallery. The work revolves very slowly, different parts of it dipping into the water. Slowness of movement is one characteristic of Bury's work.

Right *Le Cyclograveur* is an example of the work of Jean Tinguely, the Swiss sculptor. His works often feature jagged pieces of mechanized metal. In this work, which dates from 1960, a needle draws arbitrary lines on a screen.

Left *Antennae with Red and Blue Dots* (1960) by the American artist Alexander Calder illustrates one of the main types of kinetic sculpture, the mobile. Mobiles can either rely on wind to rotate them or can be powered by motors. This example does not have a motor and is made from sheet aluminum and steel wire.

s sculpture (**center**)
onstrates quite a complex
tern of movement, but is
de using readily available
erials, simple construction
niques and a single natural
rce of power – the wind.
e base of the sculpture
sists of two flat wood
tions set at right-angles to
h other. The long tail fin
hors the sculpture. The
es (**1**) are constructed by
tching plastic over a thin
od frame, cut with a jigsaw.
y are fixed to the spindle
lengths of metal rod. These
attached to the vanes with
e bound through small
led holes in the top of the
od frames. A wire is also
between the spindle and
bottom of the vane to
p it at a fixed angle.

e yellow and black paddles
mounted on stakes driven
o the ground (**11**). A piece
mild steel rod through a
led hole in the shaft allows
e movement around a
d point.

The plastic vanes are mounted on the central spindle. They activate the movement in the construction as they catch the wind and rotate (**2**, **3**). Attached to the central spindle is a circular section of wood (**4**, **5**), which transmits the movement to other sections of the sculpture. The shaped edge of the wooden wheel knocks against a metal spring, pushing the red panel back and forth between the two green flaps (**6**).

To balance the paddles, they are tied loosely with strings to wire hooks driven into the ground (**8**). Small curved pieces of wood are mounted on the flat surface of the wheel. Yellow and black paddles balanced on this move up and down over the wood as the wheel rotates (**9**, **10**).

The baseboard is fitted with small hoops of rod driven through holes drilled in the wood. The spindle slots into these and rests on a small section of angle iron screwed to the wood (**7**). The central spindle is held vertical by a wire hook halfway up. The hook attaches to a wooden stake driven into the ground.

Power sources This series of diagrams shows a number of ways movement can be created from a simple motor. The motor (**1**) turns a rod. By attaching another rod with a belt, two rods (**2**) or more (**3**) turned by one power source. Different speeds of rotation can be achieved by attaching belts to a wheel to give slower motion or by using the perimeter of a wheel to give quicker motion (**4**). Gears can create reverse motion (**5**) and cam wheels up and down movement (**6**).

Below *Two lines – Temporal 1* is an example of George Rickey's kinetic sculptures. Created between 1964 and 1977, this huge work is over 35 feet (10.5 meters) high. It consists of two stainless steel mobile blades on a stainless steel base.

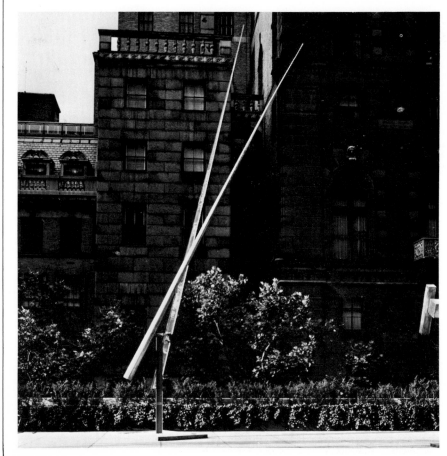

motor power or proper mechanical components are available, many scrap materials can be used to rig up some kind of system. An electric motor suitably fixed to a firm base can be used to motivate several simultaneous actions with the help of an arrangement of gears and belts. Belts will transfer the power from the drive of the motor to where the movement is needed, and the gears, if interlocked with other gear wheels, will transfer the direction of the drive. The gear cogs can be made simply from either scrap wood or metal by cutting out V-shapes for the teeth with a hacksaw, and, even if rather crude, they will serve the purpose. The gear wheels can be set together at any angle, so that a wide variety of changes can be made. If the speed of the motor is not correct for any particular action, it can be changed by gearing. A small wheel driven by a larger one, in turn driven by the motor, will speed up the motion. The opposite effect will be achieved if a large wheel is driven off a smaller one. In this way a number of different actions can be obtained from one motor, as in Moholy-Nagy's *Light Space Modulator*, where the different rotations of the plates create a kaleidoscope of reflection from the given light source.

To produce a series of connected movements from a motor, a rigid framework will be needed in which the moving parts can be set up. As long as this requirement is attained, the moving parts can be made up from the kind of scrap found in a scrap yard. Old bicycle or pram wheels are excellent, and car wheel inner tubes cut to size make very good drive belts. If these are not available, string knotted to form a chain can be used with a toothed wheel just as effectively. Plywood will make very light usable gear cogs as the criss-cross layering of the wood prevents the teeth from breaking, which may happen with ordinary wood.

A petrol engine would enable a construction to be set up independently in the open, but it is obviously too noisy and fume-producing for reasonable use indoors. Furthermore, as it is potentially more violent if left unchecked, a much more robust and rigid frame is needed than when using an electric motor. The sort of petrol motors which are ideal for an outside kinetic sculpture can be taken from old mopeds, as these are light, easy to handle, and have a small engine capacity of about 50cc, which is the best size. Secondhand electric motors are often stocked by scrap dealers. These motors, usually taken from old washing machines, are very cheap and easily fitted into a framework. Alternatively, complete washing machines can be bought from secondhand stores and the fabric of the machine can then be used as well as the motor.

Natural power sources greatly increase the

ope of kinetic sculpture and encourage inventiveness. In the studio, water falling on a wheel fitted with paddles will provide a limited amount of power. Of course, the time the system runs is dependent on the size of the water supply and the rate at which it is falling. Obviously the container supplying the water and that receiving it should be watertight and strong enough to hold the volume of water. Water can also be used in a less active way but nevertheless one which allows movement to take place as in the case of *Floating Sculpture* (1961) by the Hungarian-French artist Marta Pan (born 1923). This is a large upturned rounded form floating gracefully on a pond. On top of this, joined by a swivel joint, is another rounded form which turns independently from its partner. The sculpture is made from polyester resin, an extremely light material, so the hollow molded form easily responds to any wind. The sculpture sits in the middle of the lake by the Kröller-Müller Museum, at Otterlo in the Netherlands, surrounded by superb scenery. It is, of course, chained loosely in the middle so that it does not get beached at the side of the lake.

Air movements have been used by themselves in the mobile sculptures of Calder and Rickey to produce variations in groups of balanced objects. As long as the parts of a sculpture are finely balanced and free to move easily they will need very little breeze to move them. In both Rickey's and Calder's sculptures the same basic principle is used to catch any available breeze. Calder's mobiles are generally thin, flattish plates, and Rickey's needles are light open cross-section pieces rather than being solid.

Most of the other natural sources have been used by sculptors at one time or another, including solar energy and magnetism. However, the former requires advanced technology to make it useful and it is not really a suitable source of power for the beginner.

Electro-magnetism can be achieved in the studio with only a basic knowledge of electronics. Turning an electric current on and off produces alternate pulsations which will allow limited variations of movement. In his sculptures, Takis uses this method of turning an electric current on and off to alternately attract and repel magnets mounted upon thin rods which quiver accordingly.

Most of the power sources mentioned provide only limited possibilities for use which have been fully exploited by artists in the past. Unlike other sculptural media, kinetic techniques are usually inseparable from the idea, so further development must rely on new inventions. Nonetheless, the exploration of kinetic sculpture is still valuable in providing an understanding of real and implied movement.

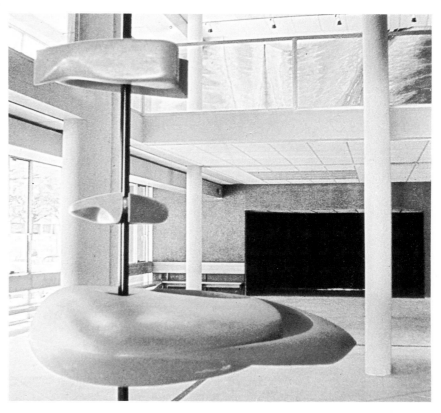

Above This sculpture by the Hungarian-French sculptor Marta Pan shows her use of organic form. In its modern architectural setting, the steel column in the sculpture echoes the perpendicular lines of the building's design.

Left Signal, also by Marta Pan, is another example of her interest in forms derived from nature. The superimposed discs bear some resemblance to the petals of a flower. Again, the artist combines curving shapes with vertical rods.

LIGHT

HISTORY

Light is a relatively new medium in the history [of] art. As a fundamental stimulus of life forms, lig[ht] has always had a magical or mystical status and [is] an important symbol in many religions. Th[e] movement of the sun was a determining factor [in] the construction of monumental edifices such [as] the Pyramids and Stonehenge. Medieval stain[ed] glass windows projected the sun's rays in[to] beautiful colored patterns to highlight architec[-]tural or sculptural features inside the buildin[g]. The Italian sculptor Bernini (1598–1680) pa[id] careful attention to the effect of light on his wor[k], both in the individual sculptures and the settin[g] in which they were displayed.

However, the technical ability to create pa[r-]ticular images and effects using light itself as t[he] medium has only become available to artis[ts] during the twentieth century. Previous expe[ri-]ments, such as the color organs of the eighteen[th] and nineteenth centuries, were unsuccessf[ul]. These attempted to link music and color sy[s-]tematically. Illumination was originally provid[ed] by candles, glowing through translucent color[ed] tapes, later by arc lamps projecting colored ligh[t]. The illuminations were linked to the keys of [a] musical instrument, and the pattern of co[lor] related directly to the musician's playing. Co[lor] organs were both technically and visually disa[p-]pointing and met with little public respons[e]. Displays of color projection devised by t[he] American Thomas Wilfred (born 1889) in t[he] early years of the twentieth century were mo[re] favorably received. These could be aptly [de-]scribed as paintings in light, although the imag[es] in his later work suggested three-dimension[al] space.

The Bauhaus artists in Germany during t[he] 1920s made a number of constructions incorpor[at-]ing movement and light. László Moholy-Na[gy] (1895–1946) became interested in patterns [of] light and shade, arising from his recognition [of] the sculptural potential of the image of citysca[pe] at night. The *Light Space Modulator* creat[ed] between 1922 and 1930, was a large metal co[n-]struction, set in motion by an electric mot[or]. Displayed in a dark room, under a changi[ng] pattern of spotlights, the effect of a fluid envir[on-]ment of light and shade was produced.

Effective technical advances in the use of li[ght] owe a great deal to work on lighting for t[he] theater and for commercial display. The devel[op-]ment of such equipment as lighting consoles a[nd] machines for bending neon tubes has given pa[in-]ters and sculptors the means to approach th[eir] traditional preoccupations with form, light a[nd] color in a new and exciting way.

Since 1945, artists have applied new technologi-
[c]al developments with great sophistication and
[ha]ve met with a far more favorable public re-
[sp]onse than did the pioneers of light art. One of
[th]e most influential figures has been the Italian
[Lu]cio Fontana (1899–1968). Writing his *White
[M]anifesto* of 1946, he defined clearly the tra-
[di]tional importance of light as a factor affecting
[w]orks of art, and proceeded both theoretically
[an]d practically to lay the ground for a positive use
[of] light in their design and construction. Sources
[of] light, such as lamps and neon strips, were
[in]corporated in his sculptural environments as
[vit]al and undisguised components of the work.

[D]uring the 1950s and 1960s, the medium of
[lig]ht was explored with the same confidence and
[sk]ill which has characterized other developments
[in] the visual arts. The German Otto Piene (born
[19]28) interpreted the sensations of his wartime
[ex]periences in work known as *Light Ballet*, which
[us]ed hand-held or mechanized apparatus to form
[im]ages within a given space. The Hungarian-
French sculptor Nicolas Schöffer (born 1912)
constructs kinetic works, of which emitted or
reflected light forms an integral part. A more
recent work detects the surrounding light level
and atmospheric conditions, systematizes the information through a computer, and projects related images. The Italian sculptor Danti Leonelli
uses light to enhance the volumetric form of his
molded plexiglass sculptures, changing the color
and mood at intervals. Chryssa (born 1933) and
Dan Flavin (born 1933) both work with neon, but
in different ways. Chryssa's free standing sculptures are linear drawings in neon, enclosed in
transparent boxes. Flavin uses straight tubes in
simple groups, but places them around the floor
and walls of a room to structure the space in terms
of light.

Laser technology is currently being explored by
artists, but as yet this work is not fully developed
or documented. Artists working with this medium
include Billy Apple and Robert Whitman. This is
a medium with considerable sculptural potential.

Below Bruce Naumann's
neon tubing sign (1967)
measures 59in (148cm) by
54in (135cm) and shows the
flexibility that this medium can
achieve. Bending the tubes is
difficult and exacting work,
which should be done by an
expert. Gentle bends are
easier to produce than sharp
ones. Several tubes will be
used to make one work.
Bottom The use of neon is
an exciting departure in light
sculpture. Closely connected
to the use of neon in
advertising, neon can create
amusing and eye-catching
images. Here three colors—
green, blue and red—have
been used to portray the
'click' of the fingers. It is
possible to see where the
individual tubes occur.

[Le]ft The north rose window
[of] Chartres Cathedral was
[bu]ilt in the thirteenth century.
[Th]is classic example of stained
[gl]ass craft and painting is
[fa]mous for its blue glass which
[is t]he result of copper being
[ad]ded to the molten glass.
[Th]e extraordinary quality of
[thi]s glass has not been
[re]peated in modern times.
[Ri]ght Nicholas Schöffer's
[To]ur Cybernétique de Liege
[is] an example of his highly
[inv]entive kinetic work. The
[ref]lected light forms an
[int]egral part of the sculpture
[as] it cuts through the space
[ar]ound.

SOURCES OF LIGHT

Natural light This is the most obvious, cheap and available source, but the quality is, of course, uncontrollable. A sculpture with reflective surface planes goes through an infinite number of changes in a day. Light through a window could also be incorporated in a sculpture, directed by mirrors or through stencils.

Light bulbs and florescent tubes The common apparatus of domestic lighting can be used to make quite complex effects. Bulbs and tubes are available in a range of colors and provide lighting of different intensities. They may be concealed within a construction to provide subtle, fixed effects, or their shapes may be positive elements in the design of the work.

Neon tubes Neon offers a greater brilliance and variety of color than florescent tubes, and can be bent into gently curving shapes. Such work must be done by a professional glass bender, working from an artist's drawing, as it requires expert technical knowledge. Neon tubes are high voltage and must be carefully installed,

with good insulation in the fittings.

Strobe lights The strobe light gives intense, white light in rapid pulsating flashes. Normal movement patterns are given a slow, eerie quality under strobe lighting.

Projectors A projector throws a strong beam of light which can be focused at a distance or close to the lens It can be used to project white light, colored light, or photographic images.

Laser beams A laser projects an almost parallel beam of light on one coherent wavelength. The visual effect is of a rod of pure light passing through space, which may be white or colored. Laser beams are used to create interwoven linear patterns in three dimensions and environments of pure light.

Laser holography This is a means of creating a three-dimensional image with light on a special photographic plate. The image is recorded on the plate by one laser, transferring information from an object. The image is not visible in normal light but must be reconstituted, in effect, by another beam. Holography is very complex and is not yet common as an art form.

Light bulbs Even ordinary light bulbs can provide the sculptor with material if used imaginatively. This type of light can be used to advantage when the sculptor wishes to exploit the reflective properties of light. The positioning of the lights shining onto a mirror sculpture, for example, will greatly affect the impression which the work gives. Some of the types of light bulb which can be used include an ordinary domestic bulb (**1**), semi-silvered (**2**), spotlight (**3**) and tinted (**4**).

MATERIALS AND TECHNIQUES
REFLECTION

Reflective surfaces react to any available light therefore no electrical work need be necessary producing a sculpture with quite complex visu effects. Pieces of mirror, glass or polished met can be glued to a basic wood construction, or s in resin.

Mirror glass is usually silvered on the back, a the thickness of the glass cuts across between t object in real space and the reflected image. Fro surfaced mirror, which may be glass, plastic stainless steel, eliminates this break. A sol object, such as a half cube, placed against t mirror, connects directly with its reflection a the image of a whole cube is created.

A semi-silvered mirror is reflective und normal lighting, but becomes translucent when from the back. It is possible to set up a sem silvered mirror, with controlled light falling dow ch side, in such a way that a reflected image xes with a view of an object on the other side of e mirror. Thus, two people looking at each her through the mirror can each see their own lection superimposed on the other's face. A gle object placed between a semi-silvered rror and a back-surfaced mirror is seen as an inite number of objects in a line receding in ace, owing to internal reflections back and forth tween the mirrors.

A multi-faceted reflective surface can be obned by setting small rectangles of mirror side side, each at a slightly different angle to the flat ne. A curved, reflective surface gives a dis-rted image.

Water can also be used to provide a reflective refractive surface, though it is no use if a given ect must be fixed or accurately repeated. fraction is a term referring to a slight change in e direction of light rays as they pass from one dium (air) into another (water). The most mmon illustration of this phenomenon is that a aight stick pushed into clear water appears to nd at the surface of the water.

Materials for making colored slides Slides on which a variety of colors move when they are projected can be made with a simple selection of materials. These include colored inks (**1**), glass slides (**2**), ether (**3**) and a dropper (**4**).

Making slides with colored inks 1. Lay out three glass slides and drop a small puddle of ink onto each one.

2. Using a clean dropper, add a little ether to each patch of different colored ink.

3. Place the slides one on top of the other, finishing with a clean one so all liquid is contained between them.

4. Put the slides into a projector and throw the image onto a white screen. The ether forms transparent patches in the ink and moves toward the edge of the slides to evaporate out. This causes the inks to flow inside the glass in constantly changing patterns.

Right When projections of the primary light colors – red, blue and green – are made by using a colored filter on each of three projectors, and combined, they form the secondary colors – yellow, magenta and turquoise or cyan – where two overlap. White light is created in the center where all three colors overlap.

Left Larry Bell's coated glass screens incorporate the spectator into the sculpture. Each pane of the glass acts as mirror, window and screen at the same time, and this unusual effect can only be demonstrated by the presence of the spectator.

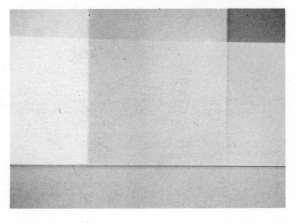

_ PROJECTION OF COLOR _

White light is composed of a spectrum of colored light waves. When a beam of white light is directed through a prism, it is refracted, but each color in the spectrum is refracted at a slightly different angle, so the beam fans out into a rainbow effect. If this is then passed through a lens and a second prism, it combines back into white light.

Color properties in light are different from those in pigments. The primary colors in light are red, blue and green. These can be mixed in pairs to produce secondary colors. Red and blue combine into magenta, blue and green form turquoise or cyan, and red and green mix into yellow.

Filters for an ordinary slide projector can be simply made by sticking colored cellophane into a cardboard slide mount. Working with three projectors, the primary colors can be made to overlap on the screen, producing the secondaries, and white light where all three primaries come together. An object placed in front of this white area casts colored shadows. The colors change across the shadow area, according to which primary is blocked by the object at any point on the screen. The shadow is black only in the center where all three projections are blocked.

Projections of moving color can be produced simply. Trap a small puddle of colored ink and a drop of ether between two clear glass slides. When this is put into a projector, the ether moves toward the edges of the slide, to evaporate out. The ether projects as a transparent 'hole' in the ink, so the effect is of a mass of color constantly

Polarizing I. Make a pattern on a glass slide by rubbing down overlapping strips of adhesive tape across the surface.

2. Cut polarizing film to the size of the slide, and sandwich it between the taped slide and a clean one.

3. When the taped slide with polarizing sheet is projected, it shows a delicate gray tracing of the pattern. A second sheet of polarizing film held in front of the projector lens causes

the light to break up, forming different colors in each section of the pattern. As the film is rotated through 360° the colors change with each new angle.

Below This photograph shows the hologram *Portrait of a Woman*, created by Harriet Casdin-Silver. It measured I foot (30cm) by 4 feet 8in (140cm). This is a pulse laser hologram. The pulse laser emits a brief flash of light and 'freezes' the action. This means that this type of laser can be used to record moving objects which otherwise would have obliterated the image.

anging shape. Two or three colors projected in
is way form a complex shifting pattern of pure
d translucently overlaid colors.

Polarizing film interferes with the pattern of
ht waves and can be used to project colors. A
sign made with strips of clear adhesive tape on
glass slide is backed with a sheet of polarizing
m. When this is projected, the design is seen as
faint, gray image. A second piece of polarizing
m held in front of the camera lens divides the
ht, and the pattern is seen in color. If the film is
tated through 360°, the colors keep changing.

CONSTRUCTION

ulpture which emits light may be very simple,
ch as a light box with an on-off switch, or highly
mplex, with interdependent sequences of light
d movement. A simple construction can easily
made with readily available electrical compo-
nts. A basic wooden framework, for instance,
n be drilled to allow wires and light sockets to
set in place.

Complicated kinetic devices with light can be
signed in careful drawings, and technical advice
ould, if necessary, be sought on making the
ulpture. Many artists now incorporate compu-
r or microprocessor systems to control the
tivity of a work. A simple device which gives a
od effect is the pressure mat. This consists of
o surfaces which are electrical conductors, held
art by insulating strips. When the viewer treads
the mat, the pressure forces the conductors
gether and completes the circuit, activating the
ulpture.

Above Each box in this construction by Rod Murray has a stainless steel sheet on the top surface which gives a mirror effect with no gap between object and reflection. When one shape is placed on another the appearance of a larger cube floating in space is created.

Below left Le Parce's continual mobile is made of painted wood, aluminum and nylon thread. It demonstrates its creator's fascination with the effects of movement and light which he first began working on in the 1960s.

SAFETY

Handling materials Handle glass, metal and mirror pieces with great care, especially if you cut them to shape yourself.
Electricity Further precautions should be taken when working with electricity. Always make sure the apparatus is unplugged while you are working on it. Cover any bare wires with insulating tape or fit them into connecting blocks. Check voltage and be sure to use the correct fuses. Do not use any equipment you are not familiar with without getting precise instructions on how it works.
Lights Strong or pulsating light can cause unpleasant effects, particularly in people subject to headaches or fits.
Lasers Lasers cannot be used by someone with merely an amateur interest. Precautions must be taken in laser installations to prevent anyone looking directly into the source of light.

Glass

MIXED MEDIA

HISTORY AND TECHNIQUES

It is nothing new for a work of art to be made from a combination of materials or objects. However, artists in the twentieth century have explored a wide range of ways of using combinations of materials or objects in sculpture. The prominence today of sculpture using mixed media, or assemblage as it is also called, seems to be the product of changing attitudes to art in the twentieth century. For the purposes of mixed media work, the technique is inseparable from the artists's approach and its content.

FORERUNNERS

Throughout the history of sculpture, examples of work using a variety of media are so common that it seems, in fact, that it is the unmixed use of a medium in the period since the Renaissance which is exceptional. For instance, bronze statues with ivory eyes made in ancient Greece still exist, and most other sculpture of that time was often brightly painted. The many different folk arts of the world also show a tendency to the use of different media in an amusing and inventive way.

In addition, the decorative arts and architecture have always concerned themselves with using a variety of materials and techniques in combination. While, in early and folk examples, the different media have mainly been used in a representational way, more contemporary mixed media works have tended to call into question the nature of art and to challenge the viewer's assumptions and existing ideas about the world.

DADA AND SURREALISM

The interest in using mixed media in the twentieth century stems, perhaps, from the use of 'real' materials by Pablo Picasso (1881–1973) and Georges Braque (1882–1963) in their revolutionary Cubist collages, which incorporated materials such as newspaper and oilcloth. The first major mixed media work, however, was one of modern art's landmarks, the *Fountain* of 1917 by the French artist Marcel Duchamp (1887–1968). Duchamp's up-ended, signed porcelain urinal caused a furore when it was exhibited at an exhibition. It was the combination of the object and the 'art' context which contributed to the outraged reaction. This type of shock has been a repeated feature of mixed media works. A par-

Below Pablo Picasso was one of the first artists to use everyday objects and materials in his works. This *Still Life*, made from many different materials, dates from 1914. One of the aims of many mixed media artists has been to shock their audiences.

rcel Duchamp was one of
e main exponents of mixed
dia work. His *Secret Noise*
ove) was made in 1916.
ving used string and metal
Secret Noise, he turned to
y different materials for a
8 work (**right**). This
consists of oil paint and silver
sheet with lead wire and a
magnifier placed between two
sheets of glass. Duchamp
made the visually striking
ready-made *Why not Sneeze,
Rose Selavy?* in 1921. (**below**).

ticular feature of much mixed media work is the
way in which it reflects the artist's particular
enthusiasms and interests, whether these are
visual or not. Duchamp's works reveal his great
sense of humor and his interests in literature and
philosophy, as well as his interests in art.

Another facet which has characterized much
mixed media work is the use of objects in ways
which remove them from their normal contexts or
present them in new or unconventional ways.

The important *Object* of 1936 by the German-
Swiss artist Maeret Oppenheim (born 1913)
showed everyday objects—a cup, saucer and
spoon—made out of fur. The idea behind the
work was related to the anti-art ideas of the
Dadaists, such as Duchamp. However,
Oppenheim's *Object* achieves its effect because
the material—fur—works against ordinary ideas
about cups, saucers and spoons. In addition, the
artist tried to use a substance which seemed as far
removed as possible from any idea of sipping. The
idea of drinking from a fur cup makes the viewer's
mouth pucker.

POTENTIAL AND
POSSIBILITIES

There is literally no limit to what material or
combination of materials can be used in mixed
media sculpture. Duchamp's urinal was only the
beginning. For instance, the American artist
Joseph Cornell (1903–1973) is best known for
making enclosed constructions consisting of various objects and clippings in picture-frame boxes.
Cornell's work in some ways follows on from the
collages and assemblages of the Dadaists and is a
precursor of the later large scale assemblages of
artists such as Robert Rauschenberg (born 1925).

Rauschenberg and his fellow American Jasper
Johns (born 1930) used a wide variety of materials
in their work. These included stuffed animals,
rubber tyres, plaster casts, paint and pillows.
Against the eclectic background of Abstract Ex-

pressionism, the predominant artistic movement
in America during the 1950s, Rauschenberg's
work is characterized by his use of associative
leaps and fascinating juxtaposition. The close
links between early and contemporary ideas of
mixed media sculpture are epitomized by what
happened when, in the late 1950s, Rauschenberg
was one of the prizewinners in an international
exhibition of painting and sculpture. His construction incorporated, among other things, an
alarm clock. One of the jurors was Marcel
Duchamp, who smiled benignly most of the way
through a public question-and-answer session
following the judging. Several members of the
audience directed slightly outraged questions to
the jurors about Rauschenberg's construction,
and it was becoming difficult for them to make
coherent replies. Finally, one of the audience
stood up and asked Duchamp if the alarm clock
actually told the time. Duchamp smiled a little

Left Robert Rauschenberg's untitled 1967 work is an example of his use of collage. Collage has been one of the main approaches to mixed media work since Picasso and Braque first used newspaper in their works in 1912. This example of Rauschenberg's work measures about 6 feet 6 inches (2 meters) square. However, collage can be done on any scale, and lends itself to both two- and three-dimensional work.

Left *Spiral Jetty* by the American artist Robert Smithson is an example of sculpture which uses the whole environment. It consists of a spiral of rock and salt crystal in the Great Salt Lake, Utah. This approach to art became popular during the late 1960s and early 1970s. The works are also called earthworks.

ore broadly and replied 'No, I tried it'.

This anecdote illustrates one of the main fac-rs in mixed media work. More than any other nd of sculpture, assemblage demands a pre-aredness on the part of the spectator to enter penly into the spirit of the work, and it also quires an informed awareness of important sues in contemporary art if the viewer is to gain e most from what such work offers.

Another feature of mixed media work is the use ade by artists of materials new to the world of t. For instance, one of the great artistic in-ovators of the twentieth century, the Hungarian ázló Moholy-Nagy (1895–1946) used plexiglass d metal discs in his *Light-Space Modulator*. nother example is the work of the German ada artist Kurt Schwitters (1887–1947). His rious *Merzbau* constructions, created through-t his career after 1919, used many everyday ousehold objects.

CONSTRUCTIONS AND ENVIRONMENTS

The *Merzbau* constructions created by Schwitters can be seen as forerunners of the extension of mixed media work into 'total' or environment art. This idea takes the notion of a work of art and extends it to take in the whole environment around the work.

For example, the American artist Ed Kienholz (born 1927) created a series of detailed environments. With scrupulous research, he produced works of uncanny realism—with surrealistic touches. His *State Hospital* had the viewer look through a peep-hole into a hospital ward which contained two bandaged figures on beds. The heads of the figures, however, were goldfish bowls with black fishes swimming in them.

Taking the idea of using the environment to an

extreme, the Bulgarian-born sculptor Christo (born 1935) put a curtain across the Grand Canyon and, on another occasion, wrapped a stretch of Australian coastline in plastic.

USING SCALE

As well as placing everyday objects in unusual contexts and making works in unconventional materials, mixed media artists have manipulated the idea of scale to create new and surprising juxtapositions. The influential American Claes Oldenburg (born 1929) has produced huge, soft sculptures of small, everyday objects. For example, his *Giant Soft Fan*, made in 1966 and 1967, consists of vinyl filled with foam rubber, wood, metal and plastic tubing. The soft version of an electric fan is some 10 feet (3 meters) high and, including the attached cord and plug, about 24 feet (8 meters) in extent. The huge scale and deflated appearance create an amusing and very visually effective image.

CREATING MIXED MEDIA WORKS

Many artists have used the possibilities offered by mixed media as a way of getting away from the traditional sculptural media, such as stone and wood carving or metal casting. While it is ve[ry] difficult to suggest any specific technique[s] because, literally, any technique can be use[d], certain approaches have become associated wi[th] mixed media work.

Collage Developed by the Cubists early in t[he] twentieth century, collage used many kinds [of] objects including newspaper cuttings and phot[o]graphs, to create a three-dimensional form on [a] flat surface. Gradually, collage developed awa[y] from its two-dimensional basis and came to i[n]clude almost any work assembled from differe[nt] sources. One of the names for mixed med[ia] work—assemblage—comes from this idea of a[s]sembling different elements.

Objets trouvés Another popular mixed med[ia] technique is using ordinary objects and juxtapo[s]ing them. Both natural and synthetic materia[ls] can be used—wood, shells, tin cans, pieces [of] commercial packaging and any other object fro[m] everyday life can be put to good use.

The idea of using many different media [in] sculpture originated partly in an attempt to bre[ak] away from traditional conventions. Much ear[ly] mixed media art was a form of mockery, but th[is] approach to sculpture has played an importa[nt] role in gaining acceptance for a large variety [of] new and exciting materials which are now [a] recognized part of the sculptor's repertoire.

Below The American artist Ed Kienholz is known for his painstaking reconstructions of scenes. This picture shows a detail from *The Portable War Memorial*, completed in 1968. The level of detail results from extensive research by the artist, who uses a wide range of materials.

Above *Wrapped Monument to Leonardo* is an example of mixed media work by Christo, an important contemporary exponent of this type of sculpture. His other works have included wrapping a stretch of Australian coastline in plastic.

Making a wax cast inside a pepper 1. Cut around the stalk and scoop out the core of the pepper. Pierce holes in the top.

2. Melt down the wax in a pan lined with tinfoil. Pour it slowly into the pepper.

3. The pepper is quite full when a little wax escapes from the holes. Replace the stalk and leave it to cool.

4. Slit open the pepper skin with a sharp knife and peel it away in sections to free the wax cast.

Making a plaster cast from a stone A mold can be made from an interesting found object, such as an oddly shaped stone, if more than

one representation of the object is required. The stone should first be thoroughly greased (**1**), and a plaster piece mold formed around it

ight *Ghetto*, a construction by the American rtist George Carter, illustrates one way of using ound objects. The American flag and eagle are xtaposed with numerous everyday objects, articularly bells and padlocks. The boxes are ifferent sizes and this contributes to the variety f the image.

(**2**). A pouring hole for the plaster must be made in one of the mold sections (**3**). When the plaster has set, the cast is released from the mold (**4**).

PRESENTATION AND DISPLAY

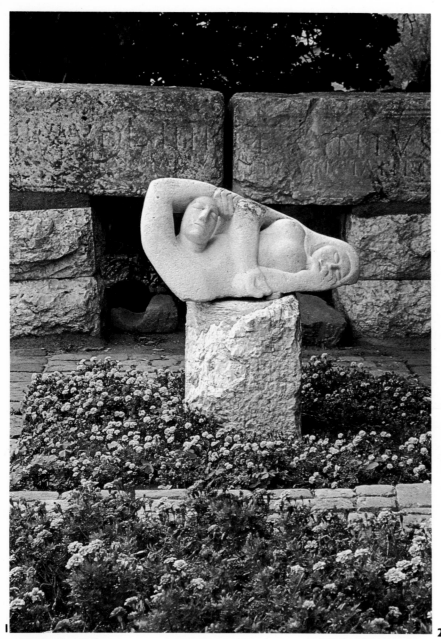

DISPLAYING SCULPTURE

It is important that sculptures are displayed to their best advantage, whether they are positioned inside or out-of-doors. This applies whether you have made the sculpture or bought it. There are several basic considerations. These include how to mount or fix the sculpture so that it is stable, where to position it and how to light it. When displaying sculpture it is vital to consider not only the space which the piece itself occupies, but also the space around it.

PLINTHS

Plinths can be used to steady a sculpture or raise it to the correct height for viewing. A plinth should always complement the piece of work which it supports, so they vary greatly in size, shape and color from one piece to another. Materials commonly used for making plinths include simple

In a private garden
In this instance, the advice of the sculptor should be obtained wherever possible. Consideration should be given to whether the work is to be seen from a distance or close to, or both. The selected site should provide a complementary—but not intrusive—setting for the piece. Modern sculpture can be displayed to great advantage, even in small town gardens, if sufficient care is taken in matching piece and site as can be seen with this Picasso piece set among flowers (**1**). Purchasers considering particular pieces can get some idea of scale by

placing garden canes to the height of the sculpture in position on site. As with interior display, the property owner must take steps to ensure that the sculpture will not injure family or friends, or vice versa. Particular care must be taken about safety in the garden in darkness; lighting or careful siting should solve this problem.

In a public outdoor location
Most of the points discussed in the section on setting in a private garden are relevant when installing a sculpture in a public exterior location. However, attention must also be given to the sculptor's

relationship with the owners of the piece as well as the site on which it is to be displayed. If the sculptor is selling the piece, but wishes to be consulted about the display arrangements, a provision to this effect should be written into the contract of sale. If the sculptor owns the piece, but is displaying it permanently or temporarily on a public site, every possible effort should be made to check that the piece is installed securely, and is adequately protected from vandals. Sculptors should take independent legal advice on the relationship between themselves and the owner or controller of the land, and on

liability should the piece cause injury to a member of the public. Here *Aston Cross* (**4**) by John Maine is displayed at the University of Aston, Birmingham, England.

In a gallery
The gallery will usually be able to provide plinths, but sculptors may wish to provide their own if those available are inappropriate. It is unlikely that a gallery would meet the cost of this, although organizers of touring shows are sometimes able to reimburse artists who provide specially constructed plinths. Gallery directors will be able to give much valuable advice on display, as they will be

thoroughly familiar with the gallery space and lighting system. It is normal for the gallery director and artist to work together on the installation of a show, but many gallery directors will expect to have the final say, and this may be specified in the exhibition contract if one is used. Galleries will usually only suggest the use of display cases for sculpture in particular circumstances. This applies, of course, to work which is particularly delicate, has special requirements (such as temperature control or special lighting) or is made of precious or semi-precious materials. This photograph of ndon's Hayward Gallery (**2**) ows how works by Anthony ro were exhibited in 1969.

a domestic setting
henever possible, owners uld seek the advice of the lptor on siting a piece of rk in a domestic interior. e work should be placed so t it can be seen to vantage, without being nfused by being too close to er objects, such as ntings, lamps and curtains. e owners should consider ether the work will be wed mainly from a standing sitting position, and site it at appropriate height. The ce around the sculpture is important element in the

work, and it is sometimes difficult to achieve adequate surrounding space in small rooms. The balance between space, sculptures and furniture can be clearly seen in this interesting arrangement (**3**).

Common-sense precautions must be taken in considering whether the piece could be damaged by any movement through the room, or whether it could cause injury, either in position or if it is dislodged. Particular care must be taken if children are likely to visit the house. Normal domestic lighting can be augmented with floor or ceiling spotlights.

Lighting a sculpture How the form of a sculpture is perceived is crucially affected by the way it is lit. Light thrown from one angle tends to accentuate curves, hollows and angles, defining changing planes. Indirect lighting from a table lamp (**1**) is directional but very soft. A downlighter (**2**) sheds a broad, clear light over the whole sculpture, illuminating the form

without exaggeration or distortion. With a combination of two spotlights on an adjustable stand (**3**), one can be thrown directly on the sculpture while the other softens the light by bouncing it off the ceiling. The glare of a ceiling mounted spotlight could be too harsh, but if the lamp is angled to bounce light off the wall (**4**), it gives a pleasant illumination.

Lighting fitments A recessed downlight (**5**) is set in the ceiling. A broad cone of clear light is shed from its fixed position. Multiple spots on a rail (**6**) can be mounted on ceiling or walls and angled to give a particular direction. Clip-on spotlights (**7**) can be attached to wall or ceiling tracks and to shelves and tables to give direct or diffused light.

Photographing sculpture An up-to-date record of work is vital, and, since slides and photographs will be sent to people who are not familiar with the sculptures, the quality of the pictures is important. If the works are small, they can be photographed adequately in the studio without much trouble. A large sheet of paper or card provides a clean, plain background for the sculpture. The camera must be mounted on a tripod so that its position is fixed and it is steady throughout the exposure. A pair of anglepoise lamps provides enough light. If the light see glaring it can be softened a diffused by placing a sheet tracing paper in front of th bulb on each lamp. Harsh shadows on or around the sculpture may obscure the form and cause difficulty fo the viewer in understandir the nature of the work. If t sculpture is in the round, it should be photographed f several angles, each view placed carefully within the viewing frame and accurat focused.

Photographing a relief sculpture A relief is best photographed placed flat on the floor, the camera fixed directly above it and lights on either side.

Plinths A plinth for a sculpture (**top**) should always complement the work. The plinth may be a solid, heavy base or a tall, narrow stand. It should be carefully chosen to place the work at the correct height and angle within the viewer's line of vision. An elaborate plinth may not be suitable unless specifically designed in conjunction with the sculpture. Plain cubic or cylindrical plinths are often used in gallery displays. Many modern sculptures, such as *Cross Bow* by Wendy Taylor (**above**) are designed to be placed directly on the floor, without a base. This is particularly common if, as in this case, they are large works with a pronounced horizontal emphasis.

painted or unpainted hardboard boxes, solid timber, stone bricks, marble, perspex, metal, concrete and paving stones.

Sculptors can profitably study the use of plinths by other artists. Look at the many different ways in which works are displayed. Note what they are made of, whether the plinth was in fact made as an integral part of the piece, whether the material harmonizes or contrasts with the work. Sculptures can also be displayed without plinths, which should, in any case, only be used if they fulfill a specific function.

PHOTOGRAPHING SCULPTURE

Slides The quality of color slides is important, and, if the sculptor is not a competent photographer, it is advisable to ask a friend or professional photographer to do this work Slides should be constantly updated. It may b necessary to produce photographs of recent wor at short notice. At least three sets of slides ar required. One set is the sculptor's master recor and should never be sent out, and the remainin two sets are for submission to galleries, compet tions and award schemes. This type of assessmen can take some time, and slides will not b returned until all decisions have been made.

Slides may be taken either in studio, gallery outdoor or domestic locations. Alternatively, th sculptor may wish to have pieces recorded in photographic studio setting which might offe many options in terms of background and lightin effects. When slides are not taken in a photc graphic studio setting, a number of points shoul be considered. Check that lighting is adequate and select the correct type of film for the lightin

Top lighting—
single spot

¾ lighting—
single spot

Side lighting—
single spot

Top lighting—
stronger
fill-in light
opposite

¾ lighting—
stronger
fill-in light
opposite

Side lighting—
stronger
fill-in light
opposite

Frontal
lighting—
single light

Soft side
lighting—
stronger fill-in
light opposite

Soft ¾ light—
light reflected
from white wall
opposite

Shield to prevent glare into
camera lens

Anglepoise lamp

Sculpture on plinth

35mm camera

Standard
tripod

Paper backdrop

Photographing a small sculpture A suitable area for photography can be set up in the studio. A paper backdrop pinned to the wall and draped over a table provides a clean background. Two anglepoise lamps, placed one on either side, give clear, strong light. A simple shield or screen should be erected to prevent glare from the lamps entering the lens. It is necessary to steady the camera on a tripod.

Lighting a sculpture There are many ways of lighting a sculpture to obtain a particular effect. A single, strong light produces a dramatic heightening of tonal contrasts. This can be countered by filling in the shadows with a second light from a different angle, or by reflecting back the light with white paper or card.

to be used. Place the work to be photographed against a plain background; plaster walls, brick walls, grass, trees, yards and playgrounds are all suitable. Photograph the work from several angles if this is necessary to give a sense of the piece. Give special attention to the placing of the work within the camera frame, and accurate focusing. Harsh shadows which may confuse the reading of the slide should be avoided. Consider including some clue as to scale—brick walls, windows, doorways, floorboards and objects of known size such as matchboxes may be helpful. One or two 'scale' slides can usefully be included in a presentation which is going to people unfamiliar with the work. In addition, installation shots, studio shots, slides of work in progress and pictures showing the artist at work can all be useful in certain circumstances, and should be taken when the sculptor feels it is appropriate.

Black and white photographs The general points about color slides also relate to black and white photographs, but greater care must be taken in selecting backgrounds which will not become confused with the work. Consideration should be given to how the tonal relationship between the sculpture and the background will translate into black and white. It is helpful if sculptors have black and white photographs available to give to the press, catalog compilers and for other publicity purposes. Artists should not rely on getting these prints back again.

RECORDING WORK

It is advisable to maintain a complete record of all the work you do. This is usually done on slide or through the use of photographs.
35mm color slides This is the most commonly used

system for recording work. Most galleries are equipped with a light box and/or projector for viewing slides, and most competitions and schemes are geared to assess work initially from slides. Some artists worry that their work does not translate well onto slide, but most administrators involved in the assessment of work are experienced in 'reading' slides carefully. 35mm slides can be mounted in glass to protect them from scratching and damage from the heat of a projector. The card mounts supplied by photographic processors sometimes do not engage properly in a carousel projector, and thicker plastic mounts are preferable. Simple color prints can be made directly from 35mm slides in certain types of photocopying machine, and high quality color prints can be made from transparencies. Full color printing, for instance for catalogs, books and private view cards, is also originated from color slides.

35mm black and white slides Some artists are attracted by the use of black and white stock for photographing sculpture. Monochrome slides are acceptable as an alternative to color slides in almost all circumstances.

2¼in square slides Slides with a 2¼in square format give excellent definition. Because of their large size, they should always be mounted in glass. Some galleries and evaluation schemes may

not have ready access to a projector for this type of slide, which may be a minor disadvantage.

Black and white prints Photographic prints should be big enough to show the work to advantage–8in × 10in (20cm × 25cm) is a popular size. Prints are often used in conjunction with slides to record work, and are necessary for press, publicity and catalogs. It is possible to make black and white prints from color slides, but black and white photographs give better quality reproduction of sculpture in magazines and catalogs. Prints supplied to press and printers should be sharply focused and have good overall contrast. Photographs should never be reproduced without permission being obtained in advance from the owner of the copyright. Negatives should be filed for possible future use.

Card index Some artists find it useful to make up a card index record of completed work. This is particularly useful when a lot of work is either being sold or loaned. Large index cards should be compiled for each piece to record basic details. These include title of the work, size/dimensions, date completed, and materials. In addition, it is useful to note down the history of the piece including the slides available (numbered for reference), prints available (numbered for reference), the buyer, buyer's address, number of invoice or bill of sale, details of any resale, loans to exhibitions, other loans and details of press coverage. Information about any repair, restoration or insurance claims should also be recorded, as should the location of the piece, if it is in store.

GALLERIES

Sculptors wishing to exhibit their work in a gallery can gain much background information at the outset by analyzing their reasons for wishing to show. Knowledge of what the artist wants out of the show provides a good starting point in looking for a gallery. For instance, if the aim is to make work available to others, think about the people who visit different types of galleries and approach those which can offer exposure to the most appropriate audience.

Local galleries are usually a good starting point. Useful information about galleries in any area of the country can be obtained locally. Galleries should be researched fully before any approach is made about showing. A gallery which an artist visits frequently because it shows interesting work may be the one which will eventually offer a show. Most galleries are either publicly funded or run as a commercial venture; this may affect the extent to which applications for exhibitions must be evaluated in terms of potential sales. A public gallery is often in a better position to exhibit non-commercial work than a small

INSURANCE

If a sculptor works on an amateur or freelance basis, it may be possible to insure work, materials and equipment by taking out or extending a normal household policy. When work is being carried out on a professional basis, or is being carried out in premises which are not already covered by a domestic insurance policy, it is necessary to take out a separate policy on the studio contents. This should cover completed work, work in progress, tools, equipment and materials. An insurance broker experienced in placing work of a fine art nature may be of assistance, as, in the event of a claim being made, an insurance company experienced in this area would be familiar with the nature of the goods. As with an ordinary domestic policy, substantiation of the value of the items lost as well as photographs would probably be required.

Work should also always be insured during exhibitions. If an artist organizes an exhibition where the work will not be covered by an existing exhibition insurance policy, it would be

wise to take out appropriate cover for the period of the exhibition. Most large insurance companies are willing to quote for such cover, or, as above, a specialized broker could help. Comparative estimates should be obtained. If the sculpture is already covered by a 'studio' insurance policy, it may be possible to obtain temporary extended coverage under the same policy to insure the work whilst on exhibition elsewhere.

When work is being shown at the invitation of another person or organization, the artist should make careful inquiries about all aspects of the arrangements offered, including what insurance cover will be effected. The sculptor needs to know whether the gallery or organizer is insuring the work, what the maximum amount claimable on each piece is, whether there is a maximum sum claimable on the whole exhibition, what period the insurance covers, which premises or locations are covered by the insurance, and whether the insurance covers all risks—theft, accidental damage, vandalism, and damage by fire and water. It is

also wise to check whether there are any exclusion clauses in the policy.

Confirmation of the insurance cover offered by the organizer, together with details of all other administrative arrangements should always be obtained in writing, preferably as an exhibition contract. If the insurance cover offered is unsatisfactory to the artist, it is wise either to reconsider the exhibition arrangements or to take out separate insurance cover. If a carrier or hired van is involved in moving the work between studio and gallery, the artist should make equally thorough inquiries about insurance arrangements while the work is in transit.

When work is to be exhibited in a public place, such as a park or garden, it is important that the artist checks that suitable arrangements are made for public liability insurance. For instance, if a child was injured as a result of falling from a piece of outdoor sculpture, the artist could be faced with a sizable claim for damages. Advice on these and other legal and insurance matters should be obtained.

recording work It is useful keep a comprehensive hotographic record of all ork. 35mm slides are the ost convenient form. These n be assembled in ansparent viewing sheets hich are kept in a file (**I**).

Administrators of galleries and exhibitions will have access to a suitable projector (**2**) or light box (**3**) for viewing the slides. A sheet of slides must be carefully packed for submission by post. If you are attending a gallery in person,

the file is a neat way of carrying the slides while they remain easily accessible and visible. It is sensible to take several slides of each work, and from all angles, as you may wish to apply to two or more places at once.

Name of artist — S. PILKINGTON — 5.10.79. — Date of work
DANIELS DEN. — Title of work
5' — Dimensions of work
← II' →
CHORLEYWOOD, HERTS, UK — Location
Medium — BRONZE — 81/C — Number of slide

Labeling slides Although the mount of a slide is small, a great deal of information about the work can be neatly recorded on it. If each slide is clearly numbered and the details are also kept in a card index, you will have an invaluable record of all work.

If slides are sent to a gallery, it is essential that they are clearly marked with the artist's name and the title and date of the work. The medium and dimensions of the sculpture also help to make it clear whether or not the work is suitable for a

particular location or purpose. If the work has been sold or is on exhibition, it is also helpful to know its location. This information is of as much help to the artist as to anyone viewing the slides. It is surprisingly easy to forget such details once a few months or years have passed.

rivate operation. Some galleries plan their prog-ms months or even years in advance, and may ot have exhibition space available at a time to it the artist applicant. Sculptors should also find ut what application procedure the gallery uses, nd comply with this. Common procedures in-ude personal recommendation, submission of ides or photographs, a formal or informal studio sit and completion of an application form.

If an application is unsuccessful, there is no eason why the artist should not ask the gallery to nlarge upon the reasons for this. The gallery may e able to redirect the artist to a more appropriate stablishment, or indicate that they would con-der a further application when the work is more eveloped. Many exhibition applications fail be-ause artists are aiming too high too soon, or have mply approached a gallery which has no interest their type of work.

UNCONVENTIONAL VENUES

culptors suffer from a lack of conventional xhibition opportunities because showing sculp-re tends to require more space and more

complex administration than displaying other types of work. One way to redress this balance is by seeking out non-gallery locations in which work can be shown. Sculpture could be exhibited in a public building such as a library or hospital, in houses open to the public, parks, gardens, offices, stores, restaurants and in the artist's own studio.

COMPETITIONS AND EXHIBITIONS

Information about competitions and exhibitions can be obtained from the many newsletters and magazines aimed at practicing artists. Local public libraries or national organizations are good sources of information. In addition, many local or regional arts' associations publish newsletters which carry this type of information. Further-more, opportunities of special regional interest would usually also be advertised in the local press.

For open exhibitions and competitions, great care should be exercised in putting together a detailed application. It is important to assess the field at the outset, follow the submission instruc-tions carefully, and not to be discouraged.

Mounting slides under glass Plastic slide mounts with glass windows are available and they provide far better protection for slides than the usual cardboard type. The thickness of the plastic keeps the slide rigid and gives extra weight to engage it in an automatic projector. Make sure the slide is clean and free of dust before clipping the halves of the plastic mount together, as any specks will show up badly when the slide is projected.

Transporting sculpture
Sculptures must be moved with great care. A small fork lift (**1**) is useful for moving large or heavy works. A simple trolley can be made from casters (**2**) mounted on a strong piece of wood (**3**).

Above right For lifting very heavy pieces, a carrying sling on a gantry may be needed. The straps should be placed carefully.

PACKING

Packing a piece of sculpture well requires almost as much effort as went into making the piece, but good packing not only protects the work but also makes the handler's job easier and underlines the professionalism of the artist. Certain general points on packing should always be assessed. Consider the function of the packing and plan accordingly. Inspect the work carefully, checking its condition and noting any points needing special attention. Photograph the work before it leaves the studio, not only for record purposes, but also in case the work is lost or damaged. If the work will be dismantled and put together again by others, compile clear assembly instructions and diagrams which will travel with the work. Keep copy in case the original is lost. Make up loa which require no more than two people to hand them. Special arrangements must be made f heavier work.

For short-term packing, the sculpture should wrapped in soft absorbent material, such as foa rubber, wood wool, shock absorbent 'bliste plastic, shaped polystyrene blocks or cotto waste, and placed within a rigid outer containe If necessary, braces or internal supports can used to keep the piece in position within the out case. There should be at least 4in (10cm) clea ance between the sculpture and the outer cas Second-hand crates can be used for the out packing.

If work is included in a touring show, loaned traveling in circumstances where it will be packed by someone other than the artist, it important to provide strong, clearly marked pac ing materials. Slatted outer crates, as describe above, can be made from sturdy softwood, asse bled with screws and fitted with padded intern braces. Alternatively, solid crates can be bu from panels of softwood boards, plywood marine ply, within a strong timber frame. Cra lids should be screwed on and marked to sho which screws are to be removed for opening. If crate is to be continually re-used, the lid shou be fitted with captive bolts or hinges and a loc Cases for long term packing should also reinforced with cleats and riding battens, but n so as to make them unnecessarily heavy. Woode battens or metal handles may make handli easier; avoid ropes as they burn hands. Painti the outside will prolong the life of a case, and al help with identification if it forms part of composite load.

Most big galleries and firms of carriers w provide a hand trolley and a set of piano whee for handling heavy pieces. Carrying slings m also be available. In smaller or temporary venue the sculptor may have to make special arrang ments in advance if this equipment is required.

Packing a sculpture for transport
1. A crate is specially made to a suitable size. The sculpture is first wrapped in tissue paper.

2. The sculpture is then wrapped completely in plastic sheeting which is firmly secured with adhesive tape.

3. Corrugated cardboard is laid in the crate and then padded cushions of paper stuffed with straw are laid in as a bed.

4. Thick layers of foam rubber are placed over the bed and are allowed to hang over the sides of the crate.

5. The wrapped sculpture is placed in the crate on the foam rubber bed.

Polystyrene granules

Packing materials It is important that packing materials provide as much protection as possible and that they do not damage the surface of the sculpture. Four good types of packing are compressed foam chips (**1**), expanded polystyrene (**2**), foam rubber (**3**) and polystyrene granules (**4**).

International signs

Battens over main support to stabilize sculpture

Padding to protect surface of sculpture

Screws used for crate and frame

Framework around main axis of work

Specially constructed wooden crate

acking a sculpture
cking a sculpture can take
me and effort, but it is well
orth while to help avoid
mage to the piece. The
cking must suit the
quirements of the work, so
fore packing, consider the
ape, weight and fragility of
e piece. It is wise to
otograph the work before
s packed in case of loss or
mage.

abels The label should state:
tist's name and address,
elivery address, exhibition
le (if applicable), title of
ork and, if appropriate, the
se number. Mark in paint,
lt marker or stencils. Mark
e top clearly.

Marking crates The top of a crate should be marked with the international symbols of an open umbrella or wineglass. Mark 'fragile' or with the broken wineglass symbol where necessary.

Transport overseas
Consult the carrier in advance about packing arrangements. In addition to the waterproof lined outer crate, an inner crate may be needed. Secure the lid carefully with screws or bolts. Label the crate carefully, but do not specify the nature of the contents on the outer crate to reduce the risk of theft.

. The overhanging foam is
ghtly packed around the
ulpture in the crate and
other layer added on top
d tucked into the sides.

7. More paper parcels stuffed with straw are laid on top and pressed firmly. Corrugated cardboard is laid over the packing and folded in to the sides of the crate.

8. The lid of the crate is put in place and nailed down around all four sides so that the crate is quite solid and secure.

9. Metal bands are passed round the reinforcing battens and tightened firmly. Instructions for handling and transporting must be clearly shown on the outside.

10. The finished package is quite secure and strong, clearly marked with instructions and given added protection by the metal bands.

GLOSSARY

A

Abrasion A technique of shaping stone, wood or plaster by rubbing the surface with an abrasive material to wear it down.

Accelerator A substance which speeds up a chemical change. An accelerator is added to polyester resin to promote curing.

Acetone A flammable solvent used to remove uncured polyester resin from tools and work surfaces.

Acrylics A range of rigid, lightweight plastics, used commonly in the form of sheets or rods. Acrylics may be transparent or opaque and are available in a range of colors.

Adze A tool used in wood carving to rough out a form. It is similar to an axe but the blade is set horizontally in the handle, sloping downwards.

Aggregate A body of granular material such as sand or gravel which is mixed with cement to make concrete.

Alloy A metal produced by combining two or more metals.

Angle grinder A heavy motorized tool with a cutting wheel, commonly used to cut or abrade the surface of metal or stone.

Annealing A process of heat treating metal to remove internal stresses and make it easier to work when cool. Mild steel and brass are allowed to cool slowly whilst other metals, such as copper, may be quenched in water. Aluminum is annealed by a slightly different process.

Armature A framework to give rigid internal support to a modeled sculpture. A basic linear form in wire can be bulked out with chicken wire or padded with wood or paper if appropriate. The medium is modeled directly onto the armature.

Assemblage A sculpture constructed from various materials not originally manufactured for artistic purposes, often including whole found objects.

Auger A tool for drilling deeply into wood, an auger is a long metal shaft with a spiral drill and cutting blades at one end.

B

Back iron A metal frame set on a wooden base, which is attached to an armature and supports the weight of the modeling material.

Ball clay An ingredient in a number of clay bodies because of its plasticity, ball clay may be black or gray in color, but fires almost white. It contracts considerably as it dries and when fired.

Ballpein hammer A hammer which has one side of the head flattened for striking, and the other rounded for flattening rivets or forming a dome.

Bandsaw A narrow, power driven blade set in heavy machinery, used to cut shapes from wood, metal or plastic sheet.

Banker A heavy wooden bench to support work being carved or modeled. The top may be fitted with a turntable so the work can be easily rotated.

Baroque This term refers to a dramatic or highly ornate style of work, originally the characteristic style of seventeenth and eighteenth century art in Europe.

Base A plinth or podium on which a sculpture is displayed, or the portion of a sculpture on which its weight rests.

Bat A thick plaster slab on which wet clay is left to lose sufficient moisture to make it workable.

Bighead bolt A threaded bolt with a broad, flat head, useful in joining two hollow cast resin sections in a resin construction.

Biscuit firing The preliminary firing of ceramic ware before a glaze is applied.

Blind mold A mold which, when fitted together, gives no access to the internal space.

Block A body of material for carving. The term is also applied to a piece of wood used to beat and consolidate large masses of clay.

Bloom A fine cloudy film which forms, for example, on the surface of melted wax or concrete cast in a plaster mold.

Blow forming A method of shaping acrylic sheet. The plastic is heated until pliable, then clamped and subjected to a blast of air which inflates it like a balloon.

Blueing Coloring the surface of metal by applying concentrated heat from a blowlamp or oxyacetylene flashlight. Oxidization gives the metal a blue tinge.

Boasting Dressing or shaping the surface of a stone block with a broad chisel.

Body A term used to refer to a mass of clay formed from a mixture of clays or clay and ceramic materials.

Brazing A method of joining two pieces of mild steel by heating to red heat and using a copper zinc alloy as a solder in the joint. This is known as hard soldering. A flux such as borax is necessary to aid the flow of the alloy.

Bronze Bronze is an alloy of copper, tin and zinc sometimes with the addition of other metals. It is commonly used in casting.

Bust peg An armature on which a portrait bust is modeled. A framework of metal loops is mounted on a central support of wood or metal.

Butterfly Two pieces of wood bound together to form a cross, suspended from an armature as an extra internal support for the weight of the modeling material.

C

Callipers An instrument used to measure a three-dimensional object, consisting of two metal arms with curved, pointed ends, hinged together.

Carbide disc An abrasive disc attachment for a power tool.

Carborundum Another name for silicon carbide, this a hard crystalline substance used as an abrasive and in refractory compounds.

Carving Carving is the technique of cutting and abrading the surface of a block of material to shape it into a particular form.

Cast, casting A cast is a sculpture produced from a mold. There are various casting processes by which a original sculpture can be reproduced exactly in a different material, or severa copies can be made.

Catalyst A substance whic provokes a chemical reactio in other materials without itself changing. Specifically, i resin sculpture, an additive which causes the resin to harden. An accelerator, usually already added to the resin, reacts with the catalys and heat is generated which sets off the hardening proce

Celluloid One of the earliest invented plastics, a cellulose nitrate which is tough and inflammable.

Cellulose A substance obtained from plant cells which is one of the basic materials used in the manufacture of plastics.

Cement A powdered substance made from calciu aluminum silicate, or alumina which is the binding ingredie in concrete.

Ceramics Pottery or hollo clay sculpture which is hardened and finished by firing.

Chamfer To cut through t thickness of a material at an angle, giving a sloping edge.

Chasing The process of finishing and refining the surface of a metal sculpture, for example, removing the protuberances on a bronze cast which necessarily form i the casting process.

Chisel A cutting tool consisting of a metal shaft bevelled at one end to form the cutting edge. A chisel is specially designed for cuttin particular material—wood, metal or stone.

ment fondu A gray-black mina cement, relatively ick-drying, used in concrete ulpture and as an ingredient refractory compounds.

rcular saw A circular othed blade which is power ven. A bench circular saw is ed for cutting timber by eding the wood into the ade, to cut across or down e length.

ladding A technique of nstruction with wood. A id shape is formed by nding thin sheets of asonite or plywood over a oden framework.

law chisel A stoneworking isel with the blade fashioned to small teeth. It is used for aping and leaves striations in e stone surface.

law hammer The head of claw hammer has a flat riking face on one side and o heavy metal prongs on e other used to trap and ver out nailheads.

lay wash A thin liquid ade by dissolving a little clay water, used to coat the ams in a plaster mold to event adhesion.

lear casting A solid cast ade from clear casting resin.

oiling A pottery technique which a pot is built up by iling thin rolls of clay into e required shape.

old chisel A toughened eel chisel used to cut metal hen it is cold.

ollage An image sembled on a flat plane by uing scraps of paper, fabric nd found materials to a round such as canvas, paper r board.

ollaring Part of the eramic technique of rowing a pot on a wheel. ollaring means constricting e top of the pot to prevent e wet clay from flaring out.

oncrete An extremely eavy, durable material when et, concrete is made from a ixture of sand, aggregate nd cement.

oning When a mass of clay worked on a potter's wheel, is repeatedly drawn up into cone shape and then attened down to center it on e wheel and shape the mass. his process is known as ning.

Construction A term referring to a sculpture made by joining together various components of different materials or of the same substance.

Constructivism A modern art movement developed in 1917 by the Russian sculptor Tatlin. The aim was to construct abstract sculpture suitable for an industrialized society and the work pioneered the use of modern technology and materials such as wood, glass, plastic and welded metal. Constructivism was introduced to Western Europe by Pevsner in Paris, and Gabo in Germany. The principles of Constructivism were highly influential in twentieth century European art, although for political reasons its influence was over in Russia by 1921.

Coping A method of splitting away stone from a block preliminary to shaping a carving. Small punches are driven into a block and hit in sequence until the stone splits between them.

Core A hollow wax sculpture to be cast in metal is filled with refractory material to give it a solid core. The wax can be modeled directly over a preformed core.

Corner clamp A device which holds together two strips or slabs of solid material at a right-angle while the joint is secured.

Crank mixture A textured stoneware body suitable for modeling terracotta sculpture. Ceramic materials mixed with stoneware clay give it the correct texture.

Crosscut saw A saw with fine teeth set and angled to cut transversely through the grain of a dense material.

Crucible A heatproof receptacle in which metal is made molten for pouring into a mold.

Cubism An influential style of art pioneered by Picasso and Braque in the early twentieth century. The form of an object was analyzed as a series of geometric units and interlocking planes describing both volume and surface.

Cure The hardening process of a material which is worked in a moist or liquid form, such as resin and concrete.

D

Dada An 'anti-art' movement which embraced sculpture, painting, theater and literature, which emerged during the First World War. Dada artists produced works which were nihilistic or reflected a cynical attitude toward social values.

Direct carving A carving technique in which the form of the sculpture evolves as the artist works into the block, or is suggested by the shape of the block.

Dolly A low platform on wheels used to move sculpture or heavy materials.

Dowel A wooden peg, which is circular in cross section, used instead of nails, bolts or screws to secure a joint.

Drawtool A metal blade with a wooden handle at either end used to strip wood.

Dummy A hammer with a rounded head, usually of iron, for striking stone carving tools.

E

Earth colors Natural pigments such as ochres, umbers and siennas, derived from metal oxides.

Earthenware Red earthenware is a clay deposit given its red color by the presence of iron oxide. A clay body based on ball clay is known as white earthenware.

Engineer's blue A blue liquid painted on metal to give a thin coating in which a scribed line can be clearly seen.

Epoxy resin A thermosetting plastic resin, used for resin casting. Epoxy is also used in the manufacture of adhesives which bond firmly.

Exothermic A material which gives off heat as it cures is described as exothermic.

F

Fettling The process of cleaning and finishing the surface of a metal sculpture, especially the seam lines on cast metal caused by the form of the mold.

File A metal tool with a rough surface used to smooth, shape or cut materials by abrasion.

Filler A powdered or ground substance added to sculpture material to give extra bulk or body. Fillers for resin also make the material opaque.

Filling compound A paste which can be spread into a break or indentation in a surface. The compound can be filed down and smoothed when hard.

Firing Baking pottery and ceramic ware in a kiln to harden it and, subsequently, to fuse decorative glazes to the surface of the ware.

Flaming A process for finishing and hardening a wax model by passing a candle flame over the surface.

Flange A metal ring which flares at the base so it can be screwed to a flat surface. A rod inserted in the flange is held at right angles to the surface.

Flat chisel A chisel with a straight cutting edge used for shaping and finishing in wood or stone carving.

Fluxing A chemical method of cleaning impurities from metal to assist fusion when metals are welded or brazed.

Former A construction usually of wood, or wood and metal, in which blocks of plaster or concrete can be formed or cast.

Futurism A movement in modern art originating among Italian artists in 1909. Futurism was a celebration of the machine age. Futurist painting and sculpture were concerned with expressing movement and the dynamics of natural and man-made forms. Some of these ideas, including the use of modern materials and techniques, were taken up later by the Constructivists.

G

Galvanized Galvanizing is a process by which steel is coated with zinc to prevent rusting.

Gantry A rigid framework which supports tackle for lifting heavy objects and materials.

G-clamp A rounded metal clamp, used to clamp materials together by adjusting a screw thread.

Gearing In Kinetic sculpture, a means of transmitting motion from a power source to the moving parts of the sculpture, utilizing either levers or interlocking gear wheels.

Gel, gel-coat When polyester resin is mixed with catalyst it begins to harden, or gel. The gel-coat is the first coat of liquid resin applied to a mold or surface when casting or laminating. It sets into a tough, plastic skin.

Gesso A mixture of whiting and glue size, gently heated. Gesso is applied with a brush to the surface of wood sculpture, forming a ground for painted decoration.

Glass fiber A light but durable sculpture material used to reinforce resin and hollow cast concrete. Thin filaments of glass are bonded into thin, flexible sheets called mats, strips of tape, or a fine, loosely stranded rope known as roving.

Glaze A transparent or colored coating which decorates and seals ceramic ware. Glazes are applied in liquid form hardened and fused to the ware by baking in a kiln.

Glue size Size crystals or powder mixed with water form a gelatinous solution which forms the binder for gesso. Glue size added to plaster retards the drying process, giving the plaster a longer working time.

Goo A creamy paste of cement mixed with water. Goo is the first coat applied to a mold in making a hollow cast concrete sculpture and forms an even surface layer for the finished cast.

Gothic A term referring to Medieval art, principally architecture, in Europe. Sculpture and architecture were closely linked during this period in monuments, tombs and church decoration.

Gouge A wood carving chisel with a curved cutting edge. A V-tool for engraving the surface of wood is a variation of the gouge.

Graphite A black mineral substance, a form of carbon, available as powder or in a stick form.

Green A term which refers to the state of wood which is unseasoned or clay before it is fired.

Grog Grog is fired clay ground into fine granules, used as an ingredient in a clay body or as a base on which clay is worked or fired which allows the form to contract freely as it dries.

Grout A liquid or paste cement mixture used to fill and seal a joint.

Guillotine A mechanical cutting apparatus with a heavy moveable blade, worked by a lever or foot pedal.

Gypsum Gypsum is calcium sulphate which is found in a variety of forms as natural deposits. When heated and deprived of its moisture it forms the substance known as plaster of Paris.

H

Hacksaw A multi-purpose saw with a narrow blade fixed at each end in a rigid curving frame.

Hardwood Certain deciduous trees yield wood which is very tough and durable when seasoned. Mahogany and oak are examples of hardwoods.

Hollow building A ceramic technique for terracotta sculpture in which the form is built up from slabs and tubes of damp clay in such a way that it is hollow throughout.

Hollow casting Casting in a mold by lining the walls of the mold with layers of the sculpture material rather than filling up the mold. The technique varies with the medium being used.

Hot air blower A hand-held electrical tool which produces a powerful jet of hot air. It is used to heat and soften acrylic rod or sheet to make it pliable.

Hot wire cutter A tool for cutting expanded polystyrene. A wire is held taut in a frame and heated, enabling it to pass cleanly through the polystyrene without undue pressure being applied. A hand-held tool or bench model may be used.

I

Indirect carving A carving technique in which the sculpture is made by copying the proportions of a small scale model.

Inflatable A sculpture made from plastic sheet or PVC which achieves its intended form when filled with air.

Investment A thick jacket of refractory material built around a wax model. This forms the mold in lost wax casting.

K

Key A small interlocking device in the seam of a mold, enabling the mold to be precisely reassembled. The term also means the slight roughening of a surface which allows a painted finish to adhere effectively.

Kiln An oven in which clay objects are baked at high temperatures, to harden them or to set surface glazing.

Kinetics A kinetic sculpture is one which moves or has moving parts. Movement may be provoked by a natural force such as wind or water, or by a motor built into the sculpture.

L

Lacquer A varnish which can be painted on a surface to produce a glossy finish.

Laminating Building up a rigid surface over a framework by applying thin layers of material. Laminating is a technique used in sculpture with wood or resin.

Latex A rubber substance used as a cold cure molding compound and also as the basis of certain adhesives.

Leather-hard This term describes the state of clay which has lost a good deal of moisture but is not yet hardened completely.

Lewis bolt An expanding metal bolt, consisting of two angled metal arms fixed on a pivot, which is used for lifting stone blocks.

Lost wax casting This is the traditional technique for producing a cast in bronze from a wax model. The wax model is jacketed in a refractory mold and fired to melt out the wax. Molten bronze is poured into the resulting space in the mold and left to set. When it is cool the mold is broken away and the bronze sculpture cleaned and finished.

do mold The refractory mold used in lost wax casting.

mp hammer A hammer with a heavy, rectangular head, usually made of iron, used to strike stone cutting tools.

M

ajolica A type of pottery glaze which produces the effect of a rich, enamelled surface.

allet A wooden hammer used to apply force to chisels in wood carving.

aquette A small sculpture, often clay, wax or plaster model, made as a preparatory study for a full scale work.

at A thin, flat sheet or strip of glass fiber material, used to reinforce laminating resin, hollow cast ciment fondu and modeled concrete sculpture. Surface mat is quite fine, chopped strand mat is a coarse, loosely woven fabric.

aul A wooden club used to strike a wood carving chisel. A maul is shaped from a single piece of wood taken from the base of a young tree.

easuring box A box devised to measure the proportions of the dry ingredients for concrete so it is possible to calculate the total volume of the mixture.

edium, media A medium is the particular material or technique with which a sculptor works. Mixed media sculptures, therefore, are those in which several materials or processes are employed.

elamine A synthetic resin or the material manufactured from that resin. Melamine can be bought in the form of a tough, non-porous sheet.

ild steel Steel which contains only a small proportion of carbon. This is the type of steel most commonly used for constructional purposes.

inimal art A style of abstract art developed, particularly by sculptors, during the 1960s. Minimal sculptures are simple, unembellished forms, often geometric. The sculpture material is undisguised and no attempt is made to represent or symbolize any other object or experience.

Mixing box A shallow wooden box, open at the top, in which concrete is mixed. A mixing box may be sealed inside to make it waterproof.

Mobile A type of kinetic sculpture, first explored by Alexander Calder. Mobiles are often constructions of flat metal shapes suspended on wires or fixed to flexible rods. The parts of the sculpture move in response to draughts of air, wind or motor power.

Modeling A process of making sculpture by building up a form in a malleable material such as clay, wax or wet plaster or concrete. The material is shaped with the fingers or with pointed and spatulate tools.

Modeling stand A turntable mounted on a tripod which can be raised or lowered, giving the sculptor access to the work from all angles. A modeling stand is only suitable for work on a small or medium scale, such as a figure under life size or a portrait bust.

Mold A negative form or impression taken from an original sculpture, in which a cast is made to copy the sculpture or reproduce it in another material.

N

Neoclassical The dominant style of European art in the late eighteenth and early nineteenth centuries. Neoclassical artists took the dignity and grandeur of ancient Greek and Roman civilizations as their model, celebrating their heroes and legends and the beauty of classical art and architecture.

O

Oilstone A stone used for sharpening and honing metal cutting tools.

P

Paddle A flat piece of wood used to beat damp clay, to remove air pockets and consolidate the mass.

Palette knife A knife with a flexible, spatulate blade, for applying or scraping off a plastic material. It is also a convenient tool for loosening a rigid layer of cured resin from a mold.

Pallet A large flat board on which materials may be stored to protect them from damp. It may be slightly raised from the floor by battens on the underside.

Paper rope Lengths of tightly rolled paper used to reinforce hollow cast resin. The paper rope is wetted out with resin and dries completely rigid.

Patina A colored coating which forms on the surface of metal sculpture owing to chemical changes induced by natural elements. These changes can also be stimulated artificially. The best known example is verdigris, the bright green deposit which forms on bronze through oxidation.

Piece mold A mold made up in interlocking sections which can be used to make several casts since the mold is easily removed each time without being damaged.

Pinching A pottery technique which involves pressing the thumb into a ball of clay and drawing the clay out into a pot shape between thumb and fingers.

Pins Long, flat headed pins which connect the core to the investment in a mold for lost wax casting. When the wax is burnt out the pins hold the core in position.

Pitching tool A broad, heavy stone carving chisel, used to strike off large pieces of stone in roughing out a carving.

Plaster of Paris A fine white powder made from heat treated gypsum, which sets hard when mixed with water and allowed to dry out, forming again as gypsum.

Plaster trap A receptacle fitted under a sink to provide a filter in the drainage system. Waste plaster is strained off when tools and mixing bowls are being cleaned.

Plasticity The quality of a material which can be modeled, molded or pressed into shape. Clay is an example of an extremely plastic material.

Plexiglas An acrylic plastic available in sheet or rod form. Plexiglas may be transparent or brightly colored.

Point A simple metal tool with a pointed end used to rough out the basic shape of a stone carving.

Pointing A mechanical means of reproducing or scaling up a three-dimensional form in correct proportion. The pointing machine is a framework of metal arms which can be fitted around a sculpture to measure the relationships between given points on the surface.

Polarizing An effect of light waves produced by limiting their normal pattern, by means of a filter. The projection of a design with changing colors is possible by this means.

Polychrome A term describing sculpture finished in or decorated with several colors, usually referring to painted decoration.

Polyester resins Synthetic plastic resins in liquid form are made to solidify by the addition of a catalyst. Resin, reinforced with glass fiber, is commonly used as casting material but may also be modeled when thickened with an inert filler such as powdered chalk. It can be cut and abraded when hard.

Polystyrene A plastic which is available in two forms— toughened polystyrene is a rigid plastic in sheet form while expanded polystyrene is a light, granular mass, usually worked in sheets or blocks but also available as loose granules.

Polythene Flexible plastic sheeting which can be sewn or welded to make the outer skin of inflatable or stuffed sculptures. Polythene may be transparent or opaque and, colored or colorless.

Pop Art A dominant style of art during the 1960s, Pop Art originated in Britain and the USA when artists began to represent the many transient products of a consumer society, revelling in bright colors and the elevation of objects such as comics and junk food to a new scale and status.

Porcelain A clay body consisting mainly of china clay, porcelain is white and often translucent when fired.

Pour The process of filling a mold with the material which will form the actual sculpture, for instance, molten bronze in lost wax casting.

Pouring ring A circular metal band attached to a long handle which holds a crucible full of molten metal for pouring in lost wax casting.

Press molding A method of making ceramic ware by pressing a sheet of clay into an open plaster mold.

Primer An undercoat applied to the surface of a sculpture to seal it and provide a ground for a painted finish.

Puddling A technique of creating even density and eliminating air bubbles in a mix of wet concrete by pushing a rod up and down through the mass.

Pug mill A machine with revolving blades which chop and mix clay. The pug mill is used to process and consolidate clay masses.

Punch A broad, pointed metal tool used in roughing out a stone carving.

PVA An abbreviation for polyvinyl alcohol. PVA is a thick white liquid which dries to a tough clear plastic skin. It is an adhesive and may also be used diluted with water as a release agent or sealant.

PVC An abbreviation for polyvinyl chloride. PVC is a flexible sheet plastic which can be sewn, glued or welded. Shapes made from PVC may be stuffed, inflated or filled with water.

Pyrometric cones Ceramic cones placed inside a kiln before firing. At a certain temperature, the cones will bend, so by constant observation it can be determined at what point particular temperatures are reached in the kiln.

R

Rasp A coarse abrasive tool made of metal. The abrasive surface has many pointed teeth shaped like tiny pyramids.

Refractory A refractory material is one which is resistant to high temperatures. Refractory materials are used for molds in lost wax casting and for kiln furniture on which ceramic ware stands while it is fired.

Release agent A substance applied to the interior or seams of a mold to prevent the adhesion of two surfaces.

Relief A sculpture developed into or on a flat plane surface. The forms of a relief sculpture are not fully rounded, but they vary from low relief, which may be only shallow undulations or incisions in the surface, to high relief in which there is considerable expression of the three-dimensional form.

Riffler A metal tool with a small filing surface at the end of a rounded shaft. The riffler is used in delicate shaping and finishing of a carving. Rifflers are made in different shapes and sizes for work in wood, metal and stone.

Ripsaw A long-bladed hand-held saw with teeth designed for cutting down the grain of the material.

Risers In lost wax casting, risers are channels through the mold which allow air to escape as molten metal is poured into the mold.

Riveting A method of joining sheets of metal using short bolts with flattened heads.

Rodding The process of attaching wax rods to the surface of a wax model in lost wax casting. The rods form the runners and risers in the mold.

Romanesque The style of art and architecture dominant in Europe in the eleventh and twelfth centuries. Like the later Gothic style, Romanesque art was mainly applied in buildings and monuments for religious purposes.

Roving A light rope made of loosely bonded glass fiber, used as reinforcement for resin sculpture.

Rubbing compound An abrasive paste used to rub down the surface of a resin sculpture to give it a polished finish.

Runners In lost wax casting, channels in the mold through which the molten bronze flows into the mold.

S

Sand molding A method of casting in metal in which a mold is made by packing layers of damp sand firmly around a sculpture. When the original is removed an exact impression is left in the sand.

Sash clamp A straight clamp with adjustable fixings, used in wood construction.

Scaling up A mechanical method of copying a small sculpture on a larger scale by increasing all the measurements proportionately, using such measuring devices as a scaling board or callipers.

Scraper A tool with a broad metal blade which is fairly rigid, but not honed to a cutting edge.

Scribe A metal tool with a sharp point used to draw fine, accurate lines on a rigid material such as metal or plastic sheet.

Scrim A coarse, loosely woven hessian fabric which acts as reinforcement for plaster models and casts.

Sculpture in the round Sculpture which is free standing and fully developed from all points of view.

Seasoning The long process of drying out most of the natural moisture in wood to make it stable and workable for carving or construction.

Separator A substance applied to the interior of a mold to prevent the adhesion of a casting material.

Setting The hardening process of plaster of Paris, concrete or resin.

Sheet saw A saw for cutting sheet metal which has no support along the top of the blade that would hinder its movement on a long cut.

Shellac A varnish made from a natural resin secreted by the lac insect.

Shim A thin brass strip used to divide the surface of a modeled sculpture into sections for a waste mold.

Silica A hard mineral substance found in various natural deposits. Silica ground to a granular form is a component of ceramic bodies and abrasives.

Silicone rubber A cold cure molding compound which can withstand the heat of molten lead. Silicone rubber is only used for small scale casting. It is mixed from a rubber base solution and a catalyst.

Slabbing A pottery technique in which a form is built up by joining shapes cut from thick sheets of damp clay.

Slip, slip casting Slip is an opaque, creamy liquid made by mixing finely ground clay with water. To form a slip cast, slip is poured into a plaster mold and left until a thick skin forms inside the mold. The excess slip is poured out and the hollow cast left to harden.

Slipstone A small abrasive stone used to sharpen the inside curve or angle of a gouge or V-tool.

Softwoods Woods from coniferous trees, some of which are suitable for carving for example, yellow pine.

Soldering A method of joining pieces of metal by melting an alloy of tin and lead to the joint to fuse the two edges together. A soldered joint will not withstand much stress.

Solvent A substance which is able to dissolve another substance.

Spatula A simple rounded or blunt modeling tool in a flat, elongated shape. Spatulas are made from wood or metal.

Spokeshave A small planing tool for wood consisting of a blade with a handle at either end. The spokeshave is drawn across the surface of wood to smooth or shape it and can be used on a flat or curved surface.

Stoneware A smooth buff, gray or brown clay which is mixed with other clays and ceramic materials to make a dense, highly plastic clay body. The term stoneware also refers to the body and objects made from it.

Superrealism A style of figurative painting and sculpture in which forms are represented in exact detail. Paintings may be copied minutely from photographs, while the sculptures usually take the form of lifesize resin or wax figures dressed in real clothes and carrying real objects.

Surform A metal abrasive tool fitted with a replaceable blade, like a grater, so that small particles of material pass through and do not clog the cutting teeth. Surforms are available in a number of shapes—flat, curved and rounded.

Surrealism A movement in fine art, literature and theater which was extremely widespread in the period between the two World Wars. Surrealist artists aimed to free themselves from the traditions of art and pursue images born of fantasy and free association of thoughts. The work included both figurative and abstract styles.

T

Tamping Consolidating a fibrous or granular material such as resin-soaked glass fiber, concrete or damp sand by pressing or packing it into shape in a mold.

Tapping Cutting a thread inside a drilled hole so it will accept a screw or plug in which a corresponding thread has been cut. Tapping is done with a tap drill. The process is used to fill pin holes in a bronze cast with fine bronze rod.

Template A pattern cut from a thin sheet of rigid material which is used as a guide for forming or cutting the shape as a three-dimensional solid.

Tenon saw A saw with a short, rectangular blade which is supported along the side opposite the cutting edge by a narrow metal grip. It is used for cutting with accuracy through small sections of wood.

Tensile strength The ability of a material to withstand the stress imposed upon it when it is stretched.

Terracotta This term means baked clay, and is generally applied to any sculpture made in clay and fired. In a more specialized sense, terracotta specifically refers to red earthenware bodies used for modeling or building hollow sculptures which are then fired to give them permanence.

Thermoplastics Plastics which soften when they are heated and harden as they cool without changing their basic properties. Acrylics are an example of this type of plastic.

Thermosetting A term which refers to plastics, such as polyester and epoxy resins, which require the presence of heat in a forming process, but which then set hard and cannot be remolded.

Throwing In pottery, throwing means forming a pot from a ball of clay on a rotating wheel.

Tinsnips Shears with short blades used to cut through thin sheets of metal.

Turning A pottery technique by which the base of a pot is trimmed and finished on the wheel. The pot is first allowed to dry to the leather-hard stage.

Turning box An open box fitted with a metal spindle used for forming a rounded solid in plaster. A metal template is attached to the top of the box and the shape is formed by applying wet plaster to the rotating spindle which is gradually shaped as it dries and scrapes against the template.

Twist drill A drill with a straight shaft incised with spiral cutting edges for boring a hole.

U

Undercut A recess or awkward angle in the surface or form of a three-dimensional object which would prevent easy removal of a cast from a mold. Molds are designed to eliminate this problem.

V

Vacuum forming A method of shaping plastic sheet over a solid relief pattern. The plastic is heated until it is pliable and when a vacuum is created under the form the plastic is drawn down onto the pattern like a skin.

Vinyl molding compound This is a type of rubber molding compound which is heated to a liquid form and contained around the original model where it sets into a flexible rubber mold. When the mold is no longer needed, it can be melted down and the rubber used again.

W

Ware A collective term for pottery and ceramic objects.

Washer A flat metal or rubber ring fitted to a bolt head or nut which helps to secure the bolt and distribute its pressure.

Waste mold A mold from which only one cast can be taken as the mold must be broken away to release the cast and is thus wasted.

Wedge A piece of wood or metal tapered at one edge, used to split wood along its grain.

Wedging A technique by which clay is thoroughly kneaded before use in modeling or pottery, to make it the correct consistency and remove air pockets.

Welding The process of joining metals by fusing them together under direct, intense heat. A commonly used source of heat for welding is an oxyacetylene flashlight. A metal rod may be applied to the joint which melts into any gaps and strengthens the bond.

Wet-and-dry paper Paper with a coating of silicon carbide, used as an abrasive. Its common name derives from the fact that it can be used wet or dry, as suitable for the materials used and the surface finish required.

MANUFACTURERS AND SUPPLIERS

Sculpture involves such a wide range of media and equipment that often one supplier will not sell all the equipment and materials required for a particular work. For most media, especially stone, wood and metal, it is always worth looking for suppliers locally – wood yards, scrap metal merchants, foundries and stone quarries or yards. Many local hardware, do-it-yourself, craft and hobby stores stock a selection of materials and tools, such as chisels, hammers or mallets, which are suitable for sculpture. Similarly, smaller, more specialized stores may also sell tools which are of use to the sculptor. These include, for instance, ships' chandlers, which may also supply fiberglass and flexible molding compounds. These lists give the names and addresses of some of the main manufacturers who are normally extremely helpful and may be able to give details of local retail outlets. Many manufacturers and suppliers also produce their own catalogs which, as well as listing retailers, often gives useful information on using materials and tools.

UNITED KINGDOM

General sculpture tools and suppliers

Brickhouse Crafts,
Cock Green,
Felsted,
Essex.

Buck and Ryan,
101 Tottenham Court Road,
London W1.

Alec Tiranti Ltd,
70 High Street,
Theale,
Reading,
Berks.

Alec Tiranti Ltd,
21 Goodge Place,
London W1.

Wengers Ltd,
Garner Street,
Etruria,
Stoke-on-Trent,
Staffs.

Clays, ceramics and pottery supplies

Deancraft Ltd,
Lovatt Street,
Stoke-on-Trent,
Staffs.

English China Clay Co,
John Keay House,
St Austell,
Cornwall.

The Fulham Pottery Co Ltd,
184 New King's Road,
London SW6.

Harrison-Meyer Ltd,
Meir,
Stoke-on-Trent,
Staffs.

Kilns and Furnaces Ltd,
Keele Street,
Tunstall,
Stoke-on-Trent,
Staffs.

Potclays Ltd,
Brickkiln Lane,
Etruria,
Stoke-on-Trent,
Staffs.

Podmore and Sons Ltd,
Shelton,
Stoke-on-Trent,
Staffs.

Podmore Ceramics Ltd,
105 Minet Street,
London SW9.

Wengers Ltd,
Etruria,
Stoke-on-Trent,
Staffs.

Wax

Candlemakers' Supplies,
28 Blythe Road,
London W14 0HA.

Brownings of Hull,
65 Aberdeen Street,
Hull,
Humberside.

Duffek Campbell Ltd,
Thames Road,
Crayford,
Kent.

Duffek Campbell Ltd,
New Hive Works,
Bury,
Lancs.

Wood

For supplies, try local timber yards or stockists and for tools a hardware, craft or do-it-yourself shop. Contact the Timber Trade Federation for advice on local stockists of particular woods.

Afro Timber & Plywood Co Ltd,
Englemere Sawmills,
London Road,
Ascot,
Berks.
(hardwoods)

D.W. Beattie & Co Ltd,
Dalhousie Estate,
Bonnyrigg,
Midlothian EH19 3HY.

Brownlee & Co Ltd,
City Saw Mills,
Port Dundas,
Glasgow.

Wm Brown's Saw Mills Ltd,
John Street,
Darlington.

Wm Brown & Co (Ipswich) Ltd,
Greyfriars Road,
Ipswich.

J.S. Fisher Ltd,
Newry Saw Mills,
Buttercrane Quay,
Newry, Co Down, NI.
(softwoods)

Gregor Bros Ltd,
Beaufort Road,
Plasmarl Industrial Estate,
Swansea,
West Glam. SA6 8HQ.

Mallinson-Denny (Scotland) Ltd,
Kalvinaugh Saw Mills,
Kalvinaugh Street,
Glasgow G3 8PG.

Montague L. Meyer Ltd,
North Dock,
Alexandra Dock,
Newport,
Gwent.

Montague L. Meyer Ltd,
Timber Terminal,
King George Dock,
Hull HU9 5QT.

Montague L. Meyer Ltd,
Western Dock,
Southampton SO9 3RT.

Vincent Murphy & Co Ltd,
74-76 Derby Road,
Liverpool L20 8LT.

George Rankin & Co Ltd,
Dock Saw Mills,
Milewater Road,
Belfast 3, NI.
(hardwoods)

Rudders & Raynes Ltd,
Studley,
Nr. Redditch,
Worcs.

The Sabah Trading Co Ltd,
Long Reach Road,
Barking, Essex.

Sabah Timber South East (Merchants) Ltd,
1 Central Road,
Worcester Park,
Surrey KT4 8DN.

John Sadd & Sons Ltd,
Station Road Wharf,
Maldon, Essex.

The Timber Trade Federation,
47 Whitcomb St,
London WC2.
(for advice on local suppliers)

Henry Venables Ltd,
Castletown Saw Mills,
Doxey,
Stafford, Staffs.

Fibreglass and resin casting

Architectural and Industrial GRP,
400 Ewell Road,
Tolworth,
Surrey.

Dufaylite Developments Ltd,
Cromwell Road,
St Neots,
Huntingdon.

Falcon Glass,
75 Maltby Street,
London SE1.

Strand Glassfibre Ltd,
Brentway Trading Estate,
Brentford,
Middlesex.
Branches in Ashford (Kent), Birmingham, Brentford, Bristol, Derby, Dublin, Glasgow, Ilford, Leeds, Norwich, Plymouth, Portsmouth, Reading, Southampton, Stockport, Stockton-on-Tees.

Metalwork and casting

Local foundries, iron- and steelworks and scrap metal dealers are always worth investigating as a source of supp for metal casting and also for advice and help on where to obtain suitable materials.

Vinatex Ltd,
Station House,
North Street,
Havant,
Hants.
(flexible moulding compound)

Park and Patterson,
Rose Hill Works,
Croft Lane,
Manchester.
(metals)

Plastics

British Industrial Plastics,
Sheet and Film Division,
Manningtree,
Essex.

B. Brown (Holborn) Ltd,
Warriner House,
32-33 Greville Street,
London EC1N 8TD.

Evode Ltd,
Common Road,
Stafford,
Staffs.
(adhesives)

Expanded Polystyrene Suppliers Assoc,
PO Box 103,
Haywards Heath,
West Sussex.

CI Plastics Division,
Welwyn Garden City,
Herts.

ennig Chemicals Ltd,
ennig House,
Masons Avenue,
Croydon.

Margros Ltd,
Monument Way West,
Woking,
Surrey.

arnall and Sons Ltd,
lastics Machinery Division,
odge Causeway,
ishponds,
ristol.

ransatlantic Plastics Ltd,
Garden Estate,
Ventnor,
le of Wight.

Welwyn Tool Co Ltd,
tonehill House,
Welwyn Garden City,
Herts.

tone and marble

or supplies, contact a local stone
ard or quarry and for tools try a
ardware or craft shop.

Ashby and Horner Masonry Ltd,
95 London Road,
Thurrock,
Essex.

Kingston Minerals Ltd,
Bumpers Lane,
Wakeham,
Portland,
Dorset.
(Portland stone)

Marble and Slate Consolidated
tone Ltd,
a Harpenden Road,
London SE27.

Noirell Ltd,
Kent House,
Regent Street,
London W1.

C.A. Pisani,
Transport Avenue,
Brentford,
Middx.
(marble, granite, tools)

The Stone Firms Ltd,
20 Manverse St,
Bath BA1 ILX.
(limestone)

The Stone Firms Ltd,
Portland,
Dorset.
(limestone)

UNITED STATES

General sculpture and suppliers

Alexander's Sculpture Services,
117 E 39 St,
New York, NY 10016.

Arlene's Artist Materials and
Ceramic Supply,
57 Fuller Road,
Colonie, NY 12205.

Art and Hobby Center,
3177 Poplar Ave,
Memphis, TN 38111.

Art Hardware,
1135 Broadway,
Boulder, CO 80302.

Buffalo Ceramic and Art Supply
Center Inc,
437 Franklin St,
Buffalo, NY 14202.

Crafts Distributing Inc,
227 NW 63 St,
Oklahoma, OK 73112.

The Craft Tool Co Inc,
2323 Reach Rd,
Williamsport, PA 17701.

ETT Studios Inc,
Byram, CT 068 30.

Kemper Mfg Co,
Box 545,
Chino, CA 91710.

Frank Mittemeier Inc,
3577 E Tremont Ave,
Bronx, NY 10465.

Pacific and Home Foreign Trade,
1336 Harrison St,
San Francisco, CA 94103.

Sax Arts and Crafts,
316 N Milwaukee St,
Milwaukee, WI 53202.

Sculpture Associates Ltd,
114 E 25 St,
New York, NY 10010.

Sculpture House,
38 E 30 St,
New York, NY 10016.

Sculpture Services Inc,
9 E 19 St,
New York, NY 10003.

Western Sculpture Supply,
2855 W Eighth Ave,
Denver, CO 80204.

The Woodshed,
No 5 Ave A,
New York, NY 10009.

Clays, ceramics and pottery supplies

American Art Clay Co,
4717 W 16 St,
Indianapolis, IN 46222.

Binney and Smith Inc,
1100 Church Lane,
Box 431,
Easton, PA 18042.

Blair Art Products Inc
3540 Summer Ave,
Box 22381,
Memphis, TN 38122.

Kilns Supply and Service Corp,
38 Bulkey Avenue,
Box 1071,
Port Chester, NY 10573.

New England School Supply,
Spring Field, MA 01101.

Newton Pottery Supply Co,
Main St,
Waltham, MA 02154.

Paragon Industries Inc,
Box 10133,
Dallas, TX 75207.

Poly Form Products Co,
9420 W Byron St,
Schiller Park, ILL.

Potter's Supply Co,
PO Box 799,
11 Washington,
East Liverpool, Ohio.

Stewart Clay Co Inc,
400 Jersey Ave,
New Brunswick, NJ 08902.

Fiberglass and resin casting

Adhesive Products,
1660 Boone Ave,
Bronx, New York, NY 10460.

Crescent Bronze Powder Co Inc,
120 W Illinois St,
Chicago, ILL 60610.

Palmer Paint Products,
1291 Rochester Rd,
Troy, MI 48084.

Stafford Reeves Inc,
622 Greenwich St,
New York, NY 10014.

Thermoset Plastics Inc,
65th at Nickel Plate RR,
Indianapolis IN.

Metalwork and casting

Airco Welding Products,
Box 486,
Union, NJ 67083.

Allcraft Tool and Supply Co,
100 Frank Rd,
Hicksville, NJ 11801.

Bartlett and Co Inc,
5 S Wabash Ave,
Chicago, ILL 60603.

Casting Supplies House Inc,
62 W 47 St,
New York, NY 10019.

McEnglevan Heat Treating and
Mfg Co,
700-708 Griggs St,
Danville, ILL 61832.

Mason Renshaw Ind,
123 Gray Ave,
Santa Barbara, CA 93101.

Plastics

Foamed Plastic Sales,
Indian Point Lane,
Riverside, CT 06830.

Fome Board Service Center,
2211 N Elston Ave,
Chicago, ILL 60614.

Poly Products Corp,
28150 Hayes Ave,
Box 42,
Roseville, MI 48066.

Stone and marble

For supplies try a local stone yard
or quarry, and for tools try a
hardware or hobby store.

New York Marble Works Inc,
1399 Park Ave,
New York, NY 10039.

The Woodshed,
No 5 Ave A,
New York, NY 10009.

Wax

Bartlett and Co Inc,
5 S Wabash Ave,
Chicago, ILL 60603.

The Crafttool Co Inc,
2323 Reach Rd,
Williamsport, PA 17701.

Frank Mittemeier,
3577 E Tremont Ave,
Bronx, NY 10465.

Wood

For supplies try a local wood yard
or stockist and for tools try a
hardware or hobby store.

Allway Tools Co,
1513 Olmstead Ave,
Bronx, NY 10460.

Loew Cornell Inc,
131 W Ruby Ave,
Palisades Park, NJ 07650.

Sander Wood Engraving Co Inc,
212 Lincoln St,
Porter, IN 46304.

The Woodshed,
No 5 Ave A,
New York, NY 10009.

INDEX

ACKNOWLEDGEMENTS

pp. 8 W. Rawlings/R. Harding Agency. **9** R. Sheridan. **12** Fogg Art Museum. **13** Christie's/Bridgeman Library. **17** Errol Jackson. **18** Iraqi Government/Visual Arts Library. **18/19** Victoria & Albert Museum/Visual Arts Library. **27** New York, Museum of Modern Art, A. Conger Goodyear Fund. **33** (tl) Victoria & Albert Museum/Visual Arts Library. **33** (tr) Bridgeman Library. **34** (tl) Bridgeman Library. **34** (bl) Visual Arts Library. **34** (r) Stoke-on-Trent Museum. **35** (t) Visual Arts Library. **35** (l) Visual Arts Library. **35** (r) Jos. Wedgwood and Sons Ltd. **36** (l) Visual Arts Library. **36** (r) Victoria & Albert Museum/Visual Arts Library. **41** Royal Doulton Tableware Ltd. **44** Visual Arts Library. **50** Victoria & Albert Museum/Bridgeman Library. **55** Victoria & Albert Museum. **58** Tate Gallery/Bridgeman Library. **60** Victoria & Albert Museum/Visual Arts Library. **61** Statens Museum for Kunst, Copenhagen. **64** (l) Visual Arts Library. **64** (r) Visual Arts Library. **65** University College/Visual Arts Library. **76** (l) Bridgeman Library. **76/77** Scala. **77** (t) Visual Arts Library. **78** (l) Victoria & Albert Museum/Visual Arts Library. **78** (r) Paris, Musée Picasso/Visual Arts Library. **79** (l) Sean Rice. **79** (r) Paris, CNAC/Visual Arts Library. **86** (l) Visual Arts Library. **86** (r) Bridgeman Library. **87** Leo Castelli/Visual Arts Library. **95** New York, Museum of Modern Art, gift of Ch. & A. Blatt. **96** (l) British Museum/Bridgeman Library. **96** (r) British Museum/Visual Arts Library. **97** (bl) Chicago Art Institute/Visual Arts Library. **97** (t) Mansell Collection. **97** (br) Victoria & Albert Museum. **98** (l) Leipzig, Karl-Marx University/Visual Arts Library. **98** (r) Bridgeman Library. **99** (l) London, Museum of Mankind/Visual Arts Library. **99** (m) New York, Museum of American Indian/Visual Arts Library. **99** (r) Paris, Musée Picasso/Visual Arts Library. **99** (b) David Nash. **111** Visual Arts Library. **112** Visual Arts Library. **114/115** Visual Arts Library. **115** Tate Gallery/Visual Arts Library. **116** (t) Victoria & Albert Museum/Visual Arts Library. **116** (b) Paris, Musées Nationaux. **117** Paul Neagu. **119** British Museum/Visual Arts Library. **120** Bridgeman Library. **121** Victoria & Albert Museum/Visual Arts Library. **123** Tate Gallery/Bridgeman Library. **139** Mansell Collection. **140** B. Jarret/Paris, Musée Rodin. **141** Visual Arts Library. **145** Visual Arts Library. **146** Paris, Musées Nationaux. **146/147** Visual Arts Library. **147** Henry Moore Foundation. **152** Paris, Musée Picasso/Visual Arts Library. **153** Paris, Musées Nationaux. **154** Visual Arts Library. **155** Tate Gallery. **156** (l) Visual Arts Library. **156** (r) New York, Metropolitan Museum, Marquand Fund, 1951. **157** (b) University College/Visual Arts Library. **158** Wilhelm Lembruck Museum, Duisburg. **159** Paris, Musées Nationaux. **160/161** Errol Jackson. **162** Visual Arts Library. **163** Dan King. **164** British Council. **164/165** John Donnat/Visual Arts Library. **166** Visual Arts Library. **168** (t) Guggenheim Museum/Visual Arts Library. **168** (b) Los Angeles County Museum/Visual Arts Library. **169** New York, Museum of Modern Art, S. & H. Janis Collection. **176** (l) St Louis Art Museum/Visual Arts Library. **176** (r) Paris, Archives Photographiques/Visual Arts Library. **177** (l) Paris, Musée Picasso/Visual Arts Library. **177** (r) Tate Gallery. **179** (t) Tate Gallery. **179** (b) Galérie Mathias Fels/Visual Arts Library. **183** Visual Arts Library. **185** (l) Visual Arts Library. **185** (tr) Tate Gallery. **185** (br) Visual Arts Library. **186** (tl) A. Campbell. **186** (bl) Tate Gallery/Visual Arts Library. **186** (tr) A. Campbell. **188** (br) New York, Museum of Modern Art, Mrs S. Guggenheim Fund. **189** Visual Arts Library. **190** Sonia Halliday. **191** (r) Rapho. **191** (tl) Visual Arts Library. **192/193** Tate Gallery. **194** (b) Visual Arts Library. **196** Tate Gallery. **197** (tl) Philadelphia Museum of Art/Visual Arts Library. **197** (tr) New York, Museum of Modern Art/Visual Arts Library. **197** (b) Philadelphia Museum of Art, L. & W. Arensberg Collection. **198** New York, Museum of Modern Art. **199** (t) Leo Castelli/Visual Arts Library. **199** (b) Visual Arts Library. **200** Visual Arts Library. **201** (t) Visual Arts Library. **201** (b) Visual Arts Library. **202** John Webb. **204** John Donnat/Visual Arts Library.

Key:
(t)   – top
(tl)   – top left
(tr)   – top right
(m)   – middle
(b)   – bottom
(bl)   – bottom left
(br)   – bottom right
(r)   – right
(l)   – left